Barry Baddock
Susie Vrobel

Down to Business

Arbeitsbuch

Max Hueber Verlag

Dieses Werk folgt der seit dem 1. August 1998 gültigen Rechtschreibreform.

€ 3. 2. 1. | Die letzten Ziffern
2006 05 04 03 02 | bezeichnen Zahl und Jahr des Druckes.
Alle Drucke dieser Auflage können, da unverändert, nebeneinander benutzt werden.
2. Auflage 2002

Umschlaggestaltung: Isabella Valdivieso (Foto), München; Parzhuber u. Partner, München
Satz/Layout: grafik & design, Bettina Kammerer, München
Gesamtherstellung: Friedrich Pustet, Regensburg
Printed in Germany
ISBN: 3-19-019474-2

Herzlich Willkommen und Down to Business!

Sie haben sich für unseren Kurs entschieden, weil Sie auf Englisch Kundengespräche führen oder Ihre Geschäftskorrespondenz abwickeln müssen. Wir wollen Ihnen dabei helfen. Bitte lesen Sie diese Einleitung aufmerksam durch, bevor Sie mit der Arbeit beginnen. Sie erhalten wichtige Hinweise zur Benutzung des Kurses.

Jede der 10 Units *behandelt einen eigenen Themenbereich, wie z.B.* „Organising a Conference" *oder* „Making and Handling Complaints". *Der Kurs ist so strukturiert, dass in jeder* Unit *alle vier Sprachfertigkeiten (Hören – Sprechen – Lesen – Verstehen) trainiert werden. Sie erwerben aber auch wichtiges fremdsprachliches* Know-How *für das Geschäftsleben: Unter anderem werden Sie lernen, Gesprächsstrategien zu entwickeln, Notizen und Berichte zu verfassen und mit Korrespondenz umzugehen.*

Darüber hinaus greift Down to Business *relevante Themen aus der Grammatik auf und hilft Ihnen, typische Fehler beim Gebrauch der englischen Sprache zu vermeiden. Ein Teil jeder* Unit *befasst sich mit den Unterschieden zwischen britischem und amerikanischem Englisch.*

Down to Business *enthält eine Vielfalt an authentischen Materialien, Grafiken und Dokumenten aus dem internationalen Geschäftsleben. Unser Kurs versetzt Sie in die Lage, mit ähnlichen Materialien sprachlich souverän im Berufsleben umzugehen.*

Entscheiden Sie selbst, ob Sie Down to Business *von A bis Z durcharbeiten oder zunächst die für Sie wichtigen Themenbereiche durchnehmen wollen. Arbeiten Sie z.B. im Finanzbereich, so wird die* Unit „Discussing and Settling Questions of Payment" *Ihnen möglicherweise den besten Einstieg bieten. Falls Sie häufig auf Geschäftsreisen gehen – wie wäre es mit einem Sprung direkt zu* „Travelling"*? Sie selbst setzen die Prioritäten und auch die Geschwindigkeit fest, mit der Sie* Down to Business *meistern werden. Die* Grammar Review *im Anhang bietet Ihnen die Möglichkeit, spezielle Grammatikfragen nachzuschlagen oder Ihre Grammatikkentnisse generell aufzufrischen.*

Soweit nicht ausdrücklich als amerikanisches Englisch gekennzeichnet (wie z.B. in den Abschnitten „The British-American Difference"*), folgt der englische Teil in* Down to Business *britischer Rechtschreibung und Terminologie. Zu Gunsten der Lesbarkeit wurde in der Grammatik und im Wortschatz die maskuline Form stellvertretend für beide Geschlechter aufgeführt.*

Neben dem Lehrbuch begleiten Sie drei CDs durch die ausführlichen Hörtexte der einzelnen Units.
Die Hörtexte zu den Übungen sind im Arbeitsbuch durch kleine schwarze Audio-Symbole gekennzeichnet. Ein blaues Symbol kennzeichnet Hörtexte, die ausschließlich dem Training des Hörverständnisses dienen, darunter auch die umfangreiche Listening Review *mit zahlreichen zusätzlichen Hörtexten.*
Die CD-Haltepunkte werden jeweils durch Nummern neben den Symbolen angegeben. Im Anhang finden Sie die schriftliche Wiedergabe aller Hörtexte sowie ein alphabetisches Wortschatzverzeichnis.

Wir wünschen viel Spaß und gutes Gelingen!

Barry Baddock
Susie Vrobel

ACKNOWLEDGEMENTS/*QUELLENVERZEICHNIS*

Die Autoren und der Verlag danken den folgenden Personen und Organisationen für die Erlaubnis, ihre Materialen in diesem Buch benutzen zu dürfen:

Umschlagfoto: Isabella Valdivieso, München; heller & partner, München

Seite 52:	Gérard Mermet *(aus: Die Europäer: Länder, Leidenschaften. Aus dem Französischen übersetzt von Fritz Glunk © für die deutschsprachige Ausgabe: 1993 Deutscher Taschenbuch Verlag, München).*
Seite 56-57:	Cairnhill Hotel, Tianjin, China.
Seite 78:	Topeka Capitol-Journal, USA.
Seite 101:	Mobile Telecom Plc, UK.
Seite 120:	Lufthansa Fluggesellschaft
Seite 132:	Air UK and Anglia Railways, UK
Seite 166:	K.W. Brock Directories, USA and Tele-Pages Directories Ltd, UK.

Die Bilder auf den Seiten 7, 23, 57, 73, 89, 121, 137, 155 stammen aus dem Archiv des Hueber Verlags.

Alle anderen Texte und Illustrationen wurden von Susie Vrobel hergestellt oder sind Teil ihrer privaten Sammlung.

ABBREVIATIONS USED IN THIS BOOK/ *IN DIESEM BUCH VERWENDETE ABKÜRZUNGEN*

eg	exempli gratia; for example
etc	et cetera; and so on
sb	somebody
sth	something
AE	American English
BE	British English
UK	United Kingdom
US	United States
etw	*etwas*
jdn/jdm	*jemanden/m*
usw.	*und so weiter*
z.B.	*zum Beispiel*

Table of Contents/*Inhaltsverzeichnis*

Appendix/*Anhang*

Meeting a Potential Customer or Partner

Getting Started

You are Lars Siebert. You are representing your company – Siebert Packaging GmbH – at the International Trades Fair in Brussels. You have arranged to meet possible agents who might market your company's goods in Europe.

This is your schedule for the Fair.

Sie sind Lars Siebert und repräsentieren Ihre Firma – Siebert Packaging GmbH – auf der Internationalen Handelsmesse in Brüssel. Sie haben sich mit potenziellen Vertretern verabredet, die die Waren Ihrer Firma vertreiben könnten.

Hier ist Ihr Terminplan für die Messe.

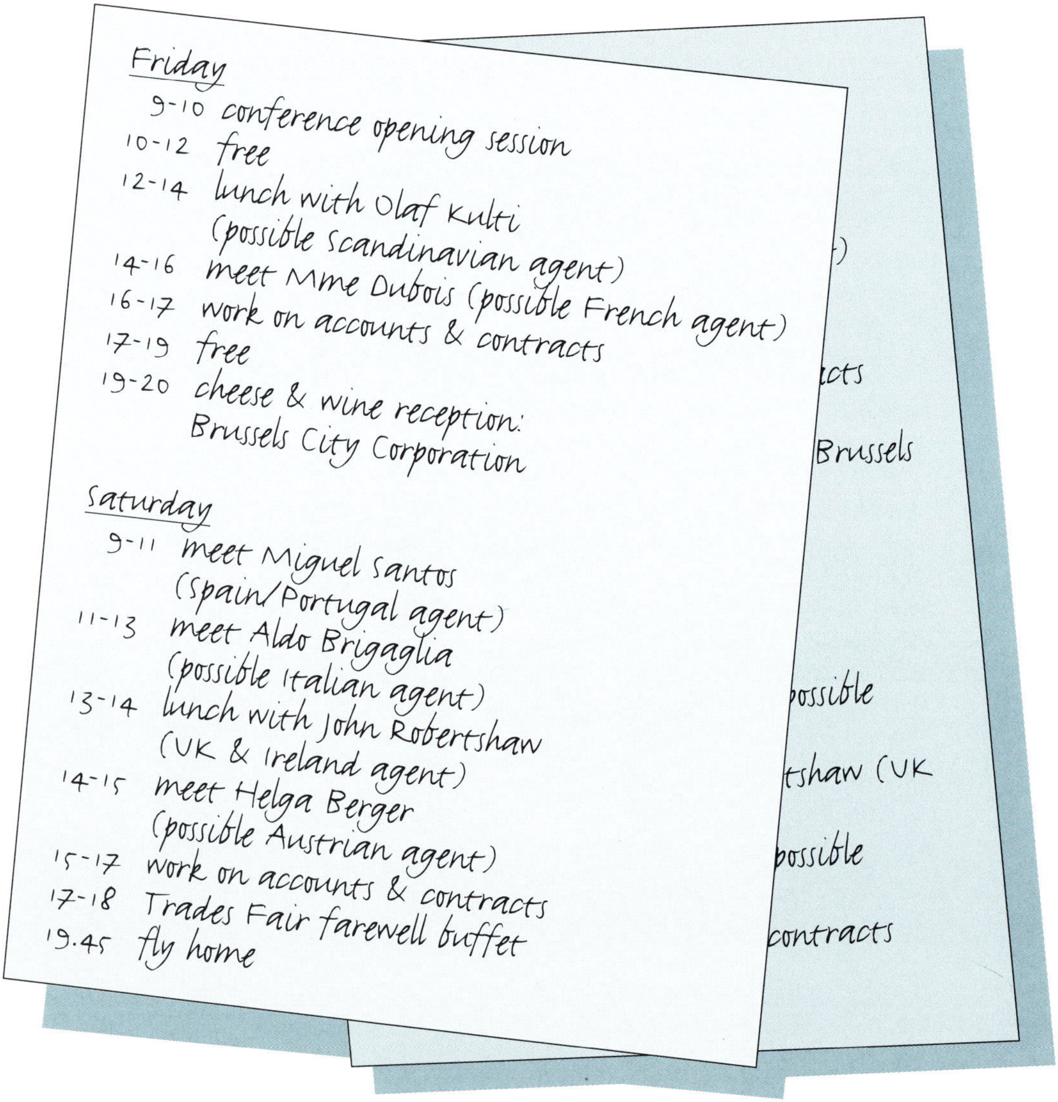

Friday
9-10 conference opening session
10-12 free
12-14 lunch with Olaf Kulti (possible Scandinavian agent)
14-16 meet Mme Dubois (possible French agent)
16-17 work on accounts & contracts
17-19 free
19-20 cheese & wine reception: Brussels City Corporation

Saturday
9-11 meet Miguel Santos (Spain/Portugal agent)
11-13 meet Aldo Brigaglia (possible Italian agent)
13-14 lunch with John Robertshaw (UK & Ireland agent)
14-15 meet Helga Berger (possible Austrian agent)
15-17 work on accounts & contracts
17-18 Trades Fair farewell buffet
19.45 fly home

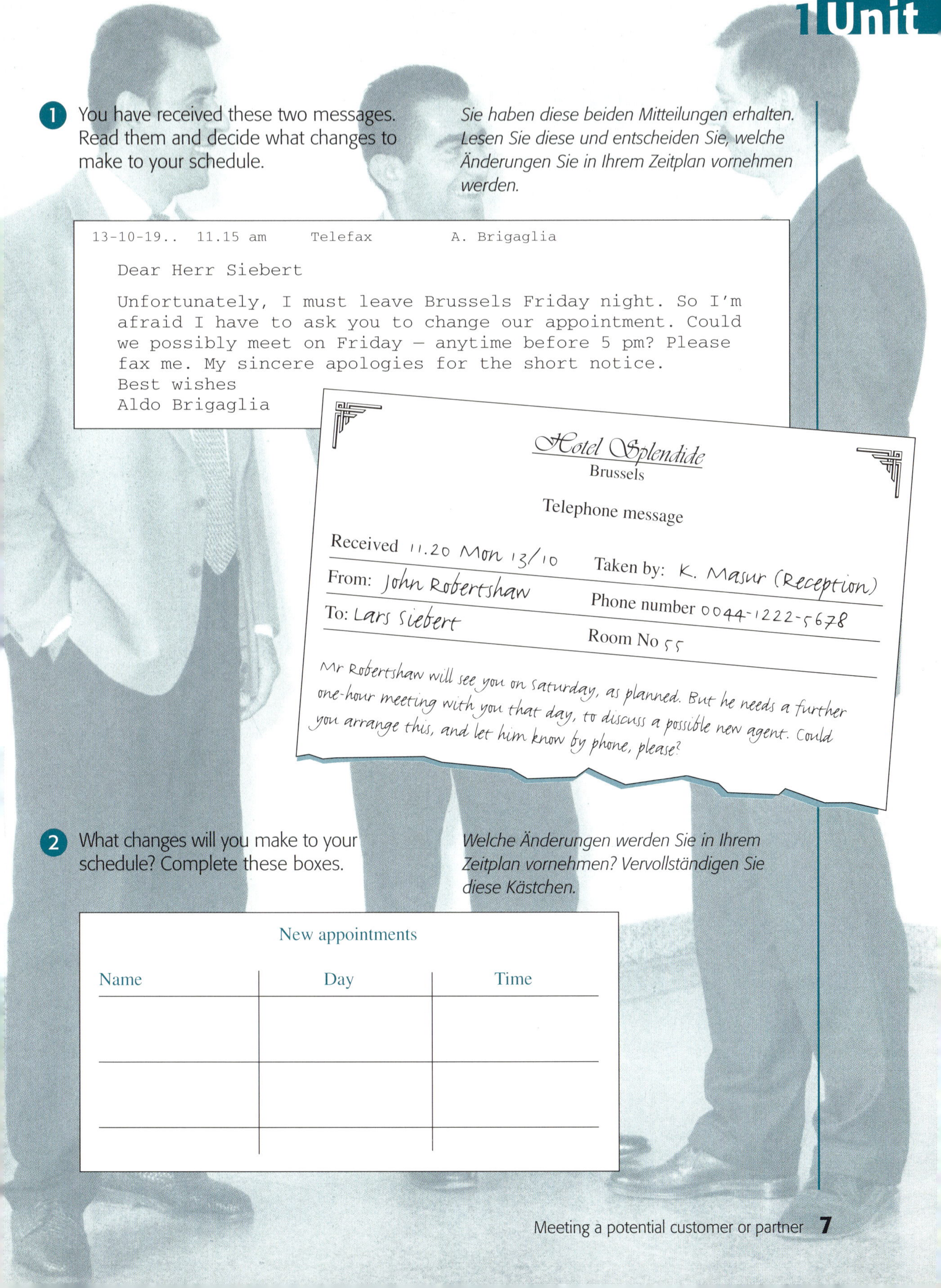

1 You have received these two messages. Read them and decide what changes to make to your schedule.

Sie haben diese beiden Mitteilungen erhalten. Lesen Sie diese und entscheiden Sie, welche Änderungen Sie in Ihrem Zeitplan vornehmen werden.

13-10-19.. 11.15 am Telefax A. Brigaglia

Dear Herr Siebert

Unfortunately, I must leave Brussels Friday night. So I'm afraid I have to ask you to change our appointment. Could we possibly meet on Friday – anytime before 5 pm? Please fax me. My sincere apologies for the short notice.
Best wishes
Aldo Brigaglia

Hotel Splendide
Brussels

Telephone message

Received 11.20 Mon 13/10 Taken by: K. Masur (Reception)
From: John Robertshaw Phone number 0044-1222-5678
To: Lars Siebert Room No 55

Mr Robertshaw will see you on Saturday, as planned. But he needs a further one-hour meeting with you that day, to discuss a possible new agent. Could you arrange this, and let him know by phone, please?

2 What changes will you make to your schedule? Complete these boxes.

Welche Änderungen werden Sie in Ihrem Zeitplan vornehmen? Vervollständigen Sie diese Kästchen.

New appointments

Name	Day	Time

Listen & Repeat

Listening Text 1/1

1.1
1.2

Lars Siebert welcomes Aldo Brigaglia at their meeting in Brussels. You will hear their conversation twice – the second time with pauses, so that you can repeat Lars Siebert's parts of the conversation.

Auf der Besprechung in Brüssel heißt Lars Siebert Aldo Brigaglia willkommen. Sie werden das Gespräch zweimal hören – beim zweiten Durchgang mit Pausen, damit Sie Lars Sieberts Dialogteil nachsprechen können.

"Would you like a cup of coffee before we begin?"

Useful Expressions

Welcoming	***Jemanden willkommen heißen***
You must be (Mr/Ms ...)	*Sie müssen (Mr/Mrs ...) sein.*
Nice to meet you.	*Schön, Sie zu treffen./Freut mich.*
Glad you could come.	*Es freut mich, dass Sie kommen konnten.*
Did you have a good trip?	*Hatten Sie eine gute Reise?*
Please take a seat.	*Bitte nehmen Sie Platz.*
Would you like a cup of coffee before we begin?	*Möchten Sie eine Tasse Kaffee, bevor wir anfangen?*
Make yourself at home.	*Fühlen Sie sich wie zu Hause.*

Listening Text 1/2

1.3
1.4

Siebert introduces Brigaglia to other members of the company staff. Again, you will hear their conversation twice – the second time with pauses, so you can repeat Lars Siebert's part of the conversation.

Siebert stellt Brigaglia den anderen Mitarbeitern vor. Sie werden das Gespräch zweimal hören – beim zweiten Durchgang mit Pausen, damit Sie Lars Sieberts Dialogteil nachsprechen können.

Useful Expressions

Introducing	***(Sich und andere) vorstellen***
I'd like you to meet ...	*Ich möchte Sie mit ... bekannt machen.*
This is ... from ...	*Das ist ... aus ...*
May I introduce ... , who handles our marketing?	*Darf ich (Ihnen) ... vorstellen, der sich um unseren Vertrieb kümmert?*
You know ... , don't you? You met in ...	*Sie kennen ... , nicht wahr? Sie haben sich in ... kennen gelernt.*

Listening Text 1/3

1.5

Lars Siebert talks about Siebert Packaging GmbH to Aldo Brigaglia. As you listen, follow his talk with the help of these notes he has made.

Lars Siebert spricht mit Aldo Brigaglia über Siebert Packaging GmbH. Verfolgen Sie den Dialog während des Zuhörens anhand dieser von ihm gemachten Notizen.

SIEBERT PACKAGING GMBH

Size
- small company in industrial packaging field
- 55 skilled + semi-skilled production workers
- 10-15 full- + part-time office staff (depending on number of orders)

Structure
3 sections, all located at Dortmund industrial site:

1. Production (includes Quality Control).
Leader: Lars Siebert.
Comments: Biggest section. High investments made to bring equipment up to state-of-the-art.

2. Sales and Marketing.
Leaders: Harold Preetz/Susie Graf.
Comments: none

3. Storage, Despatch & Transport.
Leader: Kai Vogt.
Comments: Moved to larger premises in August, due to increase in orders.

Administration
- Section leaders: policy meeting each week — make all decisions about planning & finance collectively.
- Progress report (from Lars Siebert) to Company Directors each month.

Marketing strategy
- Past 18 months: specialised in packaging for fragile goods, eg electrical equipment, glassware. Now the most profitable part of Siebert's business.
- Until last year, contracts in Germany only. Now exporting to UK & Ireland too.
- Siebert's European marketing drive — possible influx of new orders by late August/early Sept.

Useful Expressions

Talking about the company	*Über die Firma sprechen*
Size	***Größe***
Let me give you a run-down on ...	*Das Wichtigste über ... in Kürze.*
We're a small/medium-sized/large company.	*Wir sind eine kleine/mittlere/große Firma.*
We employ ... semi-skilled/skilled production workers.	*Wir haben ... angelernte/ausgebildete Arbeitskräfte in der Produktion.*
We have ... full-/part-time office staff.	*Wir haben ... Vollzeit-/Teilzeit-Bürokräfte.*
Structure	***Struktur***
The company has ... sections.	*Die Firma hat ... Abteilungen.*
The smallest/biggest is the ... section, which includes ...	*Die kleinste/größte ist die ... Abteilung, die ... einschließt.*
That's Frau ... 's part of the operation.	*Für diesen Geschäftsbereich ist Frau ... verantwortlich.*
Herr ... is in charge of ...	*Herr ... leitet ...*
Administration	***Verwaltung***
All decisions about ... are made by ...	*Alle Entscheidungen über ... werden von ... getroffen.*
We have a policy meeting every week.	*Wir haben jede Woche eine Grundsatz-/Strategiebesprechung.*
I hand in a progress report to ... each month.	*Ich reiche ... jeden Monat einen Zwischenbericht/Fortschrittsbericht ein.*
Marketing strategy	***Vertriebsstrategie***
We've specialised in ...	*Wir haben uns auf ... spezialisiert.*
This is the least/most profitable part of our business.	*Dies ist der am wenigsten profitable/profitabelste Teil unseres Geschäfts.*
Until last year ... But now ...	*Bis letztes Jahr ... Aber jetzt ...*
We are exporting to customers in ...	*Wir exportieren an Kunden in ...*

Language Study

Four tenses used in business

SIMPLE PRESENT
bezieht sich auf eine Gewohnheit, ein regelmäßiges Verfahren oder eine gängige Praxis.

He hands in a progress report to the company directors each month.
When we receive a complaint, we deal with it immediately.

In der Geschäftssprache wird es auch dazu benutzt, sich auf wirtschaftliche Prinzipien und Regeln zu beziehen.

When interest rates fall, businesses borrow more and invest more.
Prices depend on demand and supply.

"When we receive a complaint, we deal with it immediately."

PRESENT CONTINUOUS
bezieht sich auf zeitlich begrenzte Prozesse (oder solche, die als zeitlich begrenzt behandelt werden, da man nicht sicher sein kann, ob sie langfristig oder unbefristet sind).

Signor Brigaglia is considering acting as our agent in Italy.
Now we are exporting to customers in the UK and Ireland too.

Diese Zeitform eignet sich gut zur Beschreibung wirtschaftlicher Trends oder geschäftlicher Aktivitäten von kurzer Dauer.

We're borrowing heavily at the moment, but the new computers are almost paid for.
Lawsons are working at only 80% of capacity, but business is sure to pick up in the spring.

SIMPLE PAST

bezieht sich auf einen bereits beendeten Prozess und wird oft mit einer auf die Vergangenheit verweisenden Redewendung wie in August *oder* until last year *verwendet.*

They moved into larger premises in August.
Until last year, all our contracts were with German companies.

In der Geschäftssprache werden auf die Vergangenheit verweisende Redewendungen (wie die folgenden) normalerweise mit dem simple past *kombiniert.*

When we started the company	Three years ago
In 1996	After we sent the order
Soon after the committee's report	In the first quarter
Last May	On receiving your letter

PRESENT PERFECT

wird benutzt, um einen Prozess zu beschreiben, der in der Vergangenheit begann und noch in der Gegenwart andauert. Es wird oft mit auf die Vergangenheit verweisenden Redewendungen wie for the last 18 months *oder* since 1965 *kombiniert.*

For the last 18 months, we've specialised in packaging for fragile goods.

"Since 1965, the company has hired only bilingual sales staff."

Das present perfect *wird verwendet, wenn man nicht betonen will, wann, sondern dass etwas passiert ist. Es wird auch zum Verweisen auf einen bereits vergangenen Prozess, dessen Wirkung noch in der Gegenwart spürbar ist, verwendet.*

We have invested a lot there (= then), so all the equipment is state-of-the-art. (= now)

Hier zwei Beispiele dieser „resultativen" Bedeutung des present perfect *in der Geschäftssprache:*

Chile has lifted her import restrictions on video cassettes, so we can start selling there.
Mr Watson has faxed us, so we know about the problem.

Exercise

Choose the correct tenses.

Wählen Sie die passenden Zeitformen.

1. The contract (expire) ___________ at the end of last year.
2. The Christmas trade (always bring) ___________ a boost in sales.
3. Production costs (rise) ___________ , but we won't have to raise prices before April.
4. We (take part) ___________ in a lot of trade fairs, so we know how valuable they are.
5. I (hear from) ___________ Waters last week – they've sold off part of the company.
6. We (hire) ___________ extra part-time staff every summer.
7. We (appoint) ___________ five new sales staff since we expanded in January.
8. We (now build) ___________ a new extension to the plant.

Typical mistakes

Each of these sentences contains a typical mistake made by a German speaker. Can you correct them?

Jeder dieser Sätze enthält einen von einem deutschen Sprecher gemachten Fehler. Können Sie die Fehler korrigieren?

1. The bank has agreed to borrow us DM10,000.
2. It was eventually a mistake to sign the contract so quickly.
3. The news are good – all the consignments have arrived on time.
4. What's your meaning about the Schubert proposal?
5. The most people aren't interested in this brand.
6. Could we discuss about this order from Harvey & Black?
7. Perhaps you could say us something about next season's designs.
8. Herr Reinhardt can't come just at the moment – he's at the telephone.
9. How do you call *Lagerung* in English?
10. What means "premises" in this contract?

Word bank

Talking about the company	***Über die Firma sprechen***
administration	*Verwaltung*
after-sales service	*Kundendienst*
board of directors	*Vorstand*
chairperson	*Vorsitzender*
contract	*Vertrag*
equipment	*Ausrüstung/Einrichtung*

finance	*Finanzierung*
financial director	*Leiter der Finanzabteilung*
full-time	*Vollzeit*
goods (plural only)	*Ware*
industrial site	*Industriegelände*
job-sharing	*Arbeitsteilung*
management	*Unternehmensleitung*
manufacture	*herstellen*
manufacturing	*Herstellung*
marketing	*Vertrieb*
office premises	*Büroräume*
part-time	*Teilzeit*
personnel manager	*Leiter der Personalabteilung*
planning	*Planung*
policy meeting	*Strategie-/Grundsatzbesprechung*
premises	*Örtlichkeit, Räumlichkeit, Grundstück*
production manager	*Leiter der Fertigung*
progress report	*Fortschritts-/Zwischenbericht*
quality control	*Qualitätskontrolle*
sales	*Verkauf*
semi-skilled	*angelernt*
service	*Dienstleistung*
skilled	*ausgebildet*
specialise in	*sich spezialisieren auf*
state-of-the-art	*technisch auf dem neusten Stand*
storage	*Lagerung*

Down to Business

1.6

Listening Text 1/4

You will hear an office conversation at Rayner Detergents plc in Glasgow. Joyce and Brian are discussing this Internet advert.

Sie werden ein Gespräch im Büro von Rayner Detergents plc in Glasgow hören. Joyce und Brian diskutieren über diese Anzeige im Internet.

1 Test your understanding.

Prüfen Sie Ihr Leseverständnis.

a Rayner Detergents have been looking for a partner company in China. True or False?

b Brian has known about Guangzhou Lam Soon for some time. True or False?

c The Chinese company contacted Rayner Detergents at once. True or False?

d The two companies will fax each other. True or False?

2 Joyce and Brian used these expressions. Match them with their German meanings.

Joyce und Brian haben diese Ausdrücke benutzt. Kombinieren Sie diese mit den entsprechenden deutschen Ausdrücken.

a to spot sth
b to put out feelers
c to come up with sth
d to be on the ball
e to go down well with sb

(1) etw vorschlagen/einbringen
(2) die Fühler ausstrecken
(3) am Ball sein
(4) von jdm begrüßt werden
(5) etw. entdecken

3 Expand these notes into full sentences, in order to write the fax which Brian sent to Guangzhou Lam Soon.

Erweitern Sie folgende Notizen in ganze Sätze, um das Fax, das Brian an Guangzhou Lam Soon geschickt hat, zu schreiben.

Telefax

To Guangzhou Lam Soon Homecare Products Co, Ltd
Dear Manager

Having seen - advert - Internet, we - like to know - would be interested - partnership with us. Allow us - introduce ourselves.

We - small, relatively new - producing and distributing chemical detergents. Below the Management level - 68 staff - 40 skilled production workers.

More notes on the following page.

Weitere Notizen auf der nächsten Seite.

We specialize - detergents for use on industrial machinery. We - state-of-the-art equipment - this. The export of industrial detergents - most profitable part - our business - currently exporting - customers - six European countries - Japan. We - very keen - market our goods - China too.

Do - wish - market your goods - Europe? If you see any possibility of a partnership, please send us similar information about your company.

With best wishes
Brian Cull

Listening Text 1/5

1.7

Brian calls Mr Ren Yunping, and gets through to his answerphone.

Brian ruft Herrn Ren Yunping an und wird mit dessen Anrufbeantworter verbunden.

4 Here is the message Brian leaves on the answerphone. Using the diagram below, complete Brian's message.

Hier ist die Nachricht, die Brian auf den Anrufbeantworter spricht. Ergänzen Sie Brians Nachricht anhand des unten abgebildeten Diagramms.

Brian's message:
Mr Ren Yunping? This is _______ of _______ speaking. Sorry I haven't got through to you personally. I'm calling to give you some information about our company structure. Well, apart from the Management, the company has _______ sections. The biggest is _______ , which includes _______. That's _______ 's part of the operation and it has _______ skilled staff. The smallest section is _______ , which has just _______ staff. _______ in charge of that. Finally, there's _______. The Head of that section is _______. He's _______ 18 staff there. OK, that's all for now. You've got our phone and fax number. And we're very much looking forward to hearing from you again.

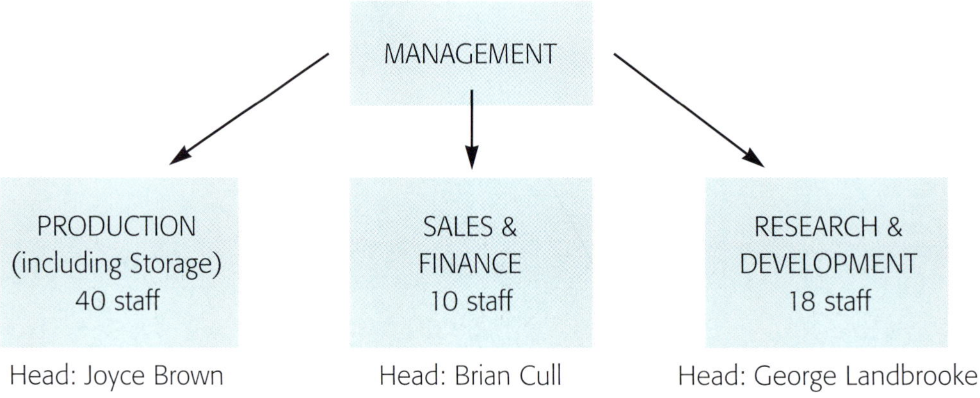

Dealing with Visual Info

Sales graphs

The two companies – Rayner Detergents and Guangzhou Lam Soon – have sent each other their sales graphs for the last three months.

Die zwei Firmen – Rayner Detergents und Guangzhou Lam Soon – haben sich gegenseitig ihre Absatzdiagramme der letzten drei Monate zugeschickt.

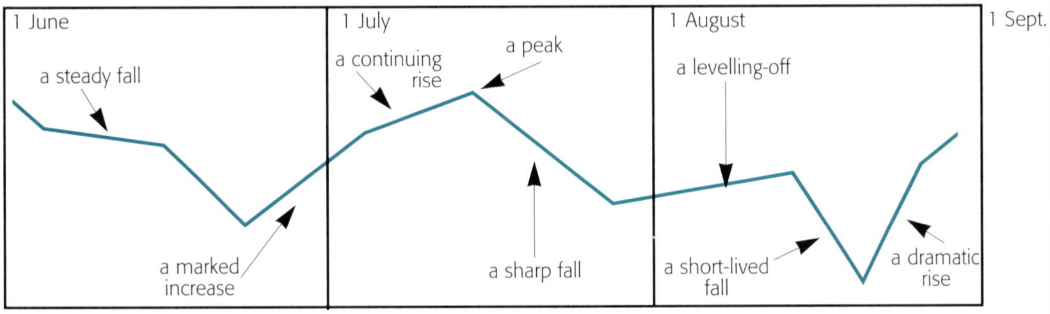

Sales Graph A (Rayner Detergents)

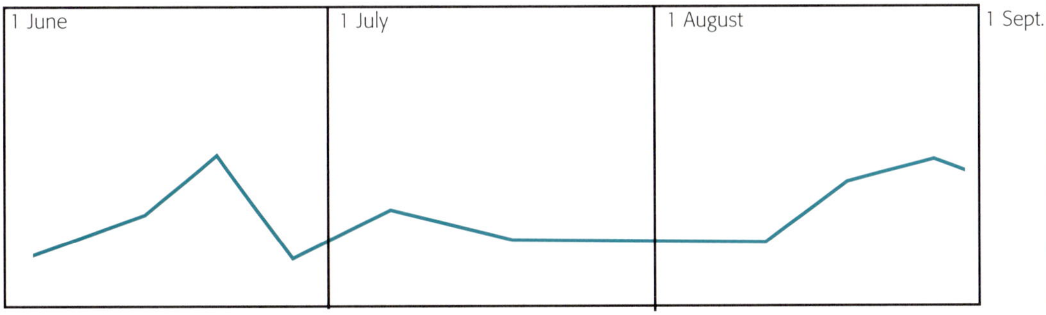

Sales Graph B (Guangzhou Lam Soon)

1 Look at this report on Sales Graph A.

Schauen Sie sich diesen Bericht über das Absatzdiagramm A an.

1.8

Sales Graph A:

Sales fell steadily during June, but there was a marked increase late in the month. They continued to rise in July, reaching their peak around mid-July. Then sales fell sharply, before levelling off in early August. Though there was another fall in sales in mid-August, this was short-lived. Towards the end of the month, they were rising dramatically.

2 Now complete this report on Sales Graph B. Use the expressions given.

Vervollständigen Sie nun diesen Bericht über das Absatzdiagramm B. Benutzen Sie die aufgeführten Ausdrücke.

1.8

> Sales Graph B:
>
> Sales ________________ (1) for most of June, before ________________ (2) late in the month. There was a short ________________ (3) in early July, then sales ________________ (4) until early August. Following this, they ________________ (5) again, and ________________ (6) in late August. But before the month ended, they ________________ (7) again.
>
> (a) levelled off (b) falling sharply (c) began to rise (d) climbed steadily
> (e) reached their peak (f) sharp increase (g) began to decline

The British-American Difference

This notice contains a number of American English expressions which can be substituted by the British English ones you can see at its side

Diese Mitteilung enthält eine Reihe von Ausdrücken in amerikanischem Englisch, die durch die britischen Ausdrücke ersetzt werden können, die daneben aufgeführt sind.

BULLETIN BOARD

Labor Union Notice

CCL has announced it is going to ax a fifth of its workforce within the next two years.

We strongly oppose this plan and call for a general meeting at 19.00 hr, Friday, July 11 to discuss further steps.

We regret the short notice but strongly encourage those members whose vacation starts on July 12th also to join the meeting.

Further topics on the agenda will include the future of the company's affirmative action program and the envisaged raise in social insurance contributions.

W. Kelsterman
Speaker

- equal opportunities programme
- Trade Union
- cut
- notice board
- rise
- holiday
- National Insurance

Last but not Least

Imagine that you're on a business visit to Britain. Work through this test, following the directions and noting down the points you score.

Stellen Sie sich vor, Sie sind auf einer Geschäftsreise in Großbritannien. Arbeiten Sie sich durch diesen Test, indem Sie den Angaben folgen und Ihre erreichte Punktzahl notieren.

1 You arranged to meet one of your British customers – Mr Lyle – at his company office. By phone, he suggested you meet at "at half-nine". When will you arrive?

Sie verabredeten eine Besprechung mit einem Ihrer britischen Kunden, Mr Lyle, in seinem Firmenbüro. Am Telefon schlug er vor, Sie „at half-nine" zu treffen. Wann treffen Sie ein?

(a) 8.30 am → Go to 8.
(b) 4.30 pm → Go to 21.
(c) 9.30 am → Go to 19.

2 Why are you reading <u>this</u>? Go to the number after your chosen answer!

Warum lesen Sie <u>diesen</u> Satz? Gehen Sie zu der Nummer, die der von Ihnen gewählten Antwort zugeordnet ist!

3 Early in the meeting, Mr Lyle says, "There's no need for formalities here – call me Harry". What do you do?

Kurz nach dem Beginn der Besprechung sagt Mr Lyle: „Wir können auf Formalitäten verzichten – nennen Sie mich Harry". Was tun Sie?

(a) Tell him your first name ("Fine. Call me ... "). → Go to 6.
(b) Say, "I'd really prefer to call you Mr Lyle for now". → Go to 4.
(c) Thank him. → Go to 13.

4 Not a good tactic. Lose 3 points. → Go back to 3.

5 No one uses this expression at the dinner table! Lose 4 points. Try again. → Go back to 24.

6 Yes, the best tactic here. Win 2 points. → Go to 11.

7 When you arrive, Mr Lyle greets you with "How do you do?" How will you reply?

Als Sie eintreffen, begrüßt Sie Mr Lyle mit „How do you do?" Was erwidern Sie?

(a) "How do you do?" → Go to 20.
(b) "How do I do what?" → Go to 9.
(c) "I'm fine, thank you. And you?" → Go to 25.

8 No – "at half-nine" doesn't mean *um halb neun!* Lose 5 points. → Go back to 1.

9 A horrible reply! Lose 5 points. → Go back to 7.

10 A bad mistake! Lose 5 points. Try again. → Go back to 14.

11 The meeting is followed by lunch with Mr Lyle at a neighbouring restaurant. One of Mr Lyle's colleagues is waiting there. What do you do?

Auf die Besprechung folgt ein Mittagessen mit Mr Lyle in einem Restaurant. Einer von Mr Lyles Kollegen wartet dort. Was tun Sie?

(a) Introduce yourself and shake hands. → Go to 15.
(b) Wait until (s)he is introduced to you. → Go to 18.
(c) Say: "Hello – and who are you, may I ask?" → Go to 23.

12 Terrible! Lose 5 points. → Go back to 24.

13 Is that all? Lose 3 points! → Go back to 3.

14 Before the meeting begins, Mr Lyle tells you: "The toilet's down the hallway on the right." What do you do?

Bevor die Besprechung beginnt, sagt Ihnen Mr Lyle: „The toilet's down the hallway on the right." *Was tun Sie?*

(a) Go immediately to examine it. → Go to 16
(b) Say: "OK. Thank you" and remain sitting. → Go to 22
(c) Say: "It's OK. I used the one at the hotel." → Go to 10

15 Not a bad tactic – but not the best one. Lose 1 point. Try again. → Go back to 11.

16 A faux-pas! Lose 3 points. Try again. → Go back to 14.

17 Good. Win 2 points. → Go to 26.

18 Good. Win 2 points. → Go to 24.

19 Yes – "half-nine" means "half past nine".
Win 2 points. → Go to 7.

20 Correct! "How do you do?" is simply a conventional greeting. Win 2 points. → Go to 14.

21 Terrible! Lose 5 points. Try again. → Go back to 1.

22 Correct. Mr Lyle was simply informing you.
Win 2 points. → Go to 3.

23 Not very discreet. Lose 2 points.
Try again. → Go back to 11.

24 The meal is on the table. You are about to eat. What do you say?

Das Essen ist auf dem Tisch. Sie werden gleich beginnen. Was sagen Sie?

(a) "Good appetite!" → Go to 5.
(b) "Dig in!" → Go to 12.
(c) "Enjoy your meal!" → Go to 17.

25 Mr Lyle was not asking about your health.
Lose 3 points. → Go back to 7.

26 End of test. How many points did you score?
Turn to the Answer Key.

Negotiating a Deal

Getting Started

Horn & Rüffin GmbH want to host a Presentation Day in Manchester to show and describe their products to potential customers there. They have seen this advertisement.

Die Horn & Rüffin GmbH möchte in Manchester einen Präsentationstag veranstalten, um dort ihre Produkte potenziellen Kunden vorzuführen und zu beschreiben. Sie haben diese Anzeige gesehen.

Let us host your conference!
Manchester Court Hotel

Full conference facilities
Bar & first-class restaurant open all day
Conference room (seating capacity 200)
Audio-visual, fax & photocopy service
Air-conditioning in all rooms
Six spacious meeting rooms

20% discount for groups of 50 or more
Call Bob Wyatt on 0161-834-1582, or Fax 0161-834-2448.

After getting further information from Manchester Court Hotel, Horn & Rüffin GmbH write this letter. Arrange the sentence parts in Lists A and B to form complete sentences.

Nachdem die Horn & Rüffin GmbH weitere Informationen vom Manchester Court Hotel erhalten hat, wird folgender Brief verfasst. Ordnen Sie die Satzteile in den Listen A und B so an, dass vollständige Sätze entstehen.

Dear Mr Wyatt

Thank you for your fax, outlining your conference terms and conditions.
We note that you allow a discount for groups of 50 or more. We are expecting 35 participants for our Presentation Day, and would need one meeting room. In view of this, we hope that you will be interested in the following proposal.

List A

1. We would be happy to sign a contract with you
2. Provided you reduced the fee,
3. Should you agree to this,
4. If you find this proposal attractive,
5. Unfortunately – since time is very short – I must add that, unless we receive your offer within two weeks,

List B

a we would also advertise your prices to the participants, who might book rooms.
b we will have to look for facilities elsewhere.
c we would also book four single rooms at your hotel for one night for our team members.
d on condition that you charge for one room and service, and not the full conference fee.
e we would very much like to receive a reduced offer from you.

Yours sincerely
pp Horn & Rüffin

Listen & Repeat

Listening Text 2/1

1.9
1.10

Herr Horn is talking to Mr Everett, one of the British visitors he has met on Presentation Day. You will hear their conversation twice – the second time with pauses, so that you can repeat Horn's parts of the conversation.

Herr Horn spricht mit Mr Everett, einem der britischen Besucher, die er am Präsentationstag kennen gelernt hat. Sie werden das Gespräch zweimal hören – das zweite Mal als Pausenversion, in der Sie Horns Dialogteil nachsprechen können.

Useful Expressions

Negotiating a deal — ***Ein Geschäft aushandeln***

Putting questions	***Fragen stellen***
Can we agree on that?	*Können wir uns darauf einigen?*
Can you keep that offer open for ... months?	*Können Sie das Angebot ... Monate aufrechterhalten?*
Would you like to place a trial order?	*Möchten Sie eine Probebestellung aufgeben?*
Couldn't you persuade your manager to ... ?	*Könnten Sie Ihren Manager nicht dazu überreden, dass ...?*
What action should be taken now?	*Wie sollten wir jetzt vorgehen?*
Could you give me the gist of it?	*Könnten Sie mir das Wesentliche erläutern?*

Proposing next steps	***Die nächsten Schritte vorschlagen***
Let's first look at ...	*Lassen Sie uns zunächst ... anschauen.*
If you ordered ... , we could ...	*Würden Sie ... bestellen, könnten wir ...*
If you give us ... , we'll ...	*Wenn Sie uns ... geben, werden wir ...*
We'd have to insist on ...	*Wir müssten darauf bestehen, dass ...*
I'd be very glad if you'd ...	*Ich wäre sehr froh, wenn Sie ... würden.*
We'll give you first option.	*Wir geben Ihnen das Vorkaufsrecht.*
Let's look into the likely costs.	*Lassen Sie uns die voraussichtlichen Kosten prüfen.*
How about ... ?	*Wie wäre es mit ... ?*

Coming to terms	***Sich einigen***
Perhaps we could come to some arrangement.	*Vielleicht könnten wir zu einer Übereinkunft kommen.*
We can agree to that.	*Wir können dem zustimmen.*
I'm willing to meet you halfway on this.	*Ich bin bereit, Ihnen auf halbem Wege entgegenzukommen.*
We are working to a tight profit margin, you know.	*Wissen Sie, wir arbeiten mit einer engen Gewinnspanne.*
Under the agreement, you'll have to ...	*Nach unserer Vereinbarung müssen Sie ...*
It's a pleasure to do business with you.	*Es ist ein Vergnügen, mit Ihnen Geschäfte zu machen.*
The pleasure's (entirely) mine.	*Das Vergnügen ist (ganz) auf meiner Seite.*
I'm glad we see eye-to-eye on this.	*Ich freue mich, dass wir der gleichen Ansicht sind.*
Thanks for your co-operation.	*Vielen Dank für Ihre Unterstützung.*

Inviting to a drink/dinner	***Zu einem Drink/zum Essen einladen***
Why don't we meet for a drink at the bar?	*Treffen wir uns doch zu einem Drink an der Bar?*
Good idea. How about 7.30?	*Gute Idee. Wie wäre es mit 7.30 Uhr?*
Right. See you there.	*In Ordnung. Wir treffen uns dort.*
May I invite you to meet me for lunch?	*Darf ich Sie zum Mittagessen einladen?*
Tomorrow maybe? Wednesday then?	*Vielleicht morgen? Dann am Mittwoch?*
Be my guest.	*Ich lade Sie ein.*

How about the El Paso Steakhouse at, say, ... ?	*Wie wäre es mit dem El Paso Steakhouse, sagen wir um ... ?*
I suggest we meet in the lounge at ...	*Ich schlage vor, wir treffen uns um ... im Foyer.*
Would 1.30 be convenient for you?	*Passt Ihnen 1.30 Uhr?*
I'll reserve a table.	*Ich reserviere einen Tisch.*

"Why don't we meet for a drink at the bar?"

Language Study

1. MAKING PREDICTIONS

Expressing possibility
It may/might be just ten units.
There is a/some possibility of ... -ing/ that ... will ...

Möglichkeit ausdrücken
It's possible that ...
Possibly ...

Expressing probability
We'll probably order five today.
There's a strong possibility that ...

Wahrscheinlichkeit ausdrücken
We may well make a follow-up order.
It is likely to be a large order.

Expressing improbability
It's (highly) improbable that we can do that.
There's (very) little chance/likelihood (that ...)

Unwahrscheinlichkeit ausdrücken
They're (highly) unlikely to accept.

Expressing certainty
We're bound/sure to get a reply soon.
You'll definitely/certainly get a 5% discount.

Gewissheit ausdrücken
I'm certain/sure we'll find ...

2. CONDITIONAL SENTENCES: TYPES I AND II

Im Geschäftsleben werden if-*Sätze oft benutzt, um über zukünftige Möglichkeiten zu sprechen.*
If you give us that follow-up order by October, we will allow the 5% discount.
If they proved to be OK, we would want more in the New Year.
Die zwei obigen Beispiele repräsentieren zwei Typen von if-*Sätzen.*

TYPE I: (Real possibility – *erfüllbare Möglichkeit)*
If you give us that follow-up order by October, we will allow the 5% discount.
(simple present) (future)
Die if-*Bedingung (= die Möglichkeit, bis Oktober eine Nachbestellung bei uns aufzugeben) ist erfüllbar.*

TYPE II: (Remote possibility – *entfernte Möglichkeit)*
If they proved to be OK, we would want more in the New Year.
(simple past) (would or could)
Hier ist unwahrscheinlicher, dass die if-*Bedingung erfüllt wird.*

In allen Fällen kann der if-*Satzteil am Anfang oder am Ende des Satzes stehen.*

If you ordered five now, we could allow that discount. *(mit Komma)*

We could allow that discount if you ordered five now. *(ohne Komma)*

Wenn Sie mehrere Vorschläge machen, können Sie, um den wiederholten Gebrauch von if *zu vermeiden,* should *benutzen.*

Should you agree to this, we would also advertise your hotel facilities. (= If you agree ...)

Provided (that) *und* on condition that *sind gewichtiger. Sie stellen eine Bedingung, die der Hörer oder Leser akzeptieren muss.*

Provided you reduced your full conference fee, we would also book four single rooms at your hotel.

We would be happy to sign a contract with you on condition that you charged for one room.

Unless *wird benutzt, um eine negative Bedingung auszudrücken.*

Unless we receive your offer within two weeks, we will have to look for facilities elsewhere. (= If we do not receive ...)

Exercises

1.9

1 Listen to Listening Text 2/1 again. Which category do the following sentences fit into?

Hören Sie noch einmal Hörtext 2/1. In welche Kategorie passen die folgenden Sätze?

certain *(gewiss)*
only possible *(nur möglich)*

probable *(wahrscheinlich)*
improbable *(unwahrscheinlich)*

1. Mr Everett will order five tools today.
2. He'll make a follow-up order for five more tools later.
3. He'll get a 5% discount for his first order.
4. His manager will agree to order all ten tools right away.
5. Mr Everett's company will want some abrasives too.
6. They'll hold off (= delay) their decision about the abrasives till the six-monthly review.
7. They'll order ten abrasives units to start with.

2 In each of the sentence pairs 1-4 below, one sentence should be completed.

In jedem der vier Satzpaare soll jeweils ein Satz vervollständigt werden.

a = real possibility

b = remote possibility

1. a) If we spend a lot more on advertising, we'll be able to sell that new model.
   b) If ____ that new model.
2. a) If salaries are increased before Christmas, all the staff will stay with the company.
   b) If ____ the company.
3. a) If ____________________ laser copier.
   b) If we could afford it, we'd get a laser copier.
4. a) If __________________________________ by August.
   b) If they advertised now, they'd find a new designer by August.

Typical Mistakes

!

Each of these sentences contains a mistake made by a German speaker. Can you correct them?

Jeder dieser Sätze enthält einen von einem deutschen Sprecher gemachten Fehler. Können Sie die Fehler korrigieren?

1. She goes often to the Far East.
2. Can you explain me the reason for the mistake?
3. We don't want to invest any more this year. Our directors don't too.
4. We'll probably hire about hundred and thirty part-timers in the summer season.
5. Owing to the unfavourable economical situation, we had to cut our sales staff.
6. Look, we need those informations by next week – can you manage that?
7. At the moment, these mowers are selling at $44.50 the piece.
8. Thank you for calling – I send you the goods immediately.
9. I look forward to hear from you.

ABC

Word Bank

Negotiating a deal	***Ein Geschäft aushandeln***
advance order	*Vorausbestellung*
agreement	*Vereinbarung*
allow a discount	*einen Rabatt gewähren*
as per contract	*laut Vertrag*
award (of a contract)	*Vergabe (eines Vertrags)*
backlog	*Rückstand*
bottom line, the	*unterm Strich*
bulk order	*Mengenbestellung*
business with foreign customers	*Geschäfte mit ausländischen Kunden*
catalogue price	*Katalogpreis*
clause (in a contract)	*Klausel (in einem Vertrag)*
co-operation	*Unterstützung*
contract of sale	*Kaufvertrag*
contracting parties	*vertragsschließende Parteien*
cost-sharing	*Kostenteilung*
deadlines	*Vertragsfristen für Leistungen*
dispute	*Streitfall*
do a deal	*ein Abkommen treffen*
draft	*Entwurf*
draw up a contract	*einen Vertrag aufsetzen*
enter into a contract	*einen Vertrag abschließen*
favourable	*günstig*
firm offer	*Festangebot*
firm order	*Festauftrag*
fixed costs	*Fixkosten, Gemeinkosten*
follow-up order	*Nachbestellung*
forecast	*Voraussage, Prognose*
fulfilment of contract	*Vertragserfüllung*
in working order	*funktionsfähig*
initial order	*Erstauftrag*
joint ventures	*Beteiligungsunternehmen*

labour charges	*Arbeitskosten, Lohnkosten*
licensing contract	*Lizenzvertrag*
likely costs	*voraussichtliche Kosten*
make headway	*vorankommen, Fortschritte machen*
negotiation	*Verhandlung*
offer	*Angebot*
operating costs	*Betriebskosten*
outlet	*Händler, Verkaufsstelle*
period of contract	*Vertragsdauer*
profit margin	*Gewinnspanne*
proposal	*Vorschlag*
repeat order	*Nachbestellung*
review (our) options	*(unsere) Optionen überprüfen*
signing (of a contract)	*Unterzeichnung (eines Vertrags)*
solution	*Lösung*
standing order	*Dauerauftrag*
stick to an agreement	*sich an eine Abmachung halten*
tool	*Werkzeug*
trading partner	*Handelspartner*
trial order	*Probeauftrag*
unfavourable	*ungünstig*
variable costs	*variable Kosten*

Down to Business

Listening Text 2/2

1.11

Horn & Rüffin GmbH have decided to open an outlet in France for some months to establish themselves in the market there. So they must hire premises in Paris. Herr Rüffin has met Monsieur Debeauvais, a Paris property dealer, to discuss this. You will hear part of their discussion.

Die Horn & Rüffin GmbH hat sich entschieden, für einige Monate eine Verkaufsstelle in Frankreich zu eröffnen, um sich dort auf dem Markt zu etablieren. Daher müssen in Paris Räumlichkeiten angemietet werden. Herr Rüffin hat sich mit Monsieur Debeauvais, einem Pariser Immobilienhändler, getroffen, um dies zu besprechen. Sie werden einen Teil ihrer Diskussion hören.

1 Listen to the discussion again and decide for each of these statements if it is correct (✔) or incorrect (**x**).

*Hören Sie die Diskussion noch einmal und entscheiden Sie für jede dieser Aussagen, ob sie richtig (✔) oder falsch (**x**) ist.*

		✔ or **x**
a	After six months in the premises, Horn & Rüffin will probably continue to rent them.	☐
b	The remodelling work in Lyon will take more than six months.	☐
c	Debeauvais' company can use the tools for ten months if they return them in working order.	☐
d	Both speakers wanted to discuss operating costs.	☐
e	Horn & Rüffin will pay fax and phone bills, but not rent.	☐
f	Debeauvais isn't sure how much the operating costs are.	☐
g	If Horn & Rüffin provide technical assistance, Debeauvais' company will pay the operating costs.	☐
h	Debeauvais' company will have to pay labour charges for the installation.	☐

2 Say out loud the responses Rüffin makes to the following remarks by Debeauvais. The Useful Expressions will help you.

Sprechen Sie Rüffins Antworten auf die folgenden Bemerkungen von Debeauvais laut. Die Useful Expressions *werden Ihnen dabei helfen.*

a Debeauvais: Right, where shall we begin?
Rüffin: Let's – the question of costs.

b Debeauvais: We could let you use the premises rent-free.
Rüffin: Can – offer open – two weeks?

c Debeauvais: I'm afraid we can't install the equipment ourselves.
Rüffin: Perhaps – arrangement.

d Debeauvais: We might need the equipment as long as ten months.
Rüffin: We – agree – that.

e Debeauvais: You'd have to provide technical assistance.
Rüffin: I'm willing – halfway – this.

f Debeauvais: So you can't provide the assistance free of charge?
Rüffin: We – tight profit margin – know.

g Debeauvais: I think we'd better go into this point more deeply.
Rüffin: May – for lunch?

h Debeauvais: Fine – where shall we meet?
Rüffin: I – meet – L'Escargot – 12.30.

3 Now, using the information you have, expand these notes into a letter which Rüffin could send to Debeauvais.

Erweitern Sie nun mit Hilfe der Ihnen zur Verfügung stehenden Informationen diese Notizen in einen Brief, den Rüffin an Debeauvais senden könnte.

Dear Monsieur Debeauvais

It was – pleasure – meet – again last week – do business with you.

As promised – am sending – summary – we agreed. This summary should – helpful – drawing up – contract.

You – give – premises rent-free – six months, after which time – decide whether – continue. During – we – pay – fax – phone – not – operating costs.

In return, we – loan – ten months maximum – equipment – remodelling your Lyon plant – condition – tools used
(a) – size and quantity – agreed –
(b) – returned – working order.
We – technical assistance – power tools – two days – Lyon – help install – equipment. For your part, you – full labour charges – installation work.

Provided – in order – please go ahead – draw up – contract, as agreed? If – keep to the time-frame of two weeks for this, we – sign by the end of the month.

Yours sincerely
B. Rüffin
for Horn & Rüffin GmbH

4 The contract has been drawn up, but not yet signed. As you read it, look up any words which are new to you.

Der Vertrag ist aufgesetzt, aber noch nicht unterschrieben. Schlagen Sie beim Lesen des Vertrags Ihnen unbekannte Wörter nach.

1.12

Contract of Agreement between Horn & Rüffin GmbH of Dortmund and SARL Labatte/Debeauvais of Paris

concerning the lease of 130 square metres of office premises at Number 8, Rue de Gorny, 75014 Paris (referred to hereafter as "the premises").

Obligations of SARL Labatte/Debeauvais

SARL Labatte/Debeauvais undertake to lease the premises to Horn & Rüffin GmbH between 1 March and 31 August of the current year.
SARL Labatte/Debeauvais further undertake

- to provide electricity and water to the premises and to have the premises cleaned and safeguarded;
- to pay the costs of the foregoing services and provisions as well as property taxes and other costs involved in the regular maintenance of the premises;
- to return in good working order, and not later than 31 December of the current year, all equipment loaned to them by Horn & Rüffin GmbH;
- to pay the costs of repair for any damage caused to the equipment during the period of loan;
- to pay (in accordance with the Scale of Fees in Appendix A) for any technical assistance provided by Horn & Rüffin GmbH at the SARL Labatte/Debeauvais plant in Lyon.

Obligations of Horn & Rüffin GmbH

Horn & Rüffin GmbH undertake to pay for

- the use of fax and telephone;
- the repair of any damage caused at the premises during the period of the lease.

Horn & Rüffin GmbH further undertake

- to lend SARL Labatte/Debeauvais new equipment for their use. The quantities and sizes of the equipment are listed in Appendix B;
- to provide two technicians to supervise and assist the installation of their equipment at the Lyon plant on 3 and 4 March of the current year.

1.13

Listening Text 2/3

5 Debeauvais and Rüffin are on the phone to each other, discussing the contract. They want to negotiate certain changes before they finally sign. As you listen, note down the changes agreed on. Then rewrite the relevant parts of the contract.

Debeauvais und Rüffin telefonieren miteinander; sie diskutieren über den Vertrag. Sie wollen über bestimmte Änderungen verhandeln, bevor sie schließlich unterschreiben. Notieren Sie beim Hören die vereinbarten Änderungen. Schreiben Sie dann die entsprechenden Teile des Vertrags um.

Dealing with Visual Info

Flow charts (1)

Horn & Rüffin are designing a new tool.

Horn & Rüffin entwerfen ein neues Werkzeug.

1 The sentences below describe how the project is being developed – but they are in the wrong order. Using the flow chart to help you, arrange the sentences into their correct order.

Die unten aufgeführten Sätze beschreiben die Entwicklung des Projekts – sie sind allerdings in der falschen Reihenfolge. Bringen Sie die Sätze mit Hilfe des Flussdiagramms in die richtige Reihenfolge.

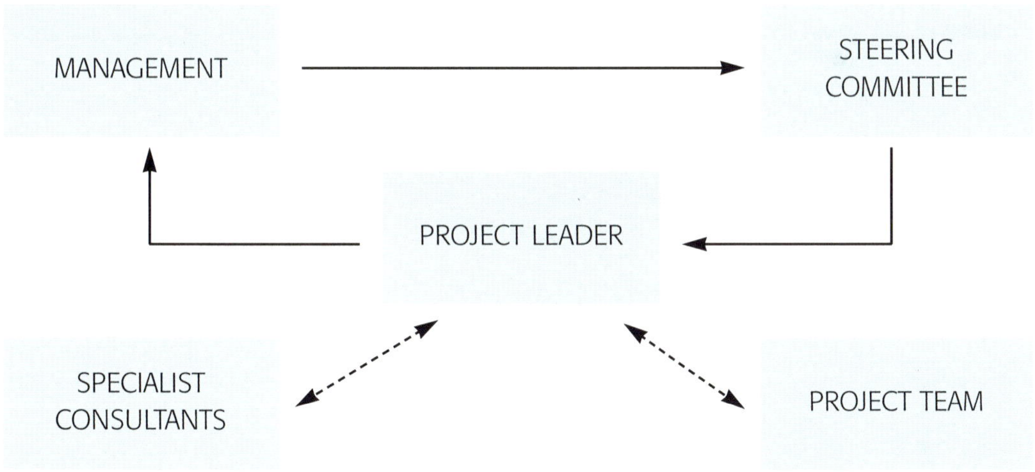

1. At this point, the responsibility passes over to the Project Leader, who has to produce his project report by the agreed deadline.
2. Finally, the Project Leader delivers his report directly to the Management.
3. First of all, the Management meet to discuss the likely production costs of the new tool and the state of the market.
4. After this, they appoint a Steering Committee – usually three or four members of the Management – to direct the project.
5. During this phase, he has a team of company employees to assist him, and he can also buy in any specialist consultant help he may need.
6. Next, the Steering Committee works out financial, marketing and technical guidelines, draws up a timetable for producing a project report and appoints a Project Leader.

2 Study these expressions used for describing processes. You will need some of them in the next exercise.

Sehen Sie sich diese Ausdrücke zur Beschreibung von Abläufen an. Sie werden einige davon in der nächsten Übung benötigen.

First (of all)	During this phase/stage	Then	In the next phase/stage
After this	Next	Later	At this point
Following this		Finally	

3 The flow chart below shows what happens at Horn & Rüffin when a customer orders a specially designed tool. Complete the text describing the process. Each blank requires at least one word.

Das Flussdiagramm stellt dar, wie Horn & Rüffin mit der Kundenbestellung für die Sonderanfertigung eines Werkzeugs umgeht. Vervollständigen Sie den Text, der den Ablauf beschreibt. Jede Leerstelle soll mit mindestens einem Wort ausgefüllt werden.

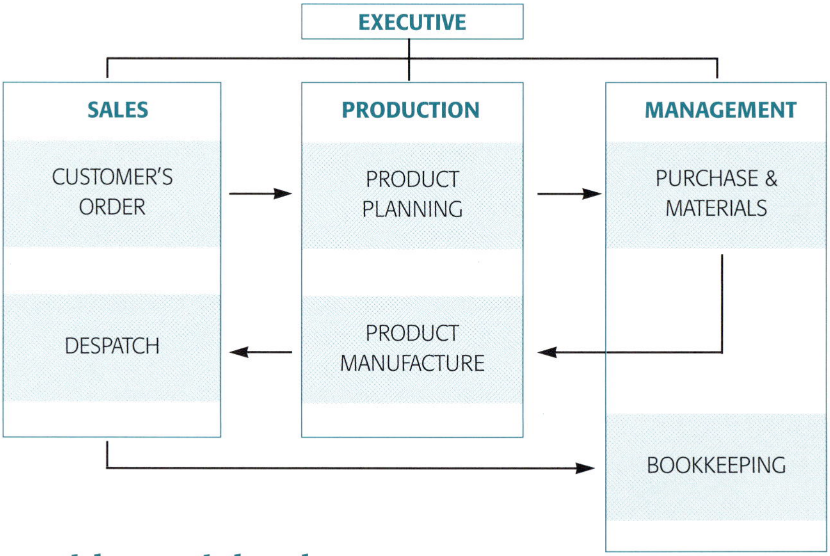

Dealing with special orders

First ________ all, when a ________ requires a specially designed tool, the order is processed by ________ Section. Next, ________ Section have the task of ________ the tool. After________, ________ acquire the materials needed, according to the production plan. Some of the materials may be in stock; others have to be ________ . Then, when the materials are ready, ________ proceed with ________ of the tool. Following ________ , ________ the finished tool to the customer. ________ , ________ pass a copy of the despatch note to ________ , ________ responsible for bookkeeping.

The British-American Difference

Write these German and American English expressions into the table below. (The first ones have already been written in for you.)

Tragen Sie diese deutschen und amerikanischen Ausdrücke in die unten aufgeführte Tabelle ein. (Die ersten wurden bereits für Sie eingesetzt.)

German

Punkt
U-Bahn
Freizeit
wiederholen
Stammaktien
Kassenbon
Vorzugsaktien
Radiergummi
für alle zahlen
Mehrwertsteuer
gegen den Uhrzeigersinn

American English

subway
period
eraser
preferred stock
leisure-time
pick up the tab
counterclockwise
common stock
proof-of-purchase
do it over
sales tax

British English	German	American English
spare-time	*Freizeit*	leisure-time
sales receipt		
pay the whole bill		
VAT		
Underground		
full stop		
ordinary shares		
preference shares		
anticlockwise		
rubber		
do it again		

Last but not Least

The following eight texts are parts of two letters, written and signed by the same person. Can you arrange the parts into their correct order – four parts to each letter? Which receiver gets the good news, and which gets the bad news?

Die folgenden acht Texte sind Teile zweier Briefe, die von derselben Person geschrieben und unterzeichnet wurden. Können Sie die Teile in die richtige Reihenfolge bringen – je vier Teile für jeden Brief? Welcher Empfänger bekommt die gute Nachricht und welcher die schlechte?

1

We were most impressed by your technical presentation, by your willingness to cooperate and by the personal relationship which resulted. We are convinced that, together, we have excellent future prospects to look forward to.

The decision is based on the draft of the Licensing Contract which is still being considered. At the moment, some slight changes in the wording still have to be dealt with. After that, you will receive the revised draft from us.

2

Even though we have not been able to decide in your favour, we would be very pleased if this atmosphere and this friendly relationship could continue. For our part, we wish to assure you of our good intention in this regard, and remain

Yours sincerely
Werner Reinhard

3

This decision has now been made. We regret to inform you that we are unable to award the Licence to your company.

4

It gives us great pleasure to convey this decision to you. I am sure that, together, we shall satisfy both the terms and the spirit of the Contract.

With best wishes
Werner Reinhard

5

Licensing Contract Negotiations

Dear Mr Watson
As we said on the occasion of our meeting in Newcastle, we intended to decide on the award of the Licence this month.

6

Following final agreement on the wording of the Contract, we would ask you to give consideration to a date on which the mutual signing might take place. We suggest around the end of next month.

7

Licensing Contract Negotiations

Dear Ms Churchyard
As our Herr Deckers has already informed you by telephone, we intend to award the Licensing Contract to your company.

8

The decision has not been an easy one to reach. As a medium-sized company, we have decided in favour of a similarly structured medium-sized applicant in Britain.

In the negotiations, we found your company particularly impressive. What especially commanded our respect was the size of your market. We would like to thank you once more for your efforts and for the friendly atmosphere in which the talks were conducted.

"We are convinced that, together, we have excellent future prospects to look forward to."

Discussing Marketing at Home and Abroad

Getting Started

Remember Horn & Rüffin GmbH from Unit 2? They now want to break into other markets in Europe, and to sell their tools there. They've spotted this advertisement in a trade journal.

Erinnern Sie sich an die Horn & Rüffin GmbH aus Unit 2? Horn & Rüffin will nun in andere europäische Märkte vordringen und dort ihre Werkzeuge verkaufen. Sie entdeckten diese Anzeige in einem Handelsjournal.

SEEKING TO EXPAND INTO GREECE?

We are experienced in serving US & European exporters who wish to market their products in Greece. All types of company served. We establish agencies and sales representatives in Greece. Over 2,000 outlets on file, including over 800 in Athens. Market research available. All enquiries treated in strictest confidence.
Contact: **Hellenic Marketing Services**

Tel: (30-1) 647-3117 Fax: (30-1)647-3117
Or e-mail us on Helms & dbnet@eb.hms.gr

Listening Text 3/1

1.14

1 Herr Horn has sent Hellenic Marketing Services a catalogue, and is now phoning them. The person receiving his call takes the following notes – but makes three mistakes. Can you spot them?

Herr Horn hat Hellenic Marketing Services einen Katalog geschickt und ruft die Firma nun an. Die Person, die sich meldet, macht die folgenden Notizen – doch auch drei Fehler. Können Sie die drei Fehler entdecken?

NOTES

Phone call from Horn
(= Horn & Rüffin, Dortmund)

H&R want
1. licensee in Greece
(= possible middle-term aim)
2. market research report (now)
- size of Greek market
- likely demand
- competition

We have H&R catalogue. H&R will also send:
- product specifications
- delivery terms (for Greece)
- product samples
- price list

Action!!! Send proposal this week. If accepted, report by end of month.

1.15

2 Hellenic Marketing Services have now prepared their market research report for Horn & Rüffin. Here is the last page of the report – but the paragraphs are in the wrong order. Put them into the correct order. Paragraph 1 is in the correct position.

Hellenic Marketing Services hat nun ihren Marktforschungsbericht für Horn & Rüffin vorbereitet. Hier ist die letzte Seite des Berichts, doch die Textblöcke befinden sich in der falschen Reihenfolge. Ordnen Sie sie in der richtigen Reihenfolge an. Absatz Nr 1 ist bereits am richtigen Platz.

Correct Order: 1 _ _ _ _ _

1. To summarise, the interior construction market in Greece has been expanding over the last two years. But the short-term outlook is that it is going to weaken. The usual summer decline has been much sharper this year. And, in view of the current recession, we don't expect the market to pick up again until the general economic climate improves. Orders will probably remain flat through the winter. The general prospects for next year are poor.
2. **Conclusions:** No Greek-based supplier is selling tools comparable with your lightweight range. We feel there is a good chance that, with good marketing literature and publicity, and with adequate agency and distribution arrangements, you could become well-established in the market in Athens.
3. On the other hand, the outlook is more encouraging in the Athens area, which contains a third of the home market. We see signs of continuing strong demand there. But it is important to examine the competition in this market.
4. If you have further questions on these findings, do not hesitate to contact us. In particular, we should like to point out that we have on file a number of possible agents and distributors for your products. We look forward to being of further service to you and await your instructions.
5. Consequently, you should look at what Sinarco are doing. They revise their marketing literature and product catalogues every few months, and have ten agents and distributors around the country – six of them in Athens. Their prices are very competitive and they offer a 12% discount on first-time orders.
6. In fact, there is only one really strong competitor – a Japanese company called Sinarco. While there are a number of other (mostly Greek) tools suppliers, Sinarco have roughly a 30% share of the market.

"We have on file a number of possible agents and distributors"

1.16

Listen & Repeat

Now listen to the repeat version of Listening Text 3/1 (Herr Horn phoning Hellenic Marketing Services). During the pauses, repeat Horn's parts of the conversation.

Hören Sie nun die Version zum Nachsprechen des Hörtext 3/1 (Herr Horn ruft Hellenic Marketing Services an). Wiederholen Sie während der Pausen Horns Teil des Gesprächs.

Useful Expressions

Discussing marketing at home and abroad

Den Vertrieb im Inland und Ausland diskutieren

Discussing market strategies	***Besprechung von Vertriebsstrategien***
May I put you in the picture/fill you in?	*Darf ich Sie ins Bild setzen?*
We're aiming to expand into ...	*Wir zielen darauf ab, in/nach ... zu expandieren.*
It's worth exploring the ... market.	*Es lohnt sich, den ... Markt zu erkunden.*
We're highlighting ... (products).	*Wir heben ... (Produkte) hervor.*
The aim would be to ...	*Ziel wäre es, ...*
That's our aim in the short-/middle-/long-term.	*Das ist unser kurz-/mittel-/langfristiges Ziel.*
We want to	*Wir wollen/möchten*
– find an agent to promote our products.	*– einen Vertreter finden, der für unsere Produkte wirbt.*
– commission a market research study.	*– eine Marktforschungsstudie in Auftrag geben.*
– see whether we ought to get into this market	*– sehen, ob wir in diesen Markt einsteigen sollten.*
– know the size of the market.	*– die Größe des Marktes kennen.*
– know the likely demand (for our products).	*– die voraussichtliche Nachfrage (nach unseren Produkten) kennen.*
Will people actually want them?	*Werden die Leute sie tatsächlich wollen?*
What about future demand?	*Wie steht es mit der zukünftigen Nachfrage?*
That's something we definitely want to know.	*Das ist etwas, das wir sicher wissen wollen.*

Discussing trends and developments	***Besprechung von Trends und Entwicklungen***
Orders are on the increase/decrease.	*Die Bestellungen nehmen zu/ab.*
The market will probably remain flat/steady.	*Der Markt wird wahrscheinlich flau/stabil bleiben.*

There's been a ... % rise over the last ... years.	*In den letzten ... Jahren gab es ein ... %-iges Wachstum.*
The market has been contracting/expanding.	*Der Markt ist geschrumpft/expandiert.*
The short-/long-term outlook is that ...	*Der kurz-/langfristige Ausblick besagt, dass ...*
The decline has been sharper/more gradual this year.	*Der Rückgang fiel in diesem Jahr stärker/schwächer aus.*
We don't expect the market to pick up again until ...	*Wir erwarten nicht, dass sich der Markt vor ... wieder erholt.*
The prospects for next year are pretty good/poor.	*Die Aussichten für das nächste Jahr sind recht gut/dürftig.*
The outlook is more/less encouraging.	*Der Ausblick ist ermutigender/weniger ermutigend.*
We see signs of continuing strong/weak demand.	*Wir sehen Anzeichen für eine fortwährend starke/schwache Nachfrage.*
How do things look right now?	*Wie sehen die Dinge jetzt aus?*

Discussing the competition	***Über die Konkurrenz diskutieren***
The main competitors are ...	*Die Hauptkonkurrenten sind ...*
They have a ... % share of the market.	*Sie haben einen ... %igen Marktanteil.*
They revise their catalogues every few months.	*Sie überarbeiten ihre Kataloge alle paar Monate.*
They have (ten) agents around the country.	*Sie haben (zehn) Vertreter im Land verteilt.*
W's prices are very competitive.	*Ws Preise sind äußerst konkurrenzfähig.*
X offers a ... % discount on first-time orders.	*X bietet einen ... %igen Rabatt auf alle Erstbestellungen.*
Y is selling ... comparable with our ...	*Y verkauft ... , vergleichbar mit unseren/m/r ...*
We should look at what Z is doing.	*Wir sollten beobachten, was Z tut.*

Offering services and advice	***Anbieten von Dienstleistungen und Beratungen***
Our market research shows ...	*Unsere Marktforschung zeigt ...*
We would be happy/delighted to ...	*Wir würden gerne ...*
We can certainly (do) ... for you.	*Wir können bestimmt ... für Sie (tun).*
We can't make any promises about ...	*Wir können hinsichtlich ... nichts versprechen.*
We feel there is little/a good chance that ...	*Wir spüren, dass es unwahrscheinlich/wahrscheinlich ist, dass ...*
We look forward to being of further service to you.	*Sehr gerne sind wir Ihnen auch weiterhin behilflich.*

We await your instructions.	*Wir warten auf Ihre Anweisungen.*
We should like to point out that ...	*Wir möchten darauf hinweisen, dass ...*
We'll ... and tell you ...	*Wir werden ... und sagen Ihnen ...*
I do need some more details.	*Ich benötige wirklich noch mehr Details.*
I'll come back to you directly.	*Ich komme sofort auf Sie zurück.*
Would that be satisfactory?	*Wäre es Ihnen so recht?*
If you ... , I can guarantee we'll ...	*Falls Sie ... , kann ich garantieren, dass wir ... (werden).*
To give you a lead, you should look at ...	*Um Ihnen einen Anhaltspunkt zu geben, sollten Sie sich ... ansehen.*
Don't hesitate to contact us.	*Zögern Sie nicht, sich mit uns in Verbindung zu setzen.*

"We await your instructions."

Language Study

1 CONNECTIVE EXPRESSIONS

Connective expressions *stehen normalerweise am Satzanfang, um das allgemeine Anliegen des Satzes aufzuzeigen. Hier sind einige Beispiele, die Sie schon kennen.*

In particular, we should like to point out that we have on file a number of possible agents.
On the other hand, the outlook is more encouraging in the Athens area.
To summarise, the interior construction market in Greece has been expanding.

2 "HOW/WHAT"-QUESTIONS

How ... ?

How do things look right now?	*Wie sehen die Dinge jetzt aus?*
How do you use this thing?	*Wie benutzt man dieses Ding?*
How old is he?	*Wie alt ist er?*
How are things (going)?	*Wie geht es?*
How much/many?	*Wie viel(e)?*
How come?/Why?	*Wieso?*

What ... ?

What is it called?/What is its name?	*Wie heißt es?*
What's the time?/What time is it?	*Wie spät ist es?*
What do you say for ...?	*Wie sagt man ...?*
What's the date today?	*Der Wievielte ist heute?*

Note: How does it look?/What does it look like? *Wie sieht es aus?*

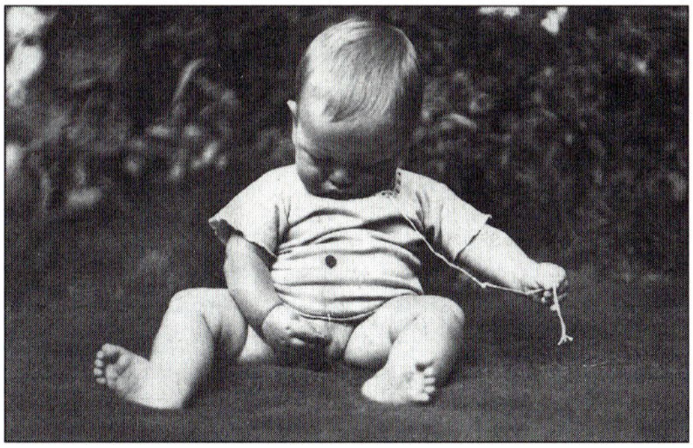

"How do you use this thing?"

Note:

Formell: Präposition am Anfang – nicht gebräuchlich: With what can I write?
Informell: Präposition am Ende – gebräuchlicher: What can I write with?

What ... with? (With what ... ?) *Womit?*
What can I write with? *Womit kann ich schreiben?*
What/Where ... from? (From what/where ... ?) *Woher?*
Where did this delivery come from? *Woher kam diese Lieferung?*
What ... on? (On what ... ?) *Worauf?*
What do you base this suspicion on? *Worauf basieren Sie diese Vermutung?*
What ... for? (For what purpose ... ?) *Wofür?/Wozu?*
What are these buttons for? *Wofür sind diese Knöpfe?*
Who ... belong to?/Whose ... ? (To whom ... belong?) *Wem/Wessen?*
Who does that belong to?/Whose is that? *Wem gehört das?/Wessen ist das?*
What sort/kind of ... ? *Was für (ein) ... ?*
What sort/kind of fax machine do you have? *Was für ein Faxgerät haben Sie?*
What does ... mean/stand for? (For what does ... stand?) *Was bedeutet ... ?*
What does CAD mean/stand for? *Was bedeutet CAD?*

Exercises

1 On the following page there is part of a report on Horn & Rüffin's recent business activities. It contains five numbered blanks. Fill each blank with a pair of connective expressions with similar meanings. Take the connective expressions from this list.

Auf der nächsten Seite sehen Sie einen Auszug aus Horn & Rüffins Geschäftsbericht. Er enthält fünf nummerierte Lücken. Setzen Sie in jede Lücke zwei connective expressions *mit ähnlicher Bedeutung ein. Entnehmen Sie die* connective expressions *dieser Liste.*

Connective expressions

By contrast,
On the whole,
Consequently,
In the meantime,
Furthermore,
In general,
As a result,
On the other hand,
Meanwhile,
Moreover,

"We hope to have the new models ready in the spring."

Horn & Rüffin GmbH
Interim Report

There has been a slump in construction work in the United States recently. ____________(1) most of our customers there are deliberately reducing their stocks. For us, this has meant a 30% fall in orders in the past six months. ____________(2) our cutting tools are selling well in Europe. We're soon opening up outlets in France and Greece. ____________(3) we've just negotiated a big order with a building company in the north of England. ____________(4) we're happy with our export position, but we've decided to reduce the amount of credit we allow our customers. It's important to prevent any repetition of the cash flow problems we had two years ago. ____________(5) we're designing new lightweight versions of some of our tools, and hope to have the new models ready in the spring.

2 Below are ten question-and-answer pairs. Fill in the expressions which are missing from the questions.

Nachfolgend sind zehn Frage-und-Antwort-Paare aufgeführt. Vervollständigen Sie die Fragesätze, indem Sie die fehlenden Ausdrücke einsetzen.

1. " __________ kind __________ communications system __________ have?"
   "It's a system based on mobile phones and fax."
2. " __________ you use the laptops for?"
   "They're for collecting data on-site, then downloading the data back at the company."
3. " __________ program called?"
   "It's called 'Electronic Transferral Net'."
4. " __________ property is this?"
   "It all belongs to Horn & Rüffin, actually."
5. " __________ CAD __________ for?"
   "Ah, that means Computer-Aided Design."
6. " __________ you allow the 5% discount __________ ?"
   "Only to customers who order on a monthly basis."
7. "How __________ produce the quotations?"
   "We have them generated automatically at the distribution office."
8. "We meet again on Wednesday. __________ next Wednesday?"
   "Wednesday? That's the 18th."
9. " __________ come __________ have no fax equipment here?"
   "Actually, we have – it's all in the next room here."
10. " __________ things __________ for the future?"
    "Well, I'm happy to say our prospects look very good indeed!"

!

Typical Mistakes

Each of these sentences contains a mistake made by a German speaker. Can you correct them?

Jeder dieser Sätze enthält einen von einem deutschen Sprecher gemachten Fehler. Können Sie die Fehler korrigieren?

1. Profits have raised by eight per cent over the past six months.
2. The directors will be meeting on the first Wednesday of the month, as usually.
3. We've received this information from a good client from us.
4. The export figures aren't particularly impressing this year.
5. So we'll see us at the Trades Fair on Friday at 10, right?
6. "Did you have lunch on the journey?" "Yes, I had."
7. The CD market grew up very rapidly during that time.
8. In former times, the company was based at Erfurt.
9. They told that they would contact us today.
10. These prices are no longer actual – we need the new catalogue.

ABC

Word Bank

Discussing marketing at home & abroad	***Den Vertrieb im Inland und Ausland diskutieren***
agency	*Agentur*
agent	*Vertreter*
bank overdraft	*Überziehungskredit*
breakthrough	*Durchbruch*
competitiveness	*Konkurrenzfähigkeit*
consumer	*Verbraucher*
consumer goods	*Verbrauchsgüter*
distributor	*Vertriebsagent, Verteiler*
diversified	*aufgefächert, diversifiziert*
main competition, the	*die Hauptkonkurrenten*
market research	*Marktforschung*
our latest model	*unser neuestes Modell*
output	*Produktionsleistung*
overestimate	*überschätzen*
overheads	*Betriebskosten*
pricing	*Preisfestsetzung*
product specifications	*Produktbeschreibung*
retailer	*Einzelhändler*
rival product	*Konkurrenzprodukt*

sales forecast	*Absatzprognose*
sales target	*Verkaufsziel*
sample	*Muster*
short-/middle-/long-term aim	*kurz-/mittel-/langfristiges Ziel*
shortage	*Fehlmenge, Engpass*
slump	*Einbruch*
special design	*Sonderanfertigung*
stocks	*Vorräte*
strengthen	*stärker werden*
trading terms	*Handelsbedingungen*
underestimate	*unterschätzen*
user-friendly	*benutzerfreundlich*
weaken	*schwächer werden*
wholesaler	*Großhändler*

Using electronic media in business	***Elektronische Medien geschäftlich nutzen***
access	*Zugang*
business application	*geschäftliche Anwendung*
compile	*kompilieren*
customized	*maßgeschneidert*
data	*Daten*
database	*Datenbank*
draft	*Entwurf*
EDP (= electronic data processing)	*EDV (= elektronische Datenverarbeitung)*
electronic payment	*elektronische Zahlung*
global village, the	*globales Dorf*
graphics	*Grafik*
icon	*Bildsymbol*
keyboard	*Tastatur*
link	*verbinden*
mailing list	*Adressenliste*
mouse	*Maus*
online	*online*
printer	*Drucker*
ready-made (+ noun)	*Fertig- (+ Nomen)*
resources	*Resourcen*

rewrite	*überarbeiten*
running charges	*laufende Kosten*
screen	*Bildschirm*
shape up	*in Form bringen*
spreadsheet	*Tabellenkalkulation*
surfing	*surfen*
typography	*Schriftarten*
word processor	*Textverarbeiter*

Many English expressions referring to modern communications are also used in German. Here are some examples.

Viele englische Ausdrücke, die sich auf moderne Kommunikation beziehen, werden auch im Deutschen benutzt. Hier einige Beispiele.

back-up pages • browser • display • download • e-mail • hardware • homepage • hyperlinks • hypermedia • hypertext • icons • Internet • Intranet • laptop • modem • newsgroup • provider • scanning • search engine • searching • server • software • URL (= User Resource Locator) • WWW (= World Wide Web) • WWW index

Down to Business

1 Barbara Steube's company has produced a new label printer. She has just demonstrated the printer to a business group in Chicago. Study these notes she made to help her with her presentation.

Barbara Steubes Firma hat einen neuen Etikettendrucker produziert. Barbara hat den Drucker gerade einer Gruppe von Geschäftsleuten in Chicago vorgeführt. Sehen Sie sich diese Notizen an, die ihr bei der Präsentation geholfen haben.

STAR LABEL PRINTER —————— Catalogue No. 443/4

- lightweight
- QWERTY keyboard
- fine graphics display
- 40 letter sizes
- 3 print styles
- barcode facility optional
- 9 mm & 18 mm widths available
- self-adhesive labels optional
- label storage capacity: 400

Suitable for offices, working from home, records & files, audio- & video-cassettes.

Method:
- tap in required characters on keyboard
- select print & lettering style(s)
- press print button to produce required label

Explain bulk discount terms.
Invite enquiries (Agency? Distributorship? Joint Venture?)

2 After the demonstration, Barbara meets Gerry Wilson, a possible distributor for the printer. With the help of the notes below, practise saying what Gerry might have said.

Nach der Vorführung trifft sich Barbara mit Gerry Wilson, einem potenziellen Vertriebsagenten für den Drucker. Versuchen Sie mit Hilfe der unten aufgeführten Notizen, Gerrys mögliches Gespräch zu führen.

(Gerry to Barbara)

OK – fill you in. We – dealers in small electronic office goods. The prospects – good – this line of business. Orders – on the increase – some months now. Our aim in the long-term – major US distributor in this field.

Now – like the look of – printer. It's user-friendly – could – attractive in the market for office goods here. We'll have to – some market research – find out the likely demand – that type of product. And we'll – look at the question of product suitability. Exactly – people – expect to buy it? What rival products – market?

Furthermore, we must also look – question of technical standards. In particular, we – to look into – US federal requirements – safety.

In the meantime – more details from you – pricing. We – your prices, including delivery, for all possible versions, with and without barcode facility – self-adhesive labels – both widths.

I can't – promises. But – definitely interested – marketing arrangement. With – right price, we think – sell – product – the States. The big question is – make the price competitive? Please let me know.

Listening Text 3/2

1.17

3 Compare your version with Gerry's actual words.

Vergleichen Sie Ihre Version mit dem von Gerry tatsächlich gesprochenen Text.

Listening Text 3/3

1.18

4 Two weeks later, back in Germany, Barbara gets an answerphone message from Gerry. Listen to it. Then (in writing) expand the following notes into a fax replying to Gerry's message.

Zwei Wochen später erhält Barbara, die inzwischen zurück in Deutschland ist, eine Nachricht von Gerry auf ihrem Anrufbeantworter. Hören Sie sich die Nachricht an und erweitern Sie dann die folgenden Notizen zu einer Faxnachricht als Antwort auf Gerrys Mitteilung.

Ref: STAR LABEL PRINTER ——————————————

Dear Gerry
Thanks – answerphone message yesterday. We – very interested – proposal.
I – confirm – bulk order – ten days – air.
As requested – despatching – immediately – air – sample of – without – facility. We hope – find – satisfactory.
I – enclosing further technical information – product.
Please – if I – more help. Looking forward – hearing – you.

With best wishes
Barbara Steube

5 Barbara's company, keen to market their product in the US, are now considering setting up a homepage in the World Wide Web. On the following page you find an advert that Barbara has seen on the Internet.

Barbaras Firma möchte ihr Produkt gerne in den USA vertreiben und erwägt jetzt, eine Homepage im World Wide Web einzurichten. Auf der folgenden Seite finden Sie eine Anzeige, die Barbara im Internet gesehen hat.

香港中華總商會
THE CHINESE GENERAL CHAMBER OF COMMERCE

中國國際網絡指南
China Internet Directory

Welcome to the CGCC Homepage

WE'LL SET UP YOUR HOMEPAGE!

Our speciality is the production of customized homepages for the WWW, together with back-up pages. Why not see some samples of the pages we've designed to get an idea of the page types possible?

Our tools
Resources: an extensive library of graphics, typographies, icons
Skills: compiling, rewriting, graphics scanning, searching

The cost
depends on the work required – minimum $100. If you can supply all the materials for your page ready-made, there'll be no further charge. The charge is higher if extensive rewriting, graphics scanning or lots of searching and compiling are necessary. Within seven days, we will have a finished draft for you to look at.

YOU PROVIDE ...

Info + materials
you want included for display.

Ideas
about basic style and contents of the homepage.

Info
about your business. Just tell us as much as you can about your work so we get to know your WWW needs.

WE PROVIDE ...

Assistance
with getting your homepage installed and properly linked.

Back-up pages

Hyper-links to places of interest to you on the WWW.

Help with registering your home-page in popular WWW indexes. We submit your new page's URL to at least six widely-used WWW indexes, so everybody can know where your page is.

6 The next day when Barbara reads the advert again, there are five additional sentences. Which five sections do you think these sentences were added to?

Am nächsten Tag liest Barbara die Anzeige noch einmal. Dort stehen nun fünf zusätzliche Sätze. Welchen Abschnitten, glauben Sie, wurden diese Sätze hinzugefügt?

a And we'll keep you informed of running charges, and estimate for you what each new step would cost.
b At any time, during or after production, you can send in further suggestions to help shape up the page.
c These are all the elements that go into making an effective and attractive Web page.
d With our guidance, you send us all the information and materials you'd like included on your Web page – text, pictures, spreadsheets.
e You'll then be part of the global village!

Dealing with Visual Info

1 Bar charts

Study these bar charts which show the consumption of beer, wine and cigarettes in a group of twelve European states.

Sehen Sie sich die Balkendiagramme an, die den Bier-, Wein- und Zigarettenkonsum in einer Gruppe von zwölf europäischen Staaten anzeigt.

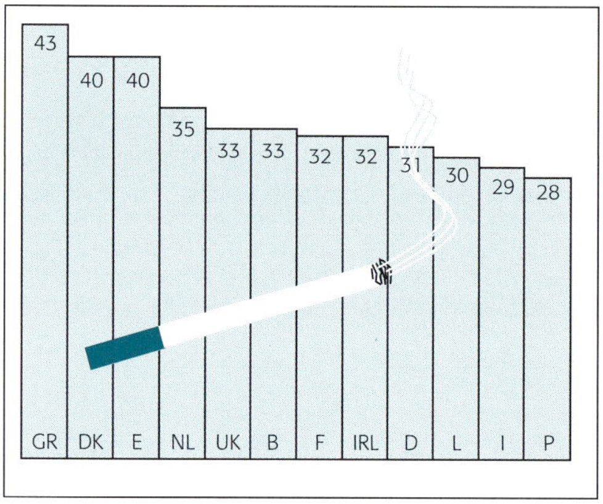

Proportion of smokers (in %)

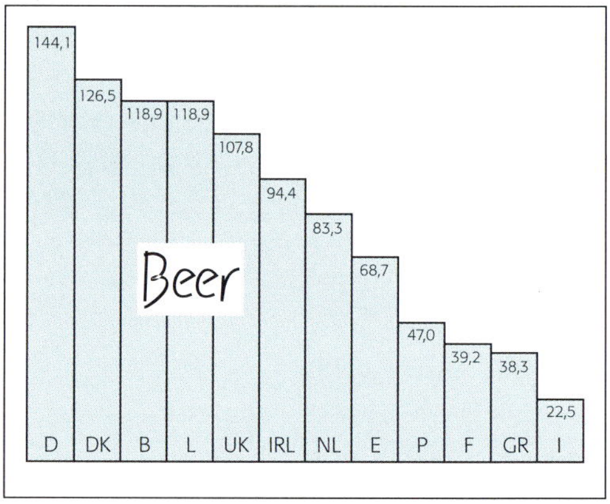

Annual consumption per head (in litres)

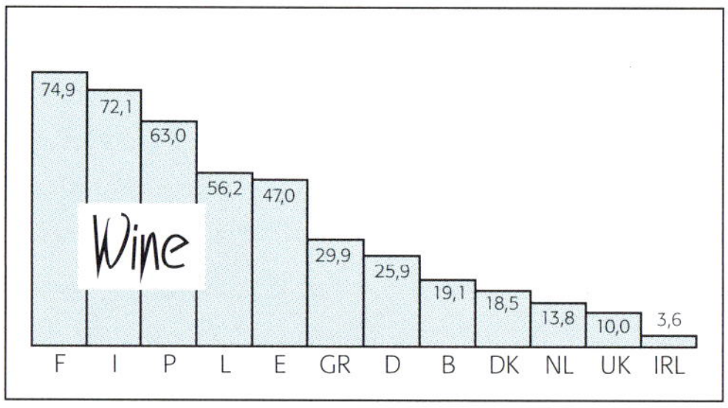

Annual consumption per head (in litres)

2

Decide if each of the following statements is true (✔) or false (**x**). The first has been done for you.

*Entscheiden Sie, ob die folgenden Aussagen richtig (✔) oder falsch (**x**) sind. Die erste Entscheidung wurde schon für Sie getroffen.*

	✔ or **x**
1. In Belgium, every third person is a smoker.	✓
2. Between a quarter and a half of the population of all twelve states are smokers.	☐
3. In nine of the twelve states, smokers comprise no more than 35% of the population.	☐

4. There are more cigarette smokers in Denmark than in Italy. ☐
5. Of all twelve states, Portugal has the fewest smokers per 100 inhabitants, and one of the lowest rates of beer consumption. ☐
6. Denmark has the second-highest consumption rate of both cigarettes and beer in the twelve states. ☐
7. In France, 74.9% of inhabitants drink wine, compared with only 25.9% in Germany. ☐
8. On average, a French person drinks more than 20 times as much wine as an Irish person. ☐
9. Italians have the lowest rate of beer consumption in the twelve states. On the other hand, they have the second-highest rate of wine consumption. ☐
10. Italians drink about three times more wine than beer, while the British drink around ten times more beer than wine. ☐
11. Greeks and Spaniards consume more beer than wine, and Italians and Portugese more wine than beer. ☐
12. In half of the twelve states, more than 90 litres of beer per individual are drunk in a year. ☐

3 Fill in the missing parts of these sentences. *Setzen Sie die fehlenden Satzteile ein.*

In________(1) of the twelve countries, between a quarter and a half of the population are smokers.

________(2) in 10 people in Denmark are smokers, compared with only three in ten in________(3).

In Spain, 40 per________(4) inhabitants are smokers.

In the United Kingdom, every________(5) person smokes.

________(6) has, on the one hand, the highest rate of wine consumption and, on the other hand, one of the lowest rates of________(7) consumption.

Italy has the________(8) rate of wine consumption, while the United Kingdom has the________(9) rate.

The average Spaniard drinks more than three times as much beer as the________(10).

On average, people living in the United Kingdom drink________(11) of wine per year, while people in________(12) drink almost three times as much.

The British-American Difference

The following list contains expressions which have to do with production, sales and documentation.

Die folgende Liste enthält Ausdrücke, die mit Produktion, Verkauf und Unterlagen zu tun haben.

German	UK	US
Materialwirtschaft	stock control	inventory control
Räumungsverkauf	clearance sale	close-out sale
abhaken	tick	check
bis	January to May	January thru (through) May
herstellen	making	fabricating
Höchstgebot	(price) or near(est) offer (o.n.o.)	(price) or best offer (o.b.o.)
Einkaufszentrum	shopping centre	(shopping) mall
Einkaufswagen	shopping trolley	shopping cart
maßgeschneidert	made-to-measure	custom-made
Aufzug	lift	elevator
Inventar	stock-taking	inventory

The following letter contains a mixture of British and American English expressions. Transform it into either all-British or all-American English.

Der folgende Brief enthält eine Mischung von Ausdrücken in britischem und amerikanischem Englisch. Wandeln Sie ihn entweder in durchgängig britisches oder amerikanisches Englisch um.

Dear Mr Kaye

As requested, we are sending you a brief statement on the stock control audit of Lukas & Sons (hereafter referred to as Lukas). The audit was carried out six weeks after Lukas' close-out sale from February thru March.

Lukas Inc. specialises in fabricating made-to-measure shopping trolleys for malls as well as elevators. According to the annual accounts, the business was booming for the first six months of last year but suddenly collapsed in mid-August. As sales had not picked up again after five months, Lukas decided to have a clearance sale and try to sell the production plant for US$ 2,600,000 o.n.o.

The inventory was carried out by means of readings of the counters attached to the production equipment. These were checked against the accounts. Our assessment concerning the stock-taking did not give rise to any queries.

With best wishes
H. Preetz
Accountant

Last but not Least

A **SWOT** Analysis looks at the **S**trengths, **W**eaknesses, **O**pportunities and **T**hreats involved in a business project. It answers questions like these.

Eine **SWOT**-*Analyse untersucht die Stärken, Schwächen, Möglichkeiten und Gefährdungen, die ein Geschäftsprojekt mit sich bringt. Sie beantwortet Fragen wie diese.*

THE COMPANY

Strengths

What products or services is the company good at making or doing?

Weaknesses

What things can the company NOT do well?

THE MARKET

Opportunities

Which parts of the market are attractive? What changes in it could the company exploit?

Threats

Which parts of (or changes in) the market could create difficulties or dangers for the company?

Here is the **SWOT** Analysis which Barbara Steube has made of her company's new label printer. Fill in the missing parts with the expressions given below.

Hier ist die **SWOT**-*Analyse, die Barbara Steube hinsichtlich des neuen Etikettendruckers ihrer Firma angefertigt hat. Setzen Sie die fehlenden Teile anhand der unten aufgeführten Ausdrücke ein.*

THE COMPANY ______________ STAR LABEL PRINTER

Strengths

1 Produces top-class lightweight electronic printers

2 ______________________

Weaknesses

1 Unable to produce custom-made printers.

2 ______________________

3 ______________________

THE MARKET

Opportunities

1 Our printers are suitable for offices + home-based deskwork.

2 ______________________

3 ______________________

Threats

1 Possible recession next year would badly damage sales drive.

2 We lack a US distributor.

3 ______________________

4 ______________________

Expressions

Limited production capacity (max 50 units per week) • Large potential market (Europe + US) • Main competitor (ElektroPro) could introduce rival printer model in the spring • Home-based deskwork is expanding in Europe (30% increase in two years) • Good reputation in the trade • Printer may fail US safety standards • 12% of technical work has to be sub-contracted

Organising a Conference or Meeting

Getting Started

Listening Text 4/1

1.19

1 Angela Parfitt and Stefan Braun are visiting China in order to represent their company. They are discussing an important meeting they have organised. Here is some information from the hotel where the meeting will take place.

Angela Parfitt und Stefan Braun sind in China, um ihre Firma zu vertreten. Sie besprechen eine wichtige Tagung, die sie angesetzt haben. Hier sind einige Informationen des Hotels, in dem die Tagung stattfinden wird.

CAIRNHILL HOTEL
TIANJIN
天津金禧大酒店

MEETING SEMINAR PACKAGE
HALF DAY
14 FLOOR

¥ 40.00 PER PERSON

The package includes the complimentary use of

- Meeting room from 9:00 am to 1:00 pm or 1:00 pm to 5:00 pm
- Potted plants for rostrum area
- Reception desk with (one) extension telephone
- One OHP or one 35mm slide projector with screen
- Delegates name tent cards (1st day)
- Chinese tea/coffee/mineral water

¥ 50.00 PER PERSON

The package includes the complimentary use of

- Meeting room from 9:00 am to 1:00 pm or 1:00 pm to 5:00 pm
- Potted plants for rostrum area
- Reception desk with (one) extension telephone
- Writing pads & pens
- One whiteboard or flip chart with marker
- One OHP and one 35mm slide projector with screen
- Delegates name tent cards (daily)
- Chinese tea/coffee/mineral water

All prices are in Chinese yuan and subject to 15% service charge

Variations of seating style
天津金禧大酒店

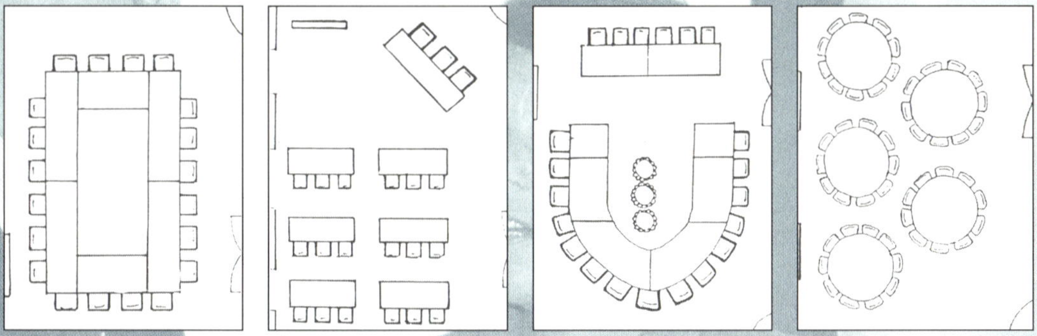

Meeting 天津金禧 | Classroom 大酒店 | Conference 20-30 Pax 津金禧 | Banquet 20-30 Pax 天津金

2 Using the information you have, complete the blanks in this fax in the most suitable way.

Vervollständigen Sie anhand der Ihnen zur Verfügung stehenden Informationen die Lücken in diesem Fax so passend wie möglich.

```
13-10-19..   11.15 am      Telefax: 0127-36 89

FAX:
Cairnhill Hotel, Tianjin
Dear Manager

Thank you for your information faxed yesterday, concerning
our meeting at the Cairnhill on ______________.
I would like to reserve a room from ______________ to
______________ for ______________ persons at Y ___________
per person. Would you please arrange the room in advance,
according to your ___________ seating style?

I look forward to your confirmation.

Many thanks
Yours faithfully

Angela Parfitt
```

Listen & Repeat

Listening Text 4/2

1.20
1.21

Listen to Stefan welcoming his clients at the Cairnhill. Then listen to the second version and repeat Stefan's words during the pauses.

Hören Sie, wie Stefan seine Kunden im Cairnhill willkommen heißt. Hören Sie dann die zweite Version und wiederholen Sie Stefans Text während der Pausen.

Useful Expressions

Organising a conference or meeting	***Eine Konferenz oder eine Tagung organisieren***
I would like to reserve a meeting room – from 9.00 am to 5.00 pm.	*Ich möchte einen Tagungsraum* *– von 9.00 Uhr bis 17.00 Uhr reservieren*
– for 15 people.	*– für 15 Personen reservieren.*
Would you please arrange the room in advance?	*Würden Sie den Raum bitte vorher herrichten?*
We prefer a frontal/round table/U-form seating arrangement.	*Wir bevorzugen eine frontal ausgerichtete/ kreisförmig angeordnete/ hufeisen-förmige Sitzordnung.*
I look forward to your confirmation.	*Bitte bestätigen Sie uns die Vereinbarungen.*

Welcoming to a conference or meeting	***Zu einer Konferenz oder Tagung willkommen heißen***
Good morning, ladies and gentlemen.	*Guten Morgen, meine Damen und Herren.*
Thank you for coming.	*Ich danke Ihnen, dass Sie gekommen sind.*
On behalf of … , I'd like to welcome you to …	*Im Namen (von/der/des) … möchte ich Sie zu/zur/zum … willkommen heißen.*
I hope you – had a pleasant journey.	*Ich hoffe, Sie* *– hatten eine angenehme Reise.*
– find everything to your satisfaction.	*– finden alles zu Ihrer Zufriedenheit vor.*
– have an enjoyable/rewarding morning.	*– verbringen einen erfolgreichen Vormittag.*

"We prefer a frontal seating arrangement."

Introducing speakers	***(Die) Redner vorstellen***
My name's X, and this is my colleague Y.	*Mein Name ist X und dies ist mein Kollege/meine Kollegin Y.*
It's my great pleasure to introduce to you ...	*Es ist mir eine große Freude, Ihnen ... vorstellen zu dürfen.*
Ms Brown represents ...	*Ms Brown vertritt ...*
Ladies and gentlemen, Ms Brown.	*Meine Damen und Herren: Ms Brown.*

Getting things started	***Einen Anfang machen***
May I have your attention, please?	*Darf ich um Ihre Aufmerksamkeit bitten?*
Can you all hear me?	*Können Sie mich alle hören?*
Just a couple of points before we begin.	*Nur ein paar Details, bevor wir beginnen.*
You should all have ...	*Sie alle sollten ... haben.*
Does anyone not have ... ?	*Hat jemand keine/n ... ?*
May I remind you that ... ?	*Darf ich Sie daran erinnern, dass ... ?*
We'll have a break at about 10.30.	*Wir werden gegen 10.30 Uhr eine Pause machen.*
Should you need any help, please see ...	*Sollten Sie Hilfe benötigen, wenden Sie sich bitte an ...*
There'll be an opportunity for ...	*Sie werden Gelegenheit zu/zur/zum ... haben.*
Feel free to raise questions at any time.	*Zögern Sie nicht, jederzeit Fragen zu stellen.*
Are there any questions?	*Gibt es Fragen?*
Let's get started.	*Lassen Sie uns beginnen.*
I'd like to begin by ...	*Ich würde gerne beginnen, indem (ich) ...*
I'd like to show you ...	*Ich würde Ihnen gerne ... zeigen.*
Now we come to an important point.	*Wir kommen jetzt zu einem wichtigen Punkt.*
I'd like to move on now to the question of ...	*Ich würde jetzt gerne zur Frage der/des ... übergehen.*

Closing a conference or meeting	***Eine Konferenz oder Tagung schließen***
I think that wraps it up.	*Ich glaube, damit kommen wir zum Schluss.*
Are there any further questions?	*Gibt es noch weitere Fragen?*
You'll get a copy of the conference report.	*Sie werden eine Kopie des Konferenzberichts erhalten.*
Have a good journey home.	*Gute Heimfahrt.*
Please make sure you take ...	*Vergewissern Sie sich, dass Sie ... mitnehmen.*

Language Study

VERB FORMS

Sehen Sie sich noch einmal diese beiden Sätze an, die dieselbe Bedeutung haben.

I think that wraps it up. ('to wrap up' = *Umgangssprache*)
I think that concludes it ('to conclude' = *formelle Sprache*)

Im Englischen kann man oft wählen zwischen
a einem (alltäglichen) Verb, das aus mehr als einem Wort besteht, und
b einem (förmlichen) Verb, das aus einem Wort besteht.

Exercise

Here are some everyday sentences from business life. Replace the verbs in brackets with more formal, one-word verbs taken from the box (below).

Hier sind einige alltägliche Sätze aus dem Geschäftsleben. Ersetzen Sie die Verben in Klammern durch die formelleren Verben aus dem Kästchen.

a complete	c submit	e open	g spoil	i suggest
b deduct	d calculate	f start	h delay	j finish

1. You'd better (put in) a claim for expenses right away.
2. Make sure you (take off) the discount before you send the invoice.
3. Just (fill in) the application form and return it to us. (BE: fill in; AE: fill out)
4. If you (work out) those estimates, I'll deal with the mail.
5. Would you (turn on) the computer so I can check those figures again?
6. I think next time we'll (take out) a house insurance policy.
7. I'm hoping you can (come up with) an idea to solve the problem.
8. I'll give you a call as soon as I (get through) with these figures.
9. We don't want to (mess up) the arrangements now they've been made, do we?
10. Shouldn't we (hold off) that decision till we've heard from the customer?

"I think next time we'll take out a house insurance policy."

Typical Mistakes

!

Each of these sentences contains a mistake made by a German speaker. Can you correct them?

Jeder dieser Sätze enthält einen von einem deutschen Sprecher gemachten Fehler. Können Sie die Fehler korrigieren?

1. London is the best example for an international city that I can think of.
2. He's studying with a great concentration for his exam.
3. I'll visit you in case I'm in Chicago.
4. Have you had any previous experiences in this line of work?
5. You have to be careful how you deal with him – he's very sensible.
6. Would you bring Herr Bracht to the station, please?
7. At last, we'd better discuss the question of bank loans.
8. When the production staff worked overtime, those orders could go out on Wednesday.
9. "Do you think we'll get a repeat order from Reynolds?" "I hope it!"
10. We really can't expect many profit in the first six months.

Word Bank

ABC

Organising a conference or meeting	***Eine Konferenz oder eine Tagung organisieren***
accommodate	*unterbringen*
accommodation	*Unterkunft*
attend	*anwesend sein*
attendance	*Anwesenheit*
book	*buchen*
booking	*Buchung*
box file	*kastenförmiger Aktenordner*
demonstration	*Vorführung*
fact sheet	*Info-Blatt*
folder	*Aktenmappe, Schreibmappe*
handouts	*Prospekte, Blätter, Handouts*
headed paper	*Papier mit Briefkopf*
logo	*Logo, Firmenzeichen*
memo (= memorandum)	*Mitteilung, Notiz*
name card/tag	*Namenskärtchen/Namensschild*
open-ended	*offen, unbefristet*
paper clip	*Büroklammer*
participant	*Teilnehmer*
participate	*teilnehmen*

punch	*Locher*
refreshments	*Erfrischungen*
seating capacity	*Sitzkapazität*
separator	*Trennfolie, Trennblatt*
session	*Sitzung*
slide	*Dia*
slide projector	*Diaprojektor*
staple	*Heftklammer*
stapler	*Hefter*
timetable	*Zeitplan/Stundenplan/Fahrplan*
transparency	*Folie*
video (cassette) recorder	*Videogerät*
video conferencing	*Videokonferencing*

Down to Business

1 You are Hanne Fuchs, organiser of a conference to take place in London in four days' time. When you arrive at your desk this morning, several communications are waiting in your in-tray. Read them quickly. Then note down what action (if any) is needed for each one.

Sie sind Hanne Fuchs, Organisatorin einer Konferenz, die in vier Tagen in London stattfinden soll. Als Sie heute Morgen in Ihr Büro kommen, warten unter „Eingänge" schon mehrere Mitteilungen auf Sie. Lesen Sie diese schnell und schreiben Sie dann auf, was aufgrund der einzelnen Notizen zu tun ist.

MEMO

From Jack Prewer, London — To Hanne Fuchs, Munich

For your information

We have a final list of 15 for the conference. 12 of them want accommodation for Friday night. I've booked them into single rooms at Pankhurst Lodge Hotel, next to the Conference Centre. We were lucky – they have no more rooms available that night.

You'll be pleased to know the name tags have arrived. They're very smart – and show the company logo really well. I'll bring them with me on Friday.

Best wishes

Jack

E-MAIL

Dear Ms Fuchs

Have just returned from five weeks in the States, so didn't get your invitation till now. I'd like to attend the conference – is there still room for me?
I'll be coming from Glasgow, so would be glad if you'd accommodate me at the same hotel as the others. Please phone.

Trevor Wiseman

FAX

From: South London Conference Centre

Dear Frau Fuchs

With reference to your event here on Friday, I can confirm that the Club Bar will be opened for your exclusive use in the evening. We need to take £80 at the Bar, otherwise we will have to make a charge for staff wages. If the Bar is open from 7.00 pm to 12 midnight, that charge would be £25.

May I remind you that we also require a returnable deposit of £30 to cover the cost of possible damage? I would like to ask you again to pay this as soon as possible.

Yours sincerely

Christine Wardingley
(Business Manager)

PHONE MESSAGE

For: HF   Taken by: BK

Michael Hurst's wife called. He has flu & can't make it to the conference. Sincere regrets. Would you please cross his name off the list and cancel his hotel reservation?

Action needed:
Phone? Send fax? Send e-mail? Send letter? Send memo? No action?

Jack Prewer:	Trevor Wiseman:
Christine Wardingley:	Michael Hurst:

Listening Text 4/3

1.22

2 Listen to Hanne's phone call to Trevor Wiseman – but Hanne's parts are missing. As you listen, use the transcript below and say what she must have said.

Hören Sie Hannes Telefongespräch mit Trevor Wiseman. Die Dialogteile von Hanne fehlen. Hören Sie den Dialog und sprechen Sie mit Hilfe der Abschrift (unten), was Hanne gesagt haben muss.

Wiseman: Hello, Trevor Wiseman here.

Fuchs: – Wiseman – Fuchs – Munich.

Wiseman: Ah, Frau Fuchs, hello. It's about the conference, isn't it?

Fuchs: Yes – your message – fit you in.

Wiseman: Ah, splendid. And how about the hotel?

Fuchs: OK – had to drop out – take over his hotel reservation.

Wiseman: Right. Good. Er ... where are we staying this year?

Fuchs: – next to – Conference Centre.

Wiseman: Oh yes, I know the Pankhurst. We used it the year before last, I think.
Will many of us be staying overnight?

Fuchs: – out of 15.

Wiseman: And will we be using the hotel bar for the get-together after the conference?

Fuchs: – this year.

Wiseman: OK. Right, thank you – and see you on Friday morning, Frau Fuchs.

Fuchs: – looking forward – Wiseman.

Wiseman: Bye for now.

3 Now listen to the complete version of the phone call which follows. How close did you get to Hanne's actual words?

1.23

Hören Sie nun die gleich darauf folgende vollständige Version des Telefongesprächs. Wie nahe kamen Sie Hannes tatsächlich gesprochenem Text?

4 Combine the parts of the broken sentences so that you have a fax to send to Christine Wardingley.

Verbinden Sie die Teile der auseinandergenommen Sätze zu einem Fax, das Sie an Christine Wardingley senden können.

FAX

To the
Business Manager, South London Conference Centre

Dear Ms Wardingley

a Many thanks for your fax of today,
b We are sending a money order
c Owing to a rather busy time here,
d I look forward

1. to seeing you in London.
2. confirming our booking of the Club Bar.
3. to cover the required deposit.
4. I regret we have been late in sending this.

Yours sincerely
Hanne Fuchs

5 As Hanne Fuchs, you are now in London, opening the conference with a speech of welcome. Invent any information you wish and use these notes to practise your speech.

Sie sind nun Hanne Fuchs und eröffnen in London die Konferenz mit einem Willkommensgruß. Üben Sie Ihre Rede anhand frei erfundener Informationen und dieser Notizen.

Fuchs — *Conference notes (speech of welcome)*

- *all hear me?*
- *introduce self*
- *welcome to conference – pleasant journey? everything to your satisfaction?*
- *couple of points:*
  - *(a) need help? see Jack Prewer (main entrance)*
  - *(b) all have folder + name tag?*
- *coffee break about 11 am*
- *lunch (restaurant) 1.00 pm*
- *questions?*

Listening Text 4/4

6 Check your speech of welcome by comparing it with the version on the CD.

Überprüfen Sie Ihren Willkommensgruß, indem Sie Ihre Version mit der auf der CD vergleichen.

1.24

Listening Text 4/5

1.25

7 Hanne is also trying to arrange a video-conference with one of her company's clients in Chicago. She's phoning Crystal Videoconferencing. As you listen, complete the boxes in this costing grid.

Hanne versucht auch, eine Videokonferenz mit einem Kunden ihrer Firma in Chicago zu verabreden. Sie ruft Crystal Videoconferencing an. Vervollständigen Sie die Kostenaufstellung, während Sie zuhören.

Crystal Videoconferencing: Scale of Fees

Room Fee:	£ ________ (Reduced by ________ if Crystal Videoconferencing's centres are used at both ends.)
Communication Fee:	£ ________
Scheduling Fee:	£ ________
Reservation Fee:	(payable if the videoconference is to be set up within ________): £ ________
Minimum hire period:	________

Dealing with Visual Info

Pie charts

1 The London Conference is over. Look at these two pie charts which compare the costs with last year's Conference.

Die Konferenz in London ist beendet. Sehen Sie sich diese beiden Kreisdiagramme an, die die Kosten mit denen der Konferenz des letzten Jahres vergleichen.

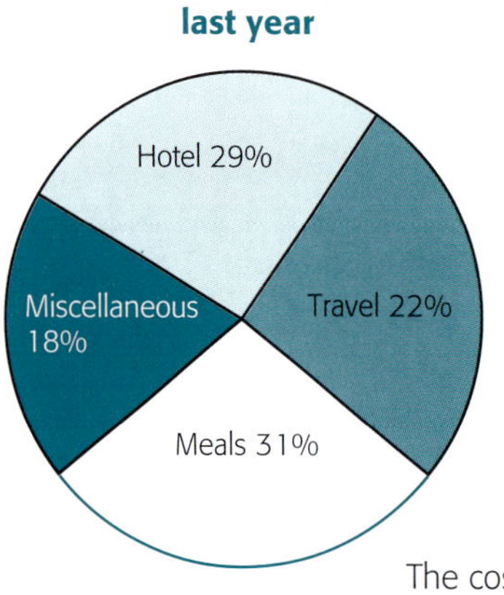

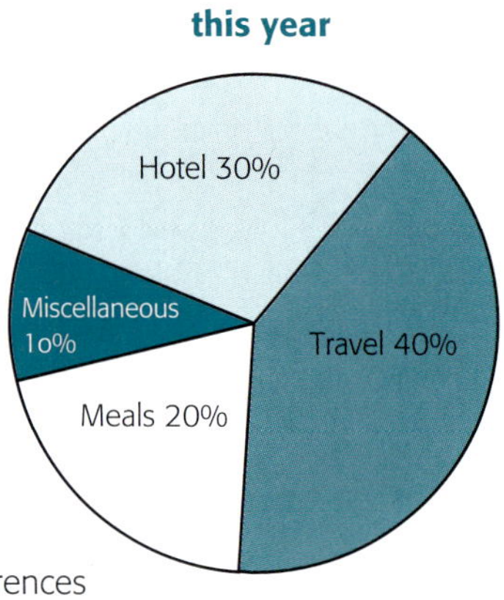

The cost of London Conferences
(Each year: total cost = 100%)

2 Hanne is discussing the charts with her Managing Director. Try to fill in the eight missing expressions.

Hanne bespricht die Diagramme mit ihrem Geschäftsführer. Versuchen Sie, die acht fehlenden Ausdrücke einzusetzen.

Managing Director: ... so we actually spent the same on last year's conference and this year's?

Hanne: Yes, practically the same amount. Almost to the penny.

Managing Director: But didn't we save a lot on ___________ (1) this year? We had a special deal, didn't we?

Hanne: Oh, yes – from that new catering service. And, as a result, we spent – let's see – we spent ___________ (2) per cent less this time.

Managing Director: And the ___________ (3) costs were only one per cent more, you say?

Hanne: That's right. And all the miscellaneous items – you know, fax and phone, materials, postage – those items are also down from ___________ (4) to ___________ (5) this year.

Managing Director: So, why wasn't the conference actually cheaper to stage this time? It was the ___________ (6) costs, I suppose.

Hanne: Right. They were just ___________ (7) per cent last year. This time they're up to ___________ (8) per cent.

Managing Director: I see. Well. Looks like we should try and economise in that area next year.

3 Listening Text 4/6

Listen to the dialogue and check your answers.

Hören Sie den Dialog und überprüfen Sie Ihre Antworten.

1.26

The British-American Difference

Complete the following adverts by filling in the missing words from the list below the adverts. The words must be in British English or American English, as appropriate. To help you, the missing words appear in German under the adverts (➔) – but not in the right order.

Vervollständigen Sie die folgenden Anzeigen, indem Sie die fehlenden Wörter aus der Liste unter den Anzeigen einsetzen. Diese müssen passend entweder in britischem oder in amerikanischem Englisch gewählt werden. Zur Hilfe finden Sie die gesuchten Wörter in Deutsch jeweils unter den Anzeigen aufgeführt (➔) – sie sind jedoch nicht in der richtigen Reihenfolge.

a)

Morris Audit Company
Birmingham ① ________

Applications are invited for the following post, available for two years in the first instance from January 1999.

② ________ ________

Applicants should have experience in applying the relevant software applications and organisational skills. The successful applicant will have at least three years' management experience.
The salary will be commensurate with the successful applicants' skills and abilities.
Application and further details from Dr. Alexander Morris Jr., Morris Audit Company, Brunswick Square, Birmingham 15 2TT, England. Tel: 01221 376 9844, Fax: 01221 376 98445, e-mail: MORRIS @ BHAM.HC. UK.

➔ *Geschäftsführer, GmbH*

b)

McCoy Real Estate
Agents ① ________

is looking for a ② ________________

We are seeking an outstanding individual to represent our business in the Toledo area. You will have the responsibility for organizing real estate sales.
McCoy Real Estate Agents offer a competitive salary commensurate with experience and working performance.

The ideal candidate will be highly motivated, independent, flexible and have extensive working experience in the real estate sector. Excellent communication and interpersonal skills are a must.
Interested individuals should send a curriculum vitae and references to McCoy Real Estate Agents, c/o R. Rettner, PO Box 10004, Toledo, Ohio 43699-0004.

→ *GmbH, Immobilienmakler*

c)

Progen Progen Progen Progen Progen Progen Progen Progen Progen

Progen Intl., ① ________ of Oligo Express ② ________., has an immediate opening for an experienced ③ ________ to supervise the ④ ____________ 's internal accountancy.

The successful candidate should be highly motivated, flexible, familiar with standard software and have at least 3 years' experience in the field. Prior experience in auditing ⑤ ________ is a merit.

Further information about the position can be obtained from
Dr. Kai V. Vasic, phone +44 (0) 171-233-4126, e.mail: k.vasic.@progen.uk
fax: +44 (0) 171-233-4127
Find more information on Progen's homepage: www-progen.coms

→ *Wirtschaftsprüfer, Dachgesellschaft, Großhändler, GmbH, Firma*

d)

① ____________ wanted for promising enterprise in Biotechnology.
Contact S.H. Qureshi, phone +31 294.486.655
e-mail: qureshi@transgen.ww.nl., fax +31 294.486.656
TRANSGEN WORLDWIDE Rilksstraatsweg 35, 3631 AC Nieuwersluis,
The Netherlands

→ *Stiller Teilhaber*

German	**UK**	**US**
Großhändler	wholesaler	jobber
Wirtschaftsprüfer	chartered accountant	certified public accountant
Immobilienmakler	estate agent	realtor *oder* real estate agent
Geschäftsführer	Managing Director	Executive Vice-President
Stiller Teilhaber	sleeping partner	silent partner
GmbH	limited (Ltd.)	incorporated (Inc.)
Dachgesellschaft	holding company	proprietary company
Firma	company	corporation

1 LAST BUT NOT LEAST

Arrange the items from Lists A & B into pairs, so that you have seven complete instructions.

Ordnen Sie die Elemente aus den Listen A & B in Paaren an, so dass Sie sieben vollständige Anweisungen erhalten.

STAYING FIT AT WORK

List A: Seven golden rules

A Work out
B Start out right
C Warm up
D Set goals
E Change your environment
F Change your posture
G Vary your computer habits

List B: Further advice

1. Adjust your screen to eye-level. Sit as far from it as you can without straining your eyes. The human body wasn't designed to sit for long periods in front of a screen.

2. You need fuel to get started each morning. A balanced breakfast combining fast- and slow-burning fuels can give you this. Make sure you include carbohydrates and proteins in your diet.

3. Determine what you want to do each day. Don't let yourself be controlled by routine.

4. Take every opportunity you can to get in the gym, to ride that indoor bike, to take a brisk walk or a swim.

5. Give yourself 15 minutes breathing space before you start your day. Relax, make lists, write in a journal, think things over.

6. If you live in a dark house or work in a dreary office, you'll become tired. So bring variety to your surroundings.

7. Vary your sitting position from time to time. Stretch out your legs. Relieve your back by using a cushion. After working at the desk for a while, do stretching exercises to prevent neck- and shoulder-ache. Roll your head slowly in a circular fashion or wheel your arms over and over.

2 Now add one more piece of information taken from List C to each of the seven pairs.

Fügen Sie nun jedem der sieben Paare eine weitere Information aus Liste C zu.

1.27

List C:

a Then you won't reach your workplace feeling rushed and tired.

b Too many or too few of these will make you drowsy in mid-afternoon.

c Try adding some music or a new colour.

d Do this first in one direction, then in the other.

e Remember: exercise actually gives you energy.

f So the simplest way to avoid discomfort is to get up occasionally.

g Decide clearly for yourself what tasks are to be completed.

"Try adding some music ... "

Dealing with Deadlines, Delivery and Supply

Getting Started

Raylene, an American, and Erika, a German, run a clothing retail business in Frankfurt. They have made the following notes about the import of garments from Bali.

Raylene, eine Amerikanerin, und Erika, eine Deutsche, führen in Frankfurt einen Kleidungseinzelhandel. Sie haben folgende Notizen für den Import von Kleidungsstücken aus Bali zusammengestellt.

Transport costs: Bali-Frankfurt
Air
– Economical for meeting urgent orders from customers (= small consignments, max 200 kg);
– 3-4 days delivery period. So customers can be supplied within 5-7 days of order;
– Delivered direct to Frankfurt airport: no costs for warehousing, wharfage, inland transport.

Ship
– Economical for bulk deliveries (= more than 200 kg);
– Approx 6 weeks delivery: OK for acquiring next summer's stock.

Listening Text 5/1

1.28

The two women are discussing garments they want to order from their supplier in Bali. Complete these boxes to show what they have agreed. (The notes above will help you.)

Die beiden Frauen diskutieren über Kleidungsstücke, die sie bei ihrem Zulieferer in Bali bestellen wollen. Vervollständigen Sie die Tabelle, so dass deutlich wird, worauf sie sich geeinigt haben. (Die oben aufgeführten Notizen werden Ihnen helfen.)

	Quantities to be ordered (in kg)	
	A2	A5
by air by sea		

Listen & Repeat

Listening Text 5/2

1.29
1.30

From Frankfurt, Raylene calls the forwarding agent in Bali. She wants to have a consignment sent by air. Raylene has the agent's list of charges (see below) in front of her. You will hear their conversation twice – the second time with pauses, so that you can repeat Raylene's parts of the conversation.

Raylene ruft den Spediteur in Bali aus Frankfurt an. Sie möchte eine Lieferung auf dem Luftweg. Raylene hat die Preisliste des Spediteurs (unten) vor sich. Sie werden das Gespräch zweimal hören – beim zweiten Durchgang mit Pausen, um Raylenes Dialogteil nachsprechen zu können.

C.V. MULIA ANWAR **List of charges**

Garment Manufacturer & Forwarding Agent
Jl Tuparev No. 12 Kuta
Bali – Indonesia
Phone/Fax: 0062-361-750666/720631

Destination Frankfurt Airline LH

Prepaid Only

Freight charges

Min weight	45 kg	100 kg	250 kg	500 kg	600 kg
Net Rate in USD	4.80	4.20	3.85	3.65	3.55

Other charges

Documents	USD	15.00 per shipment
		(by L/C USD 35.00)
Packing	USD	3.00 per box of garments
Certificate of Origin	USD	5.00 per certificate
Handling/Clearance	USD	30.00 min charges per shipment
	USD	0.30/kg (45–249 kg)
	USD	0.25/kg (250–499 kg)
	USD	0.20/kg (500 kg +)
Tax	10% of Handling/Clearance	
Insurance	2% x value of goods	

Useful Expressions

Dealing with deadlines, delivery & supply	***Sich um Termine, Lieferung & Angebot kümmern***
Discussing stock	***Über den Warenbestand diskutieren***
We need ... kg of ...	*Wir benötigen ... kg ...*
We have a lot of ... in stock.	*Wir haben eine Menge ... vorrätig.*
We can manage with what we've got till ...	*Wir kommen mit dem, was wir haben, zurecht, bis ...*
We are down to the last dozen ...	*Wir sind auf unser letztes Dutzend runter ...*
We also need to stock up on ...	*Wir müssen auch ... aufstocken.*
Arranging despatch	***Den Versand arrangieren***
I need a carrier to take this consignment from ... to ...	*Ich brauche eine Spedition, die diese Lieferung von ... zu ... bringt.*
Would you be able to send ... kilos of ... immediately?	*Wären Sie in der Lage, sofort ... Kilos ... zu schicken?*
We'll help you arrange the delivery terms.	*Wir werden Ihnen helfen, die Lieferbedingungen zu vereinbaren.*
We'll arrange the shipment.	*Wir werden den Versand arrangieren.*
We'll prepare the documentation for you.	*Wir werden die Unterlagen für Sie vorbereiten.*
What will the total cost of the shipment be?	*Wie viel wird die Lieferung insgesamt kosten?*
I can give you a close estimate.	*Ich kann Ihnen eine gute Schätzung geben.*
I'll fax you the order right now.	*Ich faxe Ihnen die Bestellung sofort (zu).*
Is the packaging included?	*Ist die Verpackung im Preis inbegriffen?*
Discussing delivery deadlines	***Besprechen von Lieferfristen***
I'd like to make this order on (the) condition that ...	*Ich möchte diese Bestellung unter der Bedingung aufgeben, dass ...*
Could you give me a guarantee on that?	*Könnten Sie mir darauf eine Garantie geben?*
We'll certainly get the goods to you by ...	*Wir werden Ihnen die Waren bis ... bestimmt zukommen lassen.*
You should allow ... days.	*Sie sollten ... Tage gewähren.*
The goods will be here in ... weeks.	*Die Waren werden in ... Wochen hier sein.*

Delivery has to be brought forward ... months.	*Die Lieferung muss ... Monate vorgezogen werden.*
Tell them it's urgent, will you?	*Sagen Sie ihnen bitte, dass es dringend ist.*

Discussing modes of despatch	***Diskutieren von Versandsarten***
We want to order ... kg of ... by air/by sea.	*Wir wollen/möchten ... kg ... per Luftfracht/ per Schiff bestellen.*
Could you send a consignment by air/by sea right away?	*Könnten Sie sofort eine Lieferung per Luftfracht/per Schiff schicken?*
What would be better – road or rail?	*Was wäre besser – Straße oder Schiene?*
What's the most efficient mode of transportation?	*Welche Transportart ist am rationellsten?*
I need to get the goods from ... to ...	*Ich muss die Waren/Güter von ... nach/zu ... bekommen.*
We can offer you door-to-door delivery.	*Wir können Ihnen (eine) Lieferung von Tür zu Tür anbieten.*
That would be the cheapest/most expensive/ slowest/quickest way.	*Das wäre der billigste/teuerste/langsamste/ schnellste Weg.*

"We can offer you door-to-door delivery."

Referring to money quantities	***Auf Geldbeträge verweisen***
$11.75	eleven dollars and seventy-five cents
	or: eleven seventy-five
£3.95	three pounds and ninety-five p (p = pence)
	or: three pounds ninety-five
$2,517	two thousand five hundred and seventeen dollars
	or: twenty-five hundred and seventeen dollars
150 kg @ $4.20 per kg	a hundred and fifty kilos at four dollars twenty per kilo
14.5%	fourteen point five per cent
14.35%	fourteen point three five per cent
14.05%	fourteen point oh five per cent
2% x $810	two per cent of eight hundred and ten dollars
$1,000,000	a (or: one) million dollars *(= eine Million)*
$1,000,000,000	a (or: one) billion dollars *(= eine Milliarde)*

Note:

a *Plural:* 20 million/billion *(= 20 Millionen/Milliarden);* 20 million dollars *(= 20 Millionen Dollar);* millions/billions of dollars *(= Millionen/Milliarden von Dollar)*

b *Bei Zahlenangaben wie* „five hundred and seventeen" *wird im amerikanischen Englisch oft das* „and" *weggelassen:* „five hundred seventeen"

c *Englisch: Punkt = Deutsch: Komma (und umgekehrt)*

10.8% = *10,8%*
$998.25 = $998,25
5,000,000 = *5.000.000*

1.31

Listening Text 5/3

Say the following quantities. Then listen to them to make sure you said them correctly.

Lesen Sie die folgenden Beträge laut. Hören Sie sie dann, um Ihre Aussprache zu überprüfen.

1. $270.85 (2 versions) 2. £15.35 (2 versions) 3. $3,150 (2 versions)
4. 65.8% 5. 85.85% 6. 20.05% 7. $12,000,000

Language Study

ACTIVE & PASSIVE

Sehen Sie sich diese zwei Satzformen an.

ACTIVE

You must deliver the goods by the 15th.
They include packaging in the price.

Das Aktiv betont den Ausführenden der Handlung (= You/They).

PASSIVE

The goods must be delivered by the 15th.
Packaging is included in the price.

Das Passiv betont die Handlung selbst (= be delivered/included).

Bei den meisten Sätzen können Sie zwischen der aktiven und passiven Form wählen.

entweder:	We'll send the goods next week.
oder	The goods will be sent next week.

Passive Sätze sind unpersönlich: Sie konzentrieren sich auf die (wichtige) Handlung, nicht auf den (unwichtigen) Ausführenden der Handlung. Daher werden sie oft in der Geschäftssprache benutzt, um Verfahren, Regeln, Methoden und Taktik hervorzuheben.

Delivery has to be brought forward three months.

Letters of Credit should be used for international payments.

The office is closed at weekends.

Exercise

Raylene has written this set of rules for the Orders & Despatch staff. Use the help given and rewrite the rules as passive, impersonal sentences.

Raylene hat dieses Regelwerk für die Mitarbeiter der Auftrags- und Versandabteilung geschrieben. Schreiben Sie die Regeln anhand der angebotenen Hilfen in passive, unpersönliche Sätze um.

KEEP COSTS DOWN!

Follow these guidelines for ordering:

1. Make sure you supply customers from stock whenever possible.
2. Don't order air freight consignments of more than 200 kg.
3. Contract only carriers who deliver direct to Frankfurt. This way, we avoid costs for warehousing, wharfage and inland transport.
4. Order large deliveries by sea.
5. You can often reduce the additional costs. For example, we don't always need a Tax Certificate and Certificate of Origin. And, often, it's possible to order cheaper packing for hard-wearing cotton goods.

1.32

KEEP COSTS DOWN!
For ordering, these guidelines should______________.

1. Make sure your customers ______________.
2. Air ______________ should not ______________.
3. Only ______________ may______________. Costs ______________ are to be ______________.
4. All ______________ must ______________.
5. The ______________ can often______________. For example, ______________ are not ______________. And, often, ______________ can ______________.

"Contract only carriers who deliver direct ..."

Typical Mistakes

!

Each of these sentences contains a mistake made by a German speaker. Can you correct them?

Jeder dieser Sätze enthält einen von einem deutschen Sprecher gemachten Fehler. Können Sie die Fehler korrigieren?

1. It's typical for them to send in their order at the last moment.
2. The most businesses close at Christmas.
3. Output fell as a result of obsolete machinery and crowding conditions.
4. It's worth to spend more on training programmes.
5. The Internet gives us more market information as the newspapers.
6. We're in danger to be left with unpaid bills.
7. The both will be going to the conference.
8. According to the contract, we have the right of withdrawing after three months.
9. The accounts office deals with bad debts on individual basis.
10. You only have heard one person's opinion.

Word Bank

ABC

Dealing with deadlines, delivery and supply	***Sich um Termine, Lieferung und Angebot kümmern***
agent	*Vertreter*
air freight	*Luftfracht*
air freight charges	*Luftfrachtkosten*
airtight packaging	*luftdichte Verpackung*
by sea	*auf dem Seeweg*
carrier	*Frachtführer/Spediteur*
clearance (customs)	*(Zoll)abfertigung*
consignment	*(Waren)sendung*
consolidations	*Sammelladungen*
credit card order	*Bestellung per Kreditkarte*
delay	*Verspätung*
delivery charge	*Liefergebühr*
delivery date	*Liefertermin*
express delivery	*Eilsendung*
forwarding agent	*Spediteur*
freight costs	*Frachtkosten*
freight rate	*Frachttarif*
freight service	*Frachtdienst*
gross weight	*Bruttogewicht*

handling	*Beförderung*
have in stock	*vorrätig haben*
inland transport	*Inlandstransport*
insurance	*Versicherung*
labelling	*Etikettierung*
mode of transportation	*Transportart*
packaging	*Verpackung*
packaging material	*Verpackungsmaterial*
packing charges	*Verpackungskosten*
point of delivery	*Zustellungsort*
postage and packing (= p&p)	*Porto und Verpackung*
raw materials	*Rohstoffe*
schedule	*Zeitplan*
shipment	*(Waren)sendung*
stock	*Lagerbestand*
supplier	*Lieferant/Zulieferer*
terms of delivery	*Lieferbedingungen*
warehousing	*Lagerhaltung*
wharfage	*Kaigeld*

Incoterms
(= International Commercial terms)

Internationale Handelsbezeichnungen

CFR	Cost and Freight	*Kosten und Fracht*
CIF	Cost, Insurance, Freight	*Kosten, Versicherung, Fracht*
CIP	Carriage and insurance paid	*frachtfrei versichert*
CPT	Carriage paid	*frachtfrei*
DAF	Delivered at frontier	*geliefert Grenze*
DDP	Delivered duty paid	*geliefert verzollt*
DDU	Delivered duty unpaid	*geliefert unverzollt*
DEQ	Delivered ex quay	*geliefert ab Kai*
DES	Delivered ex ship	*geliefert ab Schiff*
EXW	Ex works	*ab Werk*
FAS	Free alongside ship	*frei Längsseite Seeschiff*
FCA	Free carrier	*frei Frachtführer*
FOB	Free on board	*frei an Bord*

Down to Business

Listening Text 5/4

1.33

Listen to two people, Jill and Keith from Transport and Despatch, discussing this memo. It was sent from a German company's head office to its British subsidiary.

Hören Sie Jill und Keith, zwei Mitarbeiter der Transport- und Versandabteilung, die über die folgende Mitteilung diskutieren. Sie wurde von der Hauptgeschäftsstelle einer deutschen Firma an ihre britische Tochtergesellschaft geschickt.

MEMORANDUM

To: Transport & Despatch Date: 16 Nov 19..
From: Executive Office

In the last six months, we've seen a 5% increase in our transport costs. Please find out why – and how we should deal with this. Have we reached the point where rail would be more economical than road?

Please report before next Thursday.

Many thanks.

Rainer Nöth

"Have we reached the point where rail would be more economical than road?"

1.33

1 On the following page are the notes Jill makes during the discussion with Keith. Listen to it again and fill in the missing phrases.

Auf der nächsten Seite sind die Notizen, die Jill während der Diskussion mit Keith macht. Hören Sie letztere noch einmal und setzen Sie die fehlenden Ausdrücke ein.

NOTES JN/16.11.

1. Hauliers Association survey confirms our findings:
– increase in road transport costs due to____________(a)
– too many vehicles = slower, longer journeys; higher____________(b) costs
Prompt deliveries to our retail outlets: down from____________(c) in 6 months

2. Rail transport still not recommended. Our____________(d) shows:
– rail____________(e) more expensive than road
– we couldn't supervise refrigerated goods (hard to____________(f) during delays)
– danger of____________(g) in transit

3. We recommend:
– increasing stocks in retail outlets
– tighter____________(h)
– squeezing more onto____________(i) vehicles

2 Finally, complete this report which Jill and Keith could send to Executive Office.

Vervollständigen Sie schließlich diesen Bericht, den Jill und Keith an die Zentrale schicken könnten.

To Herr Nöth, Executive Office

The recent Hauliers Association survey confirms ____________ . First, there has been an increase ____________ . Second, ____________ have resulted in ____________ as well as ____________ . Consequently, ____________ have fallen ____________ to ____________ the last six months.

But we still do not recommend ____________ . Our cost analysis shows ____________ would be ____________ road. Furthermore, if we ____________ , we would not be able to ____________ . It would be hard to ____________ . There is also a danger of ____________ .

Therefore, we recommend, instead, increasing ____________ . In addition, we recommend ____________ .

Dealing with Visual Info

Timetables

TransExpress, a transport company, is demonstrating its new computerised system. Here is the timetable of the demonstration.

Die Transportfirma TransExpress führt ihr neues computergestütztes System vor. Hier ist der Zeitplan für die Vorführung.

Demonstration: Saturday, 22 April

Location: ~~TransExpress~~, Main Office
Dorint Hotel

Itinerary:

10.00-10.30: Reception, coffee, introductions

10.30-12.00: Demonstration: **TransExpress Integrated System** software

12.00-1230: Report on **TransExpress** Europe & US operations

12.30-14.00: Lunch: ~~Odysseus Restaurant~~ Dorint Hotel

~~14.00-15.30~~: Hands-on session using **TransExpress Integrated System** software,
from 1400 (Tea & coffee available)

from 15.30: Free shuttle service to station.

1 The German organiser of the demonstration is calling his British partner to tell him about the changes in the timetable. Study their (incomplete) conversation and fill in phrases that could complete it.

Der deutsche Organisator der Vorführung ruft seinen britischen Partner an, um ihm die Änderungen im Zeitplan mitzuteilen. Sehen Sie sich ihr (unvollständiges) Gespräch an und setzen Sie zur Vervollständigung passende Satzteile ein.

Partner: Right – got the original timetable in front of me. – what changes – made?
Organiser: – fill them in – I read them to you?
Partner: Yes, go ahead.
Organiser: OK. When – worked out – original timetable – expected – our offices. But – twice as many participants as we thought. – Olaf came up with – switching it – Dorint Hotel, across the road.
Partner: Ah, so I'd better change – to – .
Organiser: Exactly. – too.
Partner: Ah, so I should change – to – ?
Organiser: Right – when – have finished lunch – straight into – . – will be an open-ended session.
Partner: I see. So it won't end at 15.30?
Organiser: That's right. – change – to – please?
Partner: OK – done that.
Organiser: That means – free to stay – long as they like – our software.
Partner: Good.
Organiser: Right. – will run from – . Actually, we might start it even later in the afternoon. But – holding off – decision for the time being. You see, – want to keep participants – long as possible. – other hand – mustn't mess up – travel arrangements!

1.34

Listening Text 5/5

2 Check your version by listening to the full conversation.

Überprüfen Sie Ihre Version, indem Sie das vollständige Gespräch anhören.

THE BRITISH-AMERICAN DIFFERENCE

Can you find the matching UK and US vocabulary ? The first match has been done for you.

Können Sie die sich jeweils entsprechenden britischen und amerikanischen Vokabeln finden? Das erste Paar wurde bereits für Sie eingetragen.

motorway | freeway | car park | taxi | round trip

- single ticket
- parking lot
- streetcar
- gas *oder* gasoline
- petrol
- season ticket
- one-way ticket
- goods train
- commuter ticket
- freight train
- roundabout
- cab
- truck
- railroad
- return journey
- lorry
- baggage cart
- articulated lorry
- railway
- traffic circle
- luggage trolley
- truck-trailer
- tram

German	**UK**	**US**
Eisenbahn	railway	railroad
Straßenbahn		
Einzelfahrschein		
Saisonkarte		
Kreisverkehr		
Taxi		
Autobahn		
Lastwagen		
Güterzug		
Parkplatz		
Benzin		
Lastzug		
Kofferkuli		
Hin- und Rückfahrt		

Last but not Least

Fill in the missing abbreviations from the list which follows. Be careful – there are six abbreviations too many in the list.

Setzen Sie die fehlenden Abkürzungen aus der nebenstehenen Liste in den Brief ein. Vorsicht – die Liste enthält sechs Abkürzungen zu viel!

❑ ❑ ❑ : Mr Andropov
❑ ❑ ❑
Sales ❑ ❑ ❑

❑ ❑ : your fax dated 26.11.

Dear Sir

We have received your ❑ / ❑ and are now in a position to deliver your order of ❑ ❑ 26 for the 600 units of ❑ ❑ ❑ s (❑ ❑ ❑ : $940.00). As we only recently introduced ❑ ❑ ❑ , we had to battle with hardware installation problems. We apologize for the delay. As agreed, we will deliver 600 units for $49,200.00 ❑ ❑ ❑ Frankfurt plus ❑ ❑ ❑ .

As we also export to other ❑ ❑ ❑ countries whose ❑ ❑ ❑ s will be with us for some time yet, we have a cash-flow problem here, which forces us to sell off our ❑ ❑ - ❑ ❑ ❑ bulk (200,000 units) for a total of $66,000.00 ❑ ❑ ❑ . If you are interested in the offer, contact us ❑ ❑ ❑ ❑ .

Yours faithfully
Stephen Bender
Sound Screens ❑ ❑ ❑

❑ ❑ : 26.12. is a public holiday in Britain!

VDU	visual display unit	c/f	carried forward
plc	public limited company	R/D	Refer to Drawer
VAT	Value Added Tax	CFO	Chief Financial Officer
sae	stamped addressed envelope	CD-ROM	compact disk (Read Only Memory)
Re	refering to	RSVP	Repondez s'il vous plait
CAM	computer-aided manufacture	CIS	Commonwealth of Independent States
CIF	Cost, Insurance and Freight	PS	post scriptum
wk	week	FAO	For the attention of
L/C	Letter of Credit	asap	as soon as possible
ono	or near(est) offer	RRP	Recommended Retail Price
AOB	Any Other Business (on agenda)	APR	Annual Percentage Rate
dep	department	IOU	I owe you (statement of debt)

"26.12. is a public holiday in Britain!"

Unit 6

Dealing with Documentation

Getting Started

Ms Pia Rank, the owner of a sports goods company in Germany, has received this proforma invoice from a supplier in Pakistan.

Ms Pia Rank, die Eigentümerin einer Sportartikelfirma in Deutschland, hat diese Pro-forma-Rechnung von einem Zulieferer in Pakistan erhalten.

FAX MESSAGE
PROFORMA INVOICE
+92 - 432 - 552891

Fax No.	109/98
Dt	Jan 03, 1999
Attn	Ms Pia Rank

A/c./M/e SPORT-RANK
Gescherweg 31
61169 Friedberg 2
Germany

Through

Proforma Invoice No.
1477/98

QUANTITY	**DESCRIPTION OF GOODS**	@ USD	**AMOUNT** USD
250 PCS	MP 7012 WIMBLEDON	32.00	8,000.00
200 PCS	MP 7033 FLUSHING MEADOWS	35.50	7,100.00
100 PCS	MP 7011 ROLAND GARROS	31.00	3,100.00
100 PCS	MP 7009 CENTRECOURT	29.50	2,950.00
50 PCS	MPX 112 ATP	55.00	2,750.00
20 PCS	MPX 104 MASTERS	68.00	1,360.00
	TOTAL FOB PAKISTAN	USD	25,260.00
	(US DOLLARS TWENTY-FIVE THOUSAND TWO HUNDRED SIXTY ONLY)		

DELIVERY:	ASAP BY AIR
TERMS:	RATES ARE FOB PAKISTAN
PAYMENT:	ADVANCE THROUGH TELEGRAPHIC TRANSFER

Listening Text 6/1

2.1

Listen to Ms Rank's answerphone message and make the necessary corrections to the invoice.

Hören Sie Ms Ranks Nachricht auf dem Anrufbeantworter und nehmen Sie die notwendigen Korrekturen an der Rechnung vor.

LISTEN & REPEAT

Listening Text 6/2

2.2

To deal with her proforma invoice, Ms Rank had to refer to some calculations she had made. Listen to these calculations on the CD and repeat them as you hear them.

Um ihre Pro-forma-Rechnung zu bearbeiten, musste Ms Rank auf einige Berechnungen verweisen, die sie vorgenommen hatte. Hören Sie sich diese Berechnungen auf der CD an und wiederholen Sie diese beim Hören.

Calculating — ***Rechnen***

Subtracting/Deducting — ***Subtrahieren/Abziehen***

$500 - $9.50 — five hundred dollars minus (or: less) nine dollars fifty

Adding — ***Addieren***

£20.00 + £11.10 — twenty pounds plus (or: added to/and) eleven pounds ten

Dividing — ***Dividieren***

30 ÷ 3 = 10 — thirty divided by three makes (or: comes to/equals/is) ten

Multiplying — ***Multiplizieren***

6 x $55 — six times fifty-five dollars

$55 x 6 — fifty-five dollars multiplied by six

10% x $55 — ten per cent of fifty-five dollars

20 units @ $55 apiece — twenty units at fifty-five dollars apiece

Useful Expressions

On the phone — ***Am Telefon***

Offering to help	***Hilfe anbieten***
Shall I/Would you like me to ... for you?	*Soll ich/Hätten Sie gerne, dass ich ... für Sie ... ?*
Perhaps I can help you.	*Vielleicht kann ich Ihnen helfen.*
I can ... if you like.	*Wenn Sie möchten, kann ich ...*

Let me give you a phone number.	*Ich gebe Ihnen eine Telefonnummer.*
Let me know if you run into any difficulty.	*Lassen Sie es mich wissen, falls Sie auf irgendwelche Schwierigkeiten stoßen.*

Accepting an offer	***Ein Angebot annehmen***
Yes, I'd be happy if you would …	*Ja, ich wäre* *froh, wenn Sie … würden.*
grateful if you could do that.	*dankbar, wenn Sie das tun könnten.*
That would be very helpful.	*Das wäre sehr hilfreich.*

Declining an offer	***Ein Angebot ablehnen***
No thanks. You can leave that to me.	*Nein, danke. Sie können das mir überlassen.*
That won't be necessary, thank you.	*Das wird nicht nötig sein, danke.*

Making sure	***Auf Nummer sicher gehen***
Would you repeat that/run that through again, please?	*Würden Sie* *das bitte wiederholen/noch mal durchlaufen lassen?*
spell that word, please?	*das Wort bitte buchstabieren?*
speak up, please? (= speak louder)	*bitte (etwas) lauter sprechen?*
slow down, please? (= speak slower)	*bitte (etwas) langsamer sprechen?*
Have you got all that?	*Haben Sie das alles?*

Seeking clarification	***Um Klärung bitten***
I'm afraid I don't quite follow you.	*Ich fürchte, ich kann Ihnen nicht ganz folgen.*
By "hardware", do you mean all the computers?	*Meinen Sie mit* „hardware" *alle Computer?*
Sorry, but what exactly do you mean by "hardware"?	*Entschuldigen Sie, aber was meinen Sie genau mit* „hardware"*?*
Sorry, I didn't catch that.	*Entschuldigen Sie, ich habe das nicht mitbekommen/verstanden.*
Sorry, I'm not familiar with the expression "hardware".	*Entschuldigen Sie, der Ausdruck* „hardware" *ist mir nicht bekannt.*
May I rephrase "hardware" in the following way … ?	*Darf ich* „hardware" *anders ausdrücken, und zwar … ?*

Could you tell me what "hardware" means exactly?	*Könnten Sie* *mir sagen, was „hardware" genau bedeutet?*
put that into other words, please?	*das bitte paraphrasieren?*
explain the concept of "hardware", please?	*den Begriff „hardware" bitte erklären?*
What does "o.n.o." stand for?	*Was bedeutet „o.n.o."?*
There are one or two points I don't quite understand.	*Es gibt ein oder zwei Punkte, die ich nicht ganz verstanden habe.*

Giving phone numbers	***Telefonnummern angeben***
The country code/extension number (for ...) is ...	*Die Landesvorwahl/Durchwahl (für ...)* *lautet ...*
oh-one	01
double-oh-one	001
double-three double-six seven	33667

		UK:	US:
Country Code	*Landesvorwahl* *(geschrieben:*	0044 + 44	001 + 1)
Area Code	*Ortsnetzkennzahl*	* 01372	913
(Telephone) Number	*Rufnummer*	3067	831-3805
Extension (Number)	*Durchwahl* *(geschrieben:*	22 x 22	15 x 15)
* Omit the first 0 for international calls.	** Lassen Sie bei internationalen Gesprächen die erste 0 weg!*		

Language Study

Expressions of quantity

1. SOME/ANY

Some *und* any *werden oft benutzt, um unbestimmte Mengenangaben auszudrücken.*

some = limited, uncertain quantity *(= manche, einige)*
We'd like to do some price comparisons.
any = "it doesn't matter which" *(= ganz gleich welche, irgendwelche)*
Use your dictionary to look up any words which are new to you.

some *benutzt man auch in bejahten Sätzen:*
I can give you some information about prices.
und in Fragen, bei denen eine positive Antwort erwartet wird.
Here are the brochures – would you like some price lists too?

any *benutzt man auch in verneinten Sätzen:*
I can't give you any information about prices.
und in Fragen, bei denen eine negative Antwort möglich ist.
Excuse me – do you have any price lists?

some 30 years ago *(= vor etwa 30 Jahren)*
for some time now *(= seit einiger Zeit)*
at any time *(= zu jeder Zeit)*
at any price *(= um jeden Preis)*

2. COUNT NOUNS & MASS NOUNS

count noun = *eine einzelne Einheit*
- hat Singular- und Pluralformen
computer(s), dollar(s), machine(s)

Mengenangaben:
a lot of, a large number of, plenty of, many *(= viele)*
(comparative: more – the most)
few, not many *(= wenige)*
(comparative: fewer – fewest)

mass noun = *ein kollektives Ganzes*
- hat keine Pluralform
money, knowledge, oil

a lot of, a large amount of, plenty of, much *(= viel)*
(comparative: more – the most)
little, not much *(= wenig)*
(comparative: less – the least)

Auch:

a few *(ein paar)*
a pair of *(ein Paar)*
both *(beide)*
several *(mehrere)*

enough *(genug/genügend)*
the two *(die beiden)*
some *(einige)*
all (of) the *(alle)*

a little *(etwas/ein wenig)*
a bit of *(ein bisschen)*
enough *(genug/genügend)*
all that/this *(all jen../d.../dies..)*

3. NUMERICAL EXPRESSIONS

Ordinalzahlen:
Wenn die Zahl mit 1, 2 oder 3 endet, wird -first (= -1st), -second (= -2nd), -third (= -3rd) *benutzt.*

31st = thirty-first   22nd = twenty-second   133rd = one hundred and thirty-third

Wenn die Zahl nicht mit 1, 2 oder 3 endet, wird ein -th *angefügt.*

4th = fourth   35th = thirty-fifth   50th = fiftieth

the 50th day = *der 50ste Tag*
the 1980s (the nineteen-eighties) = *die 1980er*

Multiplizieren:

He's already phoned	once/twice	(= *einmal/zweimal)*	this morning.
	three times	(= *dreimal)*	
	four times, etc	(= *viermal usw.)*	

Sales have doubled/tripled/quadrupled over the last five years.
(= *verdoppelt/verdreifacht/vervierfacht)*
Auch: three times as many/twice as much (= *dreimal so viele/doppelt so viel)*
four times a year (= *viermal im Jahr)*

Ausdrücke mit Artikel: (= the/a(n))
- the: half the cost (= *die halben Kosten)*, twice the amount (= *die doppelte Summe)*, all the goods (= *alle Waren)*, both the deliveries (= *beide Lieferungen)*
- a/an: half a pound (= *ein halbes Pfund)*, half an hour (= *eine halbe Stunde)*, 90p a kilo (= *90p das Kilo)*

Ausdrücke mit Präpositionen:

50 metres of cable	*50 Meter Kabel*
some crates of beer	*einige Kisten Bier*
20 kilos of fax paper	*20 Kilo Faxpapier*
10% of the price	*10% des Preises*

We can save up to (= *bis zu)* 50%.
The inflation rate has fallen to (= *auf)* 2%.
The price has risen by (= *um)* $25.
We take 60 orders a week on average. (= *durchschnittlich)*
We take an average of 60 orders a week.
Germany ranks among (= *zählt zu)* the world's leading industrial nations.
London is Britain's biggest city; Birmingham ranks second (= *an zweiter Stelle stehen).*

Exercise

Using the information given in brackets, fill in the missing parts of these sentences.

Setzen Sie anhand der in Klammern aufgeführten Informationen die fehlenden Satzteile ein.

1. They didn't give us __________ about the new design. (= *viele Informationen)*
2. The depot handles 50 arrivals a day __________ average. (= *durchschnittlich)*
3. Horn & Rüffin have the __________ outlets of all the major producers. (= *alle anderen größeren Hersteller haben mehr)*
4. Each rep receives __________ of the overall profits. (= *1/30)*
5. The __________ sides will resume negotiations on Monday. (= *beide)*
6. We've had __________ complaints about Bury Division's after-sales service. (= *mehrere)*
7. Buy now, and you can save __________ 15%. (= *bis zu)*
8. The two companies amalgamated __________. (= *vor etwa 15 Jahren)*
9. The price could be increased __________. (= *zu jeder Zeit)*
10. Give me one of those files please – __________ will do. (= *ganz gleich welcher)*
11. I'd like to ask __________ questions about your discount plan. (= *einige)*
12. It cost $35 – now it's $45? You mean the price has increased __________ in six weeks? (= *um)*
13. Diner's Club still ranks __________ the world's leading credit card companies. (= *zählt zu)*
14. It would help __________ if the report didn't contain so many statistics. (= *ein wenig)*
15. After checking the installation every month for 24 months, we do a major overhaul in the __________. (= *fünfundzwanzigsten)*
16. The French are exporting __________ wine as the Germans. (= *doppelt so viel)*
17. The company will be producing __________ cartridges next year. (= *doppelt so viele)*
18. Of the ten applicants, he was __________ impressive. (= *die anderen waren eindrucksvoller)*

19. Since the price cut in June, sales have ___________. *(= vervierfacht)*

20. Packaging represents 15% ___________ the overall cost of the product. *(= 15% der Gesamtkosten)*

!

Typical Mistakes

Each of these sentences contains a mistake made by a German speaker. Can you correct them?

Jeder dieser Sätze enthält einen von einem deutschen Sprecher gemachten Fehler. Können Sie die Fehler korrigieren?

1. The modern society depends a lot on the automobile.
2. Have you paid for the bill?
3. Never we have had such a difficult problem to deal with.
4. I want that all the exams are as easy as that one.
5. In the moment, manufacturers just aren't able to cope with the demand.
6. We were forced to spend money for new office equipment.
7. I'll give you directions as soon as I've found Raynham Road on the card.
8. Welcome in Germany!
9. Exports have fallen down by a fifth during the past eight months.
10. The first priority is to spare money, then we can think about investing.

Word Bank

ABC

1. Dealing with import/export documents	***Bearbeiten von Import- & Exportunterlagen***
air waybill (= AWB)	*Luftfrachtbrief*
bill of lading (= B/L)	*Konnossement*
blanket (insurance) policy	*Generalpolice*
certificate of origin	*Ursprungszeugnis/Herkunftsbescheinigung*
certificate of seaworthiness	*Seetüchtigkeitszeugnis*
commercial invoice	*Handelsrechnung*
consignment note	*Frachtbrief*
consular invoice	*Konsulatsfaktura*
contract of carriage	*Frachtvertrag*
customs invoice	*Zollfaktura*
despatch note	*Versandschein*
document of title	*Traditionspapier*
duty-free	*zollfrei*
freight bill	*Frachtrechnung*

health certificate	*Gesundheitszeugnis*
import permit	*Importgenehmigung*
import restrictions	*Einfuhrbeschränkungen*
insurance certificate	*Versicherungszertifikat*
letter of credit (L/C)	*Akkreditiv*
open a letter of credit	*ein Akkreditiv eröffnen*
packing list	*Packliste*
proforma (or: pro-forma) invoice	*Pro-forma-Rechnung*
regulations	*Bestimmungen*
trade restrictions	*Handelsbeschränkungen*

2. Telephoning	***Telefonieren***
answerphone	*Anrufbeantworter*
call confidentiality	*Einrichtung zur Vermeidung des Abhörens Ihres Gesprächs durch Dritte*
cellular phone	*Funktelefon*
collect call	*R-Gespräch (= der Angerufene zahlt)*
credit-card call	*Telefonanruf mit Kreditkarte*
directory enquiries	*Fernsprechauskunft*
international call	*Auslandsgespräch*
local call	*Ortsgespräch*
mobile phone	*Mobiltelefon (Handy)*
occasional use	*gelegentliche Benutzung*
operator	*Vermittlung*
payphone	*Münztelefon*
phone booth/box	*Telefonzelle*
portable	*tragbar*
recall-voice messaging	*Einrichtung zur Aufnahme von Mitteilungen, wenn Ihr Telefon ausgeschaltet ist*
roam	*das Mobiltelefon bei Auslandsreisen in ausländischen Netzen benutzen*
telephone directory	*Telefonbuch*
telephone number	*Rufnummer*
Yellow Pages	*Gelbe Seiten*

3. The International Telephone Alphabet *Das internationale Telefonalphabet*

2.3

A for Andrew	N for Nellie
B for Benjamin	O for Oliver
C for Charlie	P for Peter
D for David	Q for Queenie
E for Edward	R for Robert
F for Frederick	S for Sugar
G for George	T for Tommy
H for Harry	U for Uncle
I for Isaac	V for Victory
J for Jack	W for William
K for King	X for X-Ray
L for Lucy	Y for Yellow
M for Mary	Z for Zebra

Down to Business

As Ms Rank deals with several foreign companies, she often has to discuss documentation and calculations over the phone.

Da Ms Rank mit mehreren ausländischen Firmen zu tun hat, muss sie oft Unterlagen und Berechnungen am Telefon besprechen.

1 Match the calculations in List A with the instructions given by Ms Rank in List B.

Ordnen Sie die Berechnungen in Liste A den von Ms Rank gegebenen Anweisungen in Liste B zu.

List A
I) DM 60 + DM 4
II) 568 x 4
III) $64 ÷ 4
IV) 95.5 - 4
V) 50pcs @ $4

List B
a "Multiply it all by four."
b "Add the totals together."
c "Subtract four to get the final total."
d "Now divide by four."
e "Take four dollars apiece."

Listening Text 6/3

2.4

2 Ms Rank has received another call about a shipment ordered from overseas. As you listen to it, complete the Bill of Lading on the following page by filling in the six missing pieces of information.

Ms Rank hat einen weiteren Anruf wegen einer aus Übersee bestellten Lieferung erhalten. Vervollständigen Sie das Konnossement auf der folgenden Seite, indem Sie die sechs fehlenden Informationen eintragen.

BILL OF LADING

Channel Line

For Port to Port Shipment

Harbour Lane, Wellington 5, New Zealand Tel: 055/44561 Fax: 77844

SHIPPER Baldwin Runners & Co 24-26 Main Street Wellington 10 New Zealand	**OCEAN VESSEL** ①
CONSIGNEE Sport-Rank Gescherweg 31 61169 Friedberg 2 Germany	**PORT OF LOADING** ②
NOTIFY PARTY Baldwin Runners & Co	**PORT OF DELIVERY** ③
FREIGHT TO BE PAID AT: ④	

MARKS & Nos	No & KIND OF PACKAGING DESCRIPTION OF GOODS	GROSS WEIGHT (kilos)	MEASUREMENT (cbm)
FN/221	12 boxes tennis shoes	⑤	2.2

ABOVE PARTICULARS AS DECLARED BY SHIPPER.
TOTAL NUMBER OF UNITS OR PACKAGES: ⑥

FREIGHT PAID AT DESTINATION Boyd, Brown & Co. Received by the Carrier from the Shipper in apparent good order and condition; the total numbers and quantities of packages shown for carriage from the port of loading to the port of delivery.	**PLACE AND DATE OF ISSUE** Wellington, 8 October 19.. SIGNED (FOR THE CARRIER) BY *J. Thompson* FOR BOYD, BROWN & Co AS AGENTS ONLY

"Received from the shipper in apparent good order and condition."

2.5

Listing Text 6/4

3 Sport-Rank have received another call – this time from a Japanese customer. As you listen, write down
a) the phone number given to Mr Taraki;
b) the postal address given by Mr Taraki.

Sport-Rank hat einen weiteren Anruf erhalten – dieses Mal von einem japanischen Kunden. Notieren Sie während des Zuhörens
a) die Telefonnummer, die Mr Taraki genannt wird;
b) die Postanschrift, die von Mr Taraki angegeben wird.

4 Ms Rank is speaking to a company which supplies mobile phones. Here is a transcript of their conversation – but you have to fit Ms Rank's parts (given after the dialogue) into their correct places.

Ms Rank spricht mit einer Firma, die Mobiltelefone liefert. Hier ist eine Abschrift ihres Gesprächs – Sie müssen jedoch Ms Ranks Beiträge, die Sie nach dem Dialog finden, an den richtigen Stellen einsetzen.

Phone company: ... so, as I understand it, you've got a number of mobile phones already. And now you want some more, to be installed in your cars.

Ms Rank: ______________________________
Phone company: And as your team travels a lot, I suppose they'll want to roam.

Ms Rank: ______________________________
Phone company: Ah, "to roam"means to use your phone in foreign networks when you're travelling abroad. And the model we've got right here gives you that. And it has all the facilities you'll need – fax calls, recall-voice messaging ...

Ms Rank: ______________________________
Phone company: That means that received messages are recorded even when the phone is switched off. Another big advantage is its call confidentiality.

Ms Rank: ____

Phone company: Call confidentiality. That means: no one can listen in on your conversations.

Ms Rank: __________________________________

Phone company: Er – you'll be needing three phones, you said?

Ms Rank: _______________________

Phone company: Does that include Saturdays?

Ms Rank: _________________

Phone company: I see.

Ms Rank: _________________

Ms Rank's parts (wrong order)

Ms Ranks Dialogteile (in der falschen Reihenfolge)

1. Sorry, I'm not familiar with that expression.
2. And the other – well, that'll be for occasional use. Mainly for receiving calls in the evening, actually.
3. I see. Well, that seems to be what we need.
4. That's right.
5. Oh, certainly. We do a lot of road work on Saturdays. It's the only day we can get hold of a lot of our customers.
6. Recall-voice messaging. Could you explain that, please?
7. Yes, two mainly for business ...
8. Sorry, I didn't catch that – call ...?

2.6

Listening Text 6/5

5 You will hear the conversation in full. Listen for any mistakes you have made and correct them.

Sie werden das Gespräch in voller Länge hören. Achten Sie auf mögliche Fehler, die Ihnen unterlaufen sind, und korrigieren Sie diese.

6 Answer these questions, on the basis of the conversation you have heard and the phone company's list of charges (on the following page).

Beantworten Sie die unten stehenden Fragen. Beziehen Sie sich dabei auf das gerade gehörte Gespräch und die Gebührenliste der Telefonfirma (auf der folgenden Seite).

a How many mobile phones does Ms Rank want?

Wie viele Mobiltelefone möchte Ms Rank haben?

b For how many of them should she pay "Business Call" Tariff? "Lowcall" Tariff?

Für wie viele dieser Telefone sollte sie „Business Call“ *Tarif?* „Lowcall“ *Tarif bezahlen?*

BUSINESSCALL	
Connection	£60.00
Monthly Rental	£25.00
Peak Calls	25p
Off Peak Calls	10p
Peak hours (Mon-Sat)	07.30-21.30

LOWCALL	
Connection	£30.00
Monthly Rental	£12.77
Peak Calls	50p
Off Peak Calls	20p
Peak hours (Mon-Fri) 08.00-19.00	

Dealing with Visual Info

Outlines

Listening Text 6/6

2.7

1 You will hear part of a talk by a British speaker at a seminar on "Electronic Communications". There is an outline of his talk on the following page. The spaces have to be filled with the notes given. The first space has already been filled in. Listen to the talk and fill in the remaining spaces.

Sie werden einen Teil eines Vortrags hören, den ein englischer Sprecher in einem Seminar über „Elektronische Kommunikation" hält. Auf der folgenden Seite sehen Sie ein Schema seines Vortrags. Die Lücken müssen mit den vorliegenden Notizen gefüllt werden. Die erste Lücke wurde bereits ausgefüllt. Hören Sie den Text und füllen Sie die verbleibenden Lücken.

NOTES

Wider use of English as a global language	More users of English as 2nd language than 1st language
English is used by & stored on computers	Electronic Communications
Increasingly, people have 2 languages: a native language b English (formal communication)	Internet & fax: many people can write – but not speak – English

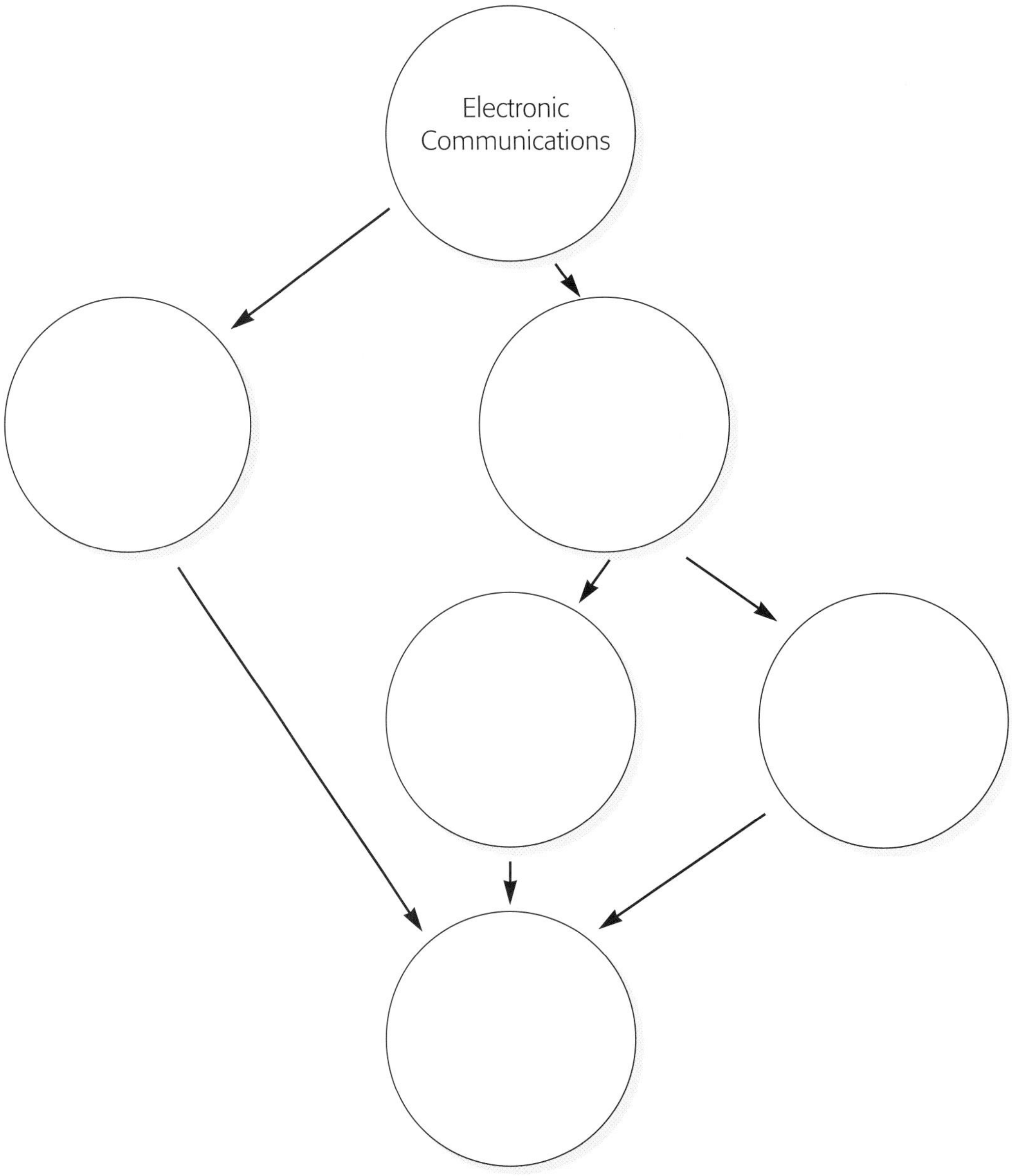

Outline of the lecture on "Electronic Communications".

Schema des Vortrags über „Elektronische Kommunikation".

2.8

Listening Text 6/7

2 Listen to this part of an economics analyst's lecture about "downsizing" and "outsourcing". Take notes on his talk by completing the boxes. The first three boxes have been completed for you.

Hören Sie diesen Teil eines Vortrags eines amerikanischen Wirtschaftsanalytikers über „downsizing" (= Stellenabbau) und „outsourcing" (= Auslagerung von Unternehmensaktivitäten). Machen Sie sich Notizen zu seinem Vortrag, indem Sie die Kästchen vervollständigen. Die ersten drei Kästchen wurden bereits für Sie beschriftet.

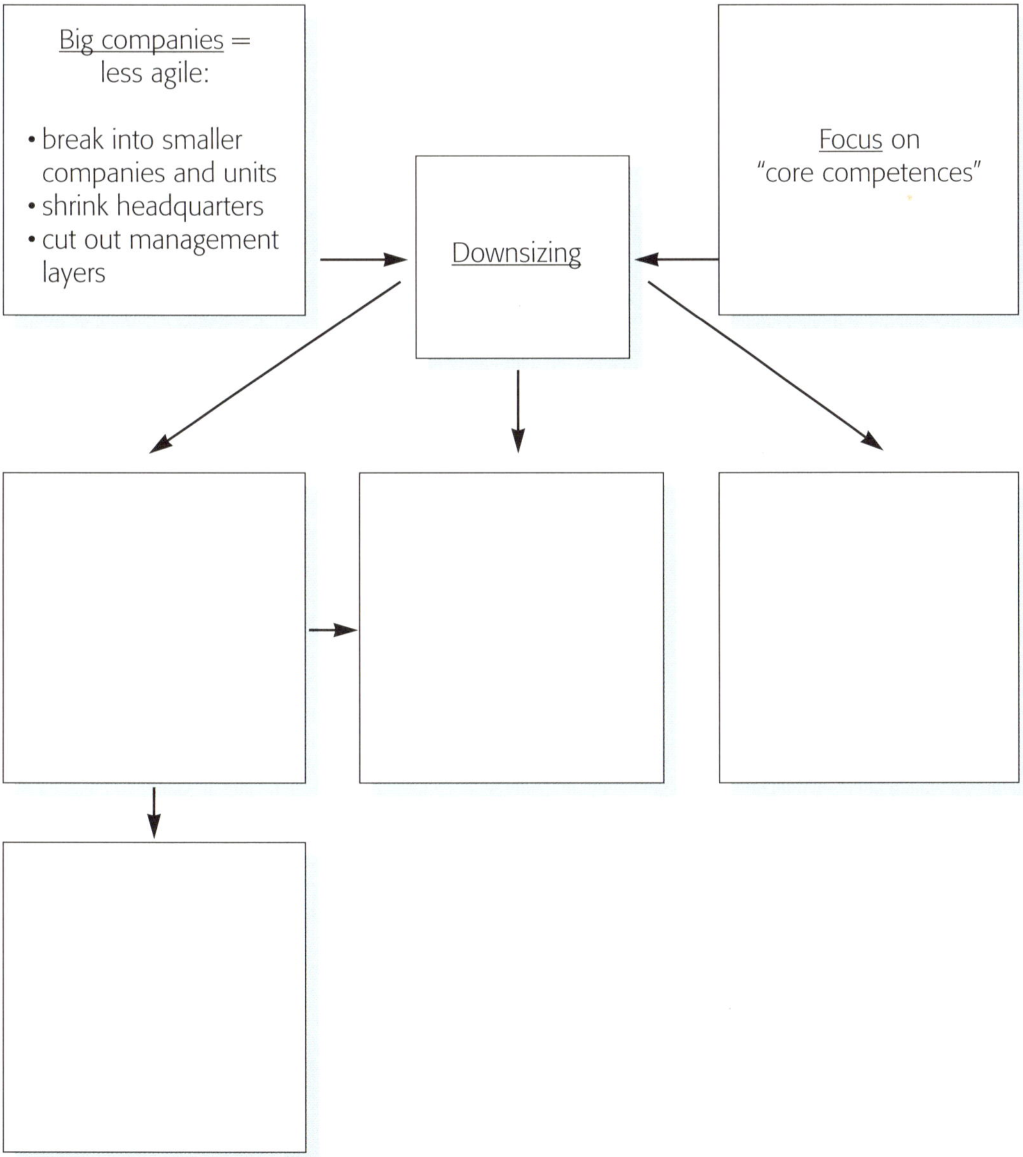

The British-American Difference

All these expressions have to do with communication.

Can you find the matching UK and US vocabulary? The first match has been done for you.

Alle folgenden Ausdrücke haben mit Kommunikation zu tun.

Können Sie die sich jeweils entsprechenden britischen und amerikanischen Vokabeln finden? Die erste Zuordnung wurde bereits für Sie vorgenommen.

German	UK	US
Postleitzahl	post(al) code	ZIP code
Nachnahme		
Post		
Briefträger		
Briefkasten		
postlagernd		
Ferngespräch		
gebührenfreie Telefonnummer		
R-Gespräch		
Stand (Messe)		
Werbezettel		
ausfüllen (Formular)		
Schwarzes Brett		

General Delivery

post restante

post(al) code

to call collect

booth

0800 or 0500 number

notice board

mailman

- trunk call
- bulletin board
- postbox
- to fill out
- to post
- to mail
- cash on delivery (COD)
- to reverse the charges
- long-distance call
- stand
- ZIP code
- publicity leafet
- mailbox
- to fill in
- 800 number
- broadside
- postman
- collect on delivery (c.o.d.)

Last but not Least

Appointments — Stellengesuche

Kai Weil, a young sales representative, is applying for a new job. He has to write the job application and CV (= Curriculum Vitae) in English. So he has written to Kate, an English friend, for help.

Kai Weil, ein junger Außendienstmitarbeiter, bewirbt sich um eine neue Stelle. Er muss eine Bewerbung und einen Lebenslauf in Englisch schreiben. Deshalb hat er Kate, einer englischen Freundin, geschrieben, um sie um Hilfe zu bitten.

1 Read Kate's reply on the following page, filling in the six missing expressions taken from the list below.

Lesen Sie auf der folgenden Seite Kates Antwort und setzen Sie die sechs fehlenden Teile aus der darunter stehenden Liste ein.

Dear Kai,

So you've decided to apply for a job in Britain!

As requested, I'm writing to give you a few tips concerning your CV. In general, you should use condensed, note-form information in the CV, ______________ (1). Ideally, it will contain only essential information which the employer can easily digest ______________ (2)! For example, give your age – not your date of birth. And there's no need to list your parents' names and professions – or your religion, unless you think it's relevant to the job. Similarly, there's no need to list all the schools you've attended ______________ (3).

You should list your previous employers, though – and each employer's type of business. But their full addresses aren't necessary – just the town or city in each case. There's no need to send a photograph , ______________ (4). And remember – if you use a German phrase, add a short translation, eg *"Abitur* (university entrance certificate)".

It's useful to mention some of your spare-time interests and activities, ______________ (5). But be specific: "secretary of local tennis club" or "playing the saxophone" are more impressive than just "sports"or "music"!

Be sure to list two or three referees, ______________ (6). Give their full addresses, as the reader may need to write to them. And make sure you ask your referees beforehand if they're willing to write references for you.

Well, that's enough, I think, Kai. Good luck – and do let me know how you get on.

With very best wishes,

Kate

(a) unless it was asked for in the advert
(b) not full sentences and paragraphs
(c) including at least one previous employer, if possible
(d) as these can show you're an interesting person
(e) – only your last one should appear on the CV
(f) – the shorter, the better

2 Kai has now written his CV. Can you arrange its six parts into their correct order?

Kai hat jetzt seinen Lebenslauf geschrieben. Können Sie die sechs Teile in die richtige Reihenfolge bringen?

```
Dear Mr Branston

I am writing about the position of International Sales
Representative advertised in Die Zeit. I would like to apply
as I would welcome the challenge and may have the
qualifications you are looking for.

I enclose a CV, written in English, as requested.
I am available for
```

1

Address Stephanweg 3, 69115 Heidelberg, Germany (Tel: 06221-5566; Fax 15566)

2

References

The following persons are willing to provide letters of reference on request:

Frau Ulrike Jüngst, Company Director, S. Bernhardt & Sohn, Jahnstrasse 38, 70176 Stuttgart

Herr Walter Dombrowski, Departmental Manager, Lehmann & Schmidt, Westring 67-69, 69115 Heidelberg

Professor Hans Ebert, Dept. of English, University of Kassel, Goethestrasse 8, 34119 Kassel

3

Curriculum Vitae

Kai Weil

4

Age 30

Marital Status single

Nationality German

5

Foreign language abilities

Advanced ability in English (speaking & writing)

Intermediate ability in Spanish (speaking only)

Outside interests and activities

Tennis (secretary of local league)

English studies (currently studying for Cambridge Certificate of Proficiency)

6

Education

1978-81	Wilhelmschule (secondary school), Friedberg	six subjects
1981-85	University of Kassel	English, Economics

Qualifications

Abitur (university entrance certificate)	1978
Diploma in English & Economics (Grade 1)	1983
Certificate in Software Applications in Business	1984

Employment record

Period	Employer	Employer's business	Position
1985-89	Lehmann & Schmidt, Heidelberg	Optical goods Manufacturer	Salesman
1989-94	S. Bernhardt & Sohn, Stuttgart	Optical instruments	Regional Sales Manager
1994 to date	T.H. Nice (US) Inc, Heidelberg	Photographic Instruments	West Europe Sales Representative

Discussing and Settling Questions of Payment

Getting Started

1 When a seller and a buyer agree on a contract, they also have to agree on the terms of payment.

Wenn ein Verkäufer und ein Käufer einen Vertrag vereinbaren, müssen sie auch die Zahlungsbedingungen vereinbaren.

Match the terms of payment in List A with the explanations in List B.

Ordnen Sie die Zahlungsbedingungen in der Liste A den Erklärungen der Liste B zu.

List A

Terms of Payment	***Zahlungsbedingungen***
1. Cash in advance	*Vorauszahlung*
2. Cash with order (CWO)	*Barzahlung bei Auftragserteilung*
3. Cash on delivery (COD)	*gegen Nachnahme*
4. Payment on receipt of invoice	*Zahlung bei Rechnungserhalt*
5. Payment on receipt of goods	*Zahlung bei Erhalt der Waren*
6. 30 days net	*30 Tage netto*
7. 3 months' credit	*3 Monate Ziel*
8. Strictly net	*rein netto*
9. 2% for cash	*2% Skonto bei Barzahlung*
10. Against 3 months' acceptance	*gegen Dreimonatsakzept*
11. Documents against payment (D/P) also known as: Cash against documents (CAD)	*Kasse gegen Dokumente*
12. Documents against acceptance (D/A)	*Dokumente gegen Akzept*

List B

Explanations	***Erklärungen***
a The buyer sends payment together with his order.	
b A third party (eg the forwarding agent or post office) collects the invoice amount.	
c The goods will be supplied if the buyer accepts a draft which is due for payment after three months.	

d The buyer pays when he has received the goods.
e The buyer pays the full amount within 30 days (= no discounts).
f The buyer pays within three months.
g The buyer may not take any discounts.
h The buyer pays for the goods before they are shipped.
i The buyer may deduct a 2% discount if he pays in cash.
j The buyer gets the documents from a bank in his country when he accepts a draft.
k The buyer gets the documents from a bank in his country when he pays.
l The buyer pays when he gets the invoice.

2 You now have twelve combinations (Terms of Payment + Explanations). Add these extra sentences to three of them.

Sie haben nun zwölf Kombinationen (Zahlungsbedingungen + Erklärungen). Fügen Sie drei dieser Kombinationen je einen der folgenden zusätzlichen Sätze hinzu.

Extra sentences
a The goods are released to the buyer after he has paid this amount.
b Then he can take the documents to the port and collect the goods.
c Then he can take the documents to the port and collect the goods, and pays the draft when it becomes due.

3 Joyce and Brian (of Rayner Detergents plc) are discussing a customer's terms of payment. Look at this transcript of their discussion. All the parts are in the wrong order except the first and last parts, which are correct. Arrange the remaining parts (2 to 8) into their correct order.

Joyce und Brian (von Rayner Detergents plc) besprechen die Zahlungsbedingungen eines Kunden. Sehen Sie sich diese Abschrift ihrer Diskussion an. Die Dialogteile sind in der falschen Reihenfolge, außer dem ersten und letzten Teil, die sich an der richtigen Stelle befinden. Ordnen Sie die verbleibenden Teile (2 bis 8) richtig an.

1. Brian, there are a few details in these accounts I'd like to clarify. For example, what about these Hallways figures?
2. But now they're asking for three months' credit.
3. Just this one – but we only issued the invoice last Tuesday.
4. Ah, we're having some difficulty with Hallways. They normally pay within 30 days.
5. That's what I thought.
6. And will they be paying this one within 30 days?
7. Three months! Hm – do they have any payments outstanding?
8. Yes, that's what we agreed.
9. Right. Well, look into this, would you, Brian? And find out as discreetly as you can why they want three months' credit now.

Listen & Repeat

Listening Text 7/1

2.9

Listen to the complete version of the conversation and correct any mistakes you have made. Then role play both parts of the conversation, for speaking practice.

Hören Sie die vollständige Version des Gesprächs und korrigieren Sie, wenn nötig, die Ihnen unterlaufenen Fehler. Spielen Sie beide Teile des Gesprächs (im Rollenspiel) – als Sprachpraxisübung.

Useful Expressions

Discussing & settling questions of payment	***Zahlungsangelegenheiten diskutieren & klären***
Who'll be responsible for paying the bank charges?	*Wer wird die Bankgebühren übernehmen?*
That's what we agreed, right?	*Darauf haben wir uns geeinigt, nicht wahr?*
Would we have to pay ... ?	*Müssten wir ... zahlen?*
How can we decide how much ... ?	*Wie können wir entscheiden, wie viel ... ?*
How much ... would have to be paid?	*Wie viel ... müssten gezahlt werden?*
We'll need to invest in ...	*Wir werden* *in ... investieren müssen.*
have to spend a lot on ...	*viel für ... ausgeben müssen.*
probably make ...	*wohl ... machen.*
be covering that payment.	*diese Zahlung vornehmen.*
There are still a few details I'd like to clarify.	*Es gibt noch einige Punkte, die ich klären möchte.*
They normally pay within 30 days.	*Normalerweise zahlen sie innerhalb von 30 Tagen.*
This time they've asked for three months' credit.	*Dieses Mal haben sie um einen dreimonatigen Kredit gebeten.*
I'm sorry, but that kind of expenditure is out of the question.	*Es tut mir Leid, aber solche Ausgaben kommen nicht in Frage.*
The money should be with you within two weeks.	*Das Geld sollte innerhalb von zwei Wochen bei Ihnen sein.*
Are there any charges other than interest?	*Entstehen außer den Zinsen noch andere Kosten?*
You have to pay the bank charges once a month.	*Sie müssen die Bankspesen einmal im Monat bezahlen.*

In this case, I think we'd better ask for payment in advance.	*Ich glaube, in diesem Fall verlangen wir besser die Zahlung im Voraus.*
About 40% of our customers pay in cash.	*Circa 40% unserer Kunden zahlen bar.*
Before I sign the letter of credit, I've got a couple of questions.	*Bevor ich das Akkreditiv unterschreibe, habe ich noch ein paar Fragen.*

"You have to pay the bank charges once a month."

LANGUAGE STUDY

CONDITIONAL SENTENCES: TYPE III

In Unit 2 wurden zwei Typen von Bedingungssätzen behandelt. Hier folgt nun ein dritter Typus, der eine „irreale Bedingung" impliziert.

If they had given us a discount, we would have paid in cash.
(Or: We would have paid in cash if they had given us a discount.)

Die if-Bedingung (= die Möglichkeit, uns einen Rabatt zu gewähren) kann nicht erfüllt werden, da die Gelegenheit verstrichen ist.

Andere Versionen dieses Bedingungssatz-Typus:

If the price had fallen, we [should / could / ought to / might] have placed an order immediately.

If we had received the order yesterday, we would be working on it now.

If we had paid the invoice, we would have the goods now.

Exercises

1

Using the examples on the preceding page to help you choose the most probable forms of the verbs in brackets.

Wählen Sie, mit Hilfe der Beispiele auf der vorangegangenen Seite, die wahrscheinlichsten Formen der Verben in Klammern.

1 If we'd been able to reassure the bank, we (get) __________ another three-year loan.

2 If the goods had been held up, we (have to pay) __________ storage costs.

3 They would have given up the venture if they (not break even) __________ after six months.

4 S&R would be selling in Korea today if they (keep) __________ their Asian sales division.

5 If you'd called earlier, I (can take) __________ you to Norwich myself.

6 We might have prepared a reception if we (know) __________ they were coming.

2

2.10

Now choose the right verb forms from the possibilities given in this description. Then, listen and check the answers on the CD.

Wählen Sie nun die richtigen Verbformen aus den in dieser Beschreibung vorgegebenen Möglichkeiten. Hören Sie im Anschluss die Lösungen auf der CD.

We make agricultural chemicals to prevent crop damage in parts of Africa. Many of our customers can't read. In the past, this was a big problem for them and us because it's important that customers understand the information on the packaging. If they'd been able to read, they 1. would have known/would know/had known whether they were buying pesticides or insecticides or fungicides or whatever.

Well, ten months ago, we came up with the idea of putting symbolic pictures onto the packaging. And this has been a great success – everyone's getting the products they want, no one's mixing them up any more, and we're gaining satisfied customers. But if we 2. had to think/had thought/would have thought of that idea at the very start, we 3. could avoid/will avoid/could have avoided the problem entirely.

And another point: we're colour-coding our packaging now – green for insecticides, red for pesticides, and so on. This, too, has proved successful. I think, if 4. we'd used/we were using/we used colour-coding right from the start, 5. we'd probably be selling/we probably sold/we've probably sold to 20 or 30 per cent more customers now. To put it another way, our competitors wouldn't have won such a substantial share of the market if we 6. would have used/had used/were using this style of packaging from the very beginning.

Typical Mistakes

German speakers of English often make mistakes with time phrases. Can you match these German phrases with the British English ones which follow? The first three have been done for you.

Deutsche Sprecher machen im Englischen oft Fehler bei den Zeitausdrücken. Können Sie diese deutschen Ausdrücke den unten aufgeführten englischen zuordnen? Die ersten drei wurden bereits für Sie zugeordnet.

today ______	*heute*
yesterday ______	*gestern*
tomorrow ______	*morgen*
______	*vorgestern*
______	*vorvorgestern*
______	*heute vor einer Woche/ heute vor acht Tagen*
______	*vor zwei Wochen*
______	*gestern vor zwei Wochen*
______	*der übernächste Tag*
______	*übermorgen*
______	*morgen in acht Tagen*
______	*in vierzehn Tagen*

today
two days later
two weeks ago
the day after tomorrow
tomorrow week
three days ago
a fortnight ago yesterday
tomorrow
yesterday
in a fortnight
the day before yesterday
a week ago today

Word Bank

Discussing & settling questions of payment	***Zahlungsangelegenheiten diskutieren & klären***
2% for cash	*2% Skonto bei Barzahlung*
3 months' credit	*3 Monate Ziel*
30 days net	*30 Tage netto*
according to our estimate	*nach unserer Schätzung*
against 3 months' acceptance	*gegen Dreimonatsakzept*

balance sheet	*Bilanz*
bank charges	*Bankgebühren*
bill of exchange	*Wechsel*
break even	*kostendeckend arbeiten*
cash against documents (= CAD)	*Kasse gegen Dokumente*
cash in advance	*Vorauszahlung*
cash on delivery (= COD)	*gegen Nachnahme*
cash with order (= CWO)	*Barzahlung bei Auftragserteilung*
creditworthy	*kreditwürdig*
discount	*Rabatt*
documents against acceptance (= D/A)	*Dokumente gegen Akzept*
documents against payment (= D/P)	*Kasse gegen Dokumente*
draft	*Wechsel*
exchange rate	*Wechselkurs*
expire	*auslaufen*
expiry	*Ablauf*
import duty	*Einfuhrzoll*
income tax	*Einkommensteuer*
increase in turnover	*Umsatzsteigerung*
interest rate	*Zinssatz*
irrevocable	*unwiderruflich*
issuing bank	*Emissionsbank*
money order	*Zahlungsanweisung*
outstanding	*unbezahlt*
overdue	*überfällig*
payment on receipt of goods	*Zahlung bei Erhalt der Waren*
payment on receipt of invoice	*Zahlung bei Rechnungserhalt*
receipt	*Quittung*
repayment	*Rückzahlung*
revocable	*widerruflich*
strictly net	*rein netto*
third party	*Dritter*
transfer	*überweisen*

Down to Business

A company in Texas has ordered a consignment of goods from a company in Hamburg. To pay for the goods, the Texas company has to open a Letter of Credit at its bank. Mrs Russell (who works for the Texas company) is completing an application for the Letter of Credit. She is calling Herr Grosskopf of the Hamburg company.

Eine Firma in Texas hat bei einer Hamburger Firma eine Warenlieferung bestellt.. Um die Waren zu bezahlen, muss die texanische Firma ein Akkreditiv bei ihrer Bank eröffnen. Mrs Russell (die für die texanische Firma arbeitet) füllt ein Antragsformular für ein Akkreditiv aus. Sie ruft Herrn Grosskopf von der Hamburger Firma an.

1 Listening Text 7/2

As you listen to the phone call, fill in as many details in the application as you can.

Tragen Sie, während Sie das Telefongespräch hören, so viele Einzelheiten wie möglich in den Antrag ein.

APPLICATION FOR A DOCUMENTARY LETTER OF CREDIT

* Delete as necessary

Please open an *IRREVOCABLE / REVOCABLE Letter of Credit
❑ By Airmail ❑ By Teletransmission

Beneficiary's Bankers:

Name and Address of Applicant	Name and Address of Beneficiary
Argus Office Supplies 14338 Katy Boulevard Houston Texas 75001 USA	Grosskopf Printers GmbH Goethestr. 14-16 22559 Hamburg Germany

Commission / Charges ❑ All our a/c ❑ All beneficiary's a/c

Amount ❑ For
❑ Up to
❑ About

Credit to expire on ________________ in the beneficiary's country

Documents to be presented within ________ days of shipment.

Transportation from:
to:
Terms & relevant place: *CIF, C&F, FOB, etc ________________________

Documents required:
Full set Bills of Lading to order marked *Freight paid / Freight payable at destination and *Notify
____

Insurance Certificate. Risks as follows: __________________________
Other documents: ____

Quantity and description of goods:

____

Special instructions:

2 Now Herr Grosskopf is calling Mrs Russell. In the transcript (below), Mrs Russell's parts are complete. But you have to work out what Herr Grosskopf must have said.

Nun ruft Herr Grosskopf Mrs Russell an. In der Abschrift (unten) sind Mrs Russells Beiträge vollständig. Sie müssen jedoch die Aussagen von Herrn Grosskopf noch herausarbeiten.

Grosskopf: Mrs Russell? It's about – Letter of – still a few details – like to clarify.
Russell: Go ahead.
Grosskopf: First, when – Letter – expire?
Russell: The 30th of November. That's what we agreed.
Grosskopf: Right. And who – responsible – bank charges?
Russell: Well, we'll be covering those – as we usually do.
Grosskopf: OK – just wanted – confirm that. Now, concerning – insurance – providing – "all risks" cover – we agreed, right?
Russell: That's right, Herr Grosskopf.
Grosskopf: OK– that's it – thanks – advise – soon as – goods have been shipped.
Russell: Thank you, Herr Grosskopf. Goodbye.

2.12

Listening Text 7/3

3 Listen to the complete version of the conversation and correct any mistakes you have made.

Hören Sie das vollständige Gespräch und korrigieren Sie, wenn nötig, die Ihnen unterlaufenen Fehler.

4 Use the information you have to fill in the missing details in the application.

Benutzen Sie die Ihnen zur Verfügung stehenden Informationen, um die fehlenden Einzelheiten in den Antrag einzutragen.

Dealing with Visual Info

Smileys

Smileys are humorous faces produced by a few strokes on the keyboard. By means of smileys, Internet users express moods to each other. Here are three examples.

Smileys sind lustige Gesichter, die mit ein paar Anschlägen auf der Tastatur produziert werden. Mit Hilfe der Smileys teilen sich Internet-Benutzer gegenseitig ihre Laune mit. Hier sind drei Beispiele.

: -) I'm smiling **8 -)** I'm wearing sunglasses! **: - C** I'm really unhappy

Here are six more smileys – try and guess the user's mood.

Hier sind sechs weitere Smileys – versuchen Sie, die Laune des Benutzers zu erraten.

1.	2.	3.	4.	5.	6.
: - #	**: - (**	**: - &**	**I - O**	**: -D**	**: - O**

The British-American Difference

1 Put a cross in the boxes to show which words match. One box has been done for you.

Markieren Sie die Kästchen mit einem Kreuzchen, um anzuzeigen, welche Wörter korrespondieren. Ein Kästchen wurde bereits für Sie angekreuzt.

Money

UK / US	deposit account	interim payment	note	current account	compen-sation	invoicing	bill	part payment	go into liquidation	tax allowance
checking account										
billing										
remuner-ation										
partial payment										
tax exemption										
progress payment										
savings account										
go bankrupt									X	
check										
bill										

2 Can you make a list of the ten corresponding German terms?

Können Sie eine Liste der zehn entsprechenden deutschen Ausdrücke anfertigen?

Last but not Least

1 Can you insert the five missing nationalities and seven missing currencies?

Können Sie die fünf fehlenden Nationalitäten und die sieben fehlenden Währungen einfügen?

The European Union

The Original Six	Nationality	National Currency
Belgium	Belgian (a Belgian) (plural: the Belgians)	Belgian Franc (BFr or Bf or FB)
Germany	German (a German) (plural: the Germans)	____________
France	French (a ________) (plural: the French)	French Franc (Fr or F or FF)
Italy	Italian (an Italian) (plural: the Italians)	____________
Luxembourg	Luxembourg (a Luxembourger) (plural: the Luxembourgers)	Luxembourg Franc (LFr)
the Netherlands	Dutch (a Dutchman/ Dutchwoman) (plural: the ________)	Guilder or Gulden or Florin (HFl or DFL or Gld or Fl)
Admitted 1973		
Denmark	Danish (a Dane) (plural: the ________)	Danish Krone (DKr or DKK)
Republic of Ireland	Irish (an Irishman /-woman) (plural: the Irish)	____________
United Kingdom	British (a ________) (plural: the British)	Pound (Sterling) (£ or £Stg)
Admitted 1981		
Greece	Greek (a Greek) (plural: the Greeks)	____________
Admitted 1986		
Portugal	Portugese (a Portuguese) (plural: the Portuguese)	____________
Spain	Spanish (a ________) (plural: the Spanish)	____________

Admitted 1995

Austria	Austrian (an Austrian) (plural: the Austrians)	______________
Finland	Finnish (a Finn) (plural: the Finns)	Markka or Finnmark (Fmk)
Sweden	Swedish (a Swede) (plural: the Swedes)	Swedish Krone (SKr)

2 Match the items in List A and List B.

Ordnen Sie die Ausdrücke der Liste A den Erklärungen der Liste B zu.

List A: Expressions

1. The Economic and Monetary Union (EMU)
2. Member States
3. The European Central Bank (ECB)
4. The Euro
5. The Euro Zone
6. Continuity of Contracts
7. The Conversion Rate

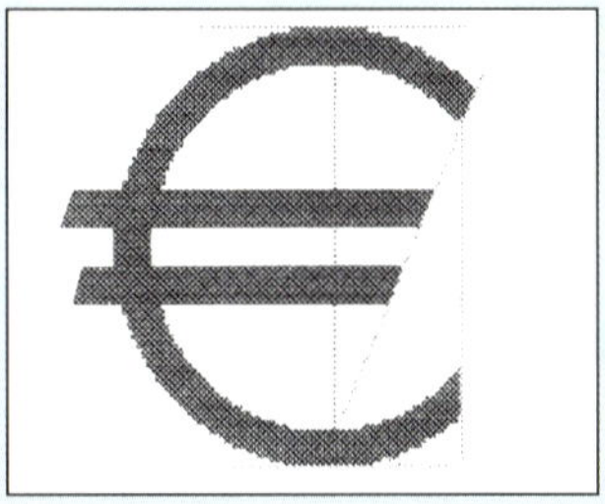

List B: Definitions

a The countries in the European Union who share the same monetary policy and the euro.
b The geographic area shared by the "participating" Member States.
c The fixed rate of exchange at which the euro is the equivalent of the national currency.
d The euro zone's official and single currency, to replace the currencies of the participating Member States.
e The countries in the European Union – those also in the EMU are called "participating" Member States.
f The institution which monitors monetary policy in the EMU.
g An agreement that (national and international) contracts remain unaffected by the currency changeover to the euro.

3 You now have seven combinations (List A + List B). Add these extra sentences to four of them.

Sie haben nun sieben Kombinationen (Liste A + Liste B). Fügen Sie vier dieser Kombinationen je einen der folgenden zusätzlichen Sätze hinzu.

Extra sentences

A It was also given the task of introducing euro notes and coins in the EMU.
B The deadline for this was set for July 2002.
C The beginning point for this was fixed at 1 January 1999.
D This means that they cannot be changed or ended on the basis of the change to the euro.

Travelling

→ Getting Started

Olaf Schubert works with a German company and has to go to England to take part in talks there.

Olaf Schubert arbeitet bei einer deutschen Firma und muss nach England reisen, um dort an Gesprächen teilzunehmen.

1 You will have to complete Schubert's travel schedule. To do this, you must look at these flight schedules and this fax.

Ihre Aufgabe ist es, Schuberts Reisezeitplan zu vervollständigen. Um dies zu tun, müssen Sie diese Flugpläne und dieses Fax ansehen.

Frankfurt, Main

Scheduled Airlines:

British Airways

Lufthansa

Scheduled Flights between Birmingham International Airport and Frankfurt,

Scheduled Departures:

FLIGHT NO	TIME	M	T	W	T	F	S	S	DATES
BA 5360	0840	✓	✓	✓	✓	✓	✓	✓	
BA 5358	1145	✓	✓	✓	✓	✓	-	-	
BA 5362	1630	✓	✓	✓	✓	✓	-	✓	
LH 4093	1750	✓	✓	✓	✓	✓	✓	✓	

Scheduled Arrivals:

FLIGHT NO	TIME	M	T	W	T	F	S	S	DATES
BA 5361	1235	✓	✓	✓	✓	✓	✓	✓	
BA 5359	1545	✓	✓	✓	✓	✓	-	-	
LH 4050	1710	✓	✓	✓	✓	✓	✓	✓	
BA 5363	2030	✓	✓	✓	✓	✓	-	✓	

If there is an entry in the Dates column, the flight runs on only those dates of this month. Passengers are advised to check with their travel agent, tour operator or the airline concerned before finalisi

Frq	Dep	Arr	Flight	Aircr	Stops
Manchester					+ 01:00 MAN
→ **Bayreuth** BYU					+ 02:00
Xe67	1150	– 1755	4015n)FRA/EW905		C
→ **Berlin** BER, T Tegel TXL					+ 02:00
X	0715	– 1225T	5213n)MUC/2505 01Jul–31Aug		C
X	0715	– 1225T	5213n)MUC/2531 01Sep–26Okt		C
Xe5	0845	– 1335T	4103n)FRA/2414		C
X	1150	– 1840T	4015n)FRA/2400		C
Xe67	1150	– 1635T	4015n)FRA/2410		C
X	1455	– 2010T	5205n)MUC/2513 01Jul–31Aug		C
Xe6	1455	– 2010T	5205n)MUC/2535 01Sep–26Okt		C
Xe7	1455	– 2035T	5205n)MUC/2533 02Sep–26Okt		C
X	1750	– 2235T	4075n)FRA/2458		C
→ **Bonn** BNJ					+ 02:00
5	0635	– 1243	4103n)FRA/1058(2A)		C
Xe5	0845	– 1443	4103n)FRA/1062(2A)		C
X	1150	– 1743	4015n)FRA/1068(2A)		C
X	1750	– 2344	4075n)FRA/1080(2A)		C
→ **Bremen** BRE					+ 02:00
Xe5	0845	– 1355	4103n)FRA/186		C
X	1150	– 1820	4015n)FRA/194		C
X	1750	– 2225	4075n)FRA/176		C
→ **Dresden** DRS					+ 02:00
2345	0715	– 1415	5213n)MUC/974 01Jul–12Jul		C
2345	0715	– 1415	5213n)MUC/974 20Aug–26Okt		C
Xe5	0845	– 1415	4103n)FRA/318		C
X	1150	– 1750	4015n)FRA/300		C
Xe6	1455	– 2020	5205n)MUC/4423		C
X	1750	– 2230	4075n)FRA/320		C
→ **Düsseldorf** DUS					+ 02:00
Xe7	**0925**	**– 1150**	**4055n)**	**737**	**0**
Xe6	**1850**	**– 2115**	**4057n)**	**737**	**0**
→ **Frankfurt** FRA					+ 02:00
5	**0635**	**– 0930**	**4103n)**	**737**	**0**
Xe5	**0845**	**– 1140**	**4103n)**	**737**	**0**
X	**1150**	**– 1445**	**4015n)**	**737**	**0**
X	**1750**	**– 2045**	**4075n)**	**737**	**0**
→ **Friedrichshafen** FDH					+ 02:00
X	1150	– 1755	4015n)FRA/222		C

FAX

Llewellin & Pankhust plc 27 April

Herr Schubert
As promised, I've reserved a room for you. You're booked at Aston Olympic Hotel for the night of 2-3 May.
Should you need any help with further travel arrangements, please let me know. If not, I'll pick you up at 9 am on Friday at the hotel.
Have a good trip.

Bob Llewellin

PS We're going to bring out the new model in July. You'll have a chance to see it when you're here.

Listening Text 8/1

2.13

2 Listen to a phone call from Herr Schubert and use the information you have to complete all the missing parts in his travel schedule.

Hören Sie sich einen Anruf von Herrn Schubert an und benutzen Sie die Ihnen zur Verfügung stehenden Informationen, um alle fehlenden Teile in seinem Reisezeitplan zu ergänzen.

Travel Schedule: Olaf Schubert

Thursday, 2 May

17.50: Depart Frankfurt: Flight LH ______________ (a)

17.55: Arrive ______________(b)

Taxi to ______________ (c)

Friday, 3 May

______ (d): Pick-up at hotel (Bob Llewellin)

09.30-11.00: Talks at Llewellin & Pankhust plc (Company Office)

12.01: Depart ______________ (e) (rail)

14.15: Arrive ______________ (f)

Lunch & talks with Wardingley & Brown at ______________ (g) Restaurant

To airport (Wardingley)

______ (h): Depart ______________ (i): Flight LH ______________ (j)

20.45: Arrive ______________ (k)

3 Can you arrange the parts of this telephone call into their correct order? The first and last parts are already in their correct positions.

Können Sie die Teile dieses Anrufs in die richtige Reihenfolge bringen? Der erste und der letzte Teil befinden sich bereits an der richtigen Stelle.

Speaker A: 1. I'll meet you at the station on Tuesday morning. You're coming on the eleven fourteen, aren't you?
2. Yes, I've made the arrangements for your visit there.
3. Then, afterwards, I'll take you back to the station myself.
4. I'll be wearing a blue coat and carrying a copy of "The Economist".
5. In good time for the three thirty-four to Leeds, I hope?
6. Thanks very much.
7. Oh, certainly. Would that arrangement be convenient for you?
8. Then I'll certainly be able to find you. Then we'll go on to the Design Centre?
9. Yes, I am. Er ... how will I recognise you?

Speaker B: 10. Yes, indeed. That sounds fine.

Listen & Repeat

2.14

Listening Text 8/2

You will hear the complete conversation – with pauses. During the pauses, repeat what the speakers say, imitating their stress and intonation as closely as possible.

Sie werden das vollständige Gespräch hören – mit Pausen. Wiederholen Sie während der Pausen das, was die Sprecher sagen. Imitieren Sie dabei bitte deren Betonung und Satzmelodie so gut wie möglich.

Useful Expressions

Travelling — ***Reisen***

Arranging travel & accommodation	***Reisen & Unterkunft planen***
You're coming from ... , aren't you?	*Sie kommen aus ... , nicht wahr?*
I'm coming on the 12.01 (train).	*Ich komme mit dem 12.01 Uhr (Zug).*
Would you make a provisional reservation for me on that flight?	*Würden Sie diesen Flug vorläufig für mich buchen?*
The flight arrives at 8.35.	*Der Flug kommt um 8.35 Uhr an.*
Isn't there a service direct to ... ?	*Gibt es keine Linie direkt nach ... ?*
You will be in good time for the flight.	*Sie werden die Maschine rechtzeitig erreichen.*
I'll take you to the airport myself.	*Ich bringe Sie selbst zum Flughafen.*

You said you'll be there to meet me at the airport?	*Sie sagten, Sie werden dort sein, um mich am Flughafen zu treffen?*
I'll pick you up at the hotel.	*Ich hole Sie im/vor dem Hotel ab.*
I'd like to reserve a room for the nights of ... to ...	*Ich möchte für die Nächte vom ... bis ... buchen.*
I've reserved a room for you/a table for lunch.	*Ich habe ein Zimmer/einen Tisch zum Mittagessen für Sie reserviert.*
You're booked at Hotel Iris for the night of ...	*Wir haben für Sie die Nacht zum ... im Hotel Iris reserviert.*
Should you need any help, please let me know.	*Sollten Sie Hilfe benötigen, lassen Sie es mich bitte wissen.*
I've made the arrangements.	*Ich habe die Vorbereitungen getroffen.*
How's that?	*Wie gefällt Ihnen das?/Was halten Sie davon?*
Would that arrangement be convenient for you?	*Würde Ihnen diese Vereinbarung/ Verabredung passen?*
I'll confirm all this for you by fax.	*Ich werde dies alles für Sie per Fax bestätigen.*
How will I recognise you?	*Wie werde ich Sie erkennen?*
I'll be wearing a red cap/carrying a copy of "The Observer".	*Ich werde eine rote Mütze tragen/eine Ausgabe des „Observers" bei mir haben.*

"I'll pick you up at the hotel."

Checking-in at the airport	Am Flughafen einchecken
Smoking, please.	*Raucher, bitte.*
A window seat, if possible.	*Wenn möglich, einen Fensterplatz.*
Is this flight due to leave on time?	*Wird die Maschine pünktlich abfliegen?*
Can I board now?	*Kann ich jetzt an Bord gehen?*

Checking-in at the hotel	Sich im Hotel anmelden
I have a reservation.	*Ich habe reserviert.*
I reserved by fax two weeks ago.	*Ich habe vor zwei Wochen per Fax reserviert.*
A single room with bath, for two nights.	*Ein Einzelzimmer mit Bad, für zwei Nächte.*
Would it be possible to have some coffee, please?	*Könnte ich möglicherweise einen Kaffee bekommen?*

Making contact on arrival	Bei Ankunft Kontakt aufnehmen
Excuse me, are you Mr/Ms ... ?	*Entschuldigen Sie, sind Sie Herr/Frau ... ?*
I'm expecting to meet a Mr/Ms ... here.	*Ich erwarte, Herrn/Frau ... hier zu treffen.*
Has there been a message for me, please?	*Wurde eine Nachricht für mich hinterlassen?*
Could you tell me where I could find ... ?	*Könnten Sie mir sagen, wo ich ... finden kann?*

Getting around	Unter die Leute kommen
Would you take me to the station, please?	*Würden Sie mich bitte zum Bahnhof bringen?*
Where can I buy ... , please?	*Wo kann ich bitte ... kaufen?*
I'd like to make a phone call.	*Ich möchte gerne telefonieren.*
What's the best way to get to ... ?	*Wie kommt man am besten nach ... ?*
I'd like a/some ... , please.	*Ich hätte gerne ein/ein paar/einige ...*
Could you tell me the price?	*Könnten Sie mir den Preis nennen?*
Yes, I'll take it, please.	*Ja, bitte, ich nehme es.*

Confirming time and place of next contact	Ort und Zeit des nächsten Zusammentreffens bestätigen
We'll meet/see you next ... at/in ...	*Wir treffen/sehen Sie das nächste Mal ... am/beim/im ...*

We meet again in ... months, don't we?	*Wir treffen uns in ... Monaten wieder, nicht wahr?*
Is 5.30 still OK?	*Ist 5.30 Uhr noch o.k.?*
We'd better meet at ...	*Wir treffen uns besser in/an/bei ...*
Our next appointment is on ...	*Unser nächster Termin ist am ...*
I'll just check my diary.	*Ich sehe in meinem Terminkalender nach.*

Saying goodbye	***Verabschieden***
See you on ... !	*Bis zum ... !*
I've enjoyed it.	*Es hat mir gut gefallen.*
I'll be in touch again after ...	*Ich werde wieder Kontakt mit Ihnen aufnehmen, nachdem ...*
I'll see you again in ... weeks.	*Ich sehe Sie in ... Wochen wieder.*
Give my regards to ...	*Grüßen Sie bitte ...*
And don't forget: ...	*Und vergessen Sie nicht: ...*
Goodbye for now.	*Bis später.*

LANGUAGE STUDY

1. REFERRING TO THE FUTURE

Hier sind einige Sätze, die Sie in dieser Unit bereits gesehen oder gehört haben. Sie zeigen verschiedene Möglichkeiten, sich auf die Zukunft zu beziehen.

The flight arrives at 8.35.
You are coming from Birmingham on Friday, aren't you?
You will be in good time for the flight.
We're going to bring out the new model in July.

Wie Sie sich auf die Zukunft beziehen, hängt von der (jeweiligen) Situation ab. Hier einige Richtlinien.

SIMPLE PRESENT
um Aussagen über feste Fahr- oder Zeitpläne zu machen.

The flight arrives at 8.35.
The guarantee expires at the end of the month.

PRESENT CONTINUOUS (be + -ing)
um sich auf einen im Voraus vereinbarten Vorgang zu beziehen, insbesondere, wenn dabei eine Zeit in der Zukunft angegeben wird.

You are coming from Birmingham on Friday morning, aren't you?
He's taking over the hardware section in the New Year.

FUTURE SIMPLE (will/shall)
um einen zukünftigen Sachverhalt darzulegen oder um ein Versprechen zu geben.

You will be in good time for the flight.
I'll pick you up at 9 am.

"GOING TO"
um Absicht auszudrücken.

We're going to bring out the new model in July.
Halsteads are going to open a branch in Leipzig.

FUTURE CONTINUOUS (will be + -ing)
um sich auf einen Vorgang zu beziehen, dessen Eintritt im Laufe der Zeit erwartet wird.

(I expect) Davidsons will be bringing out their new Christmas catalogue soon.
(I'm sure) he'll be speaking at the Convention again this year.

Present Continuous (be + -ing?) *und* Future Continuous (will be + -ing?) *werden auch in Fragen benutzt, um sich höflich nach zukünftigen Plänen zu erkundigen.*

Are you ordering/Will you be ordering any more supplies before Christmas?

2. TIMES AND DATES

(I). Sehen Sie sich diese unterschiedlichen Möglichkeiten an, das Datum schriftlich darzustellen:

British English:	day – month – year.	10.12.99 (= 10 December, 1999)
American English:	month – day – year.	10.12.99 (= October 12, 1999)

Im internationalen Schriftverkehr können Sie Verwechslungen vermeiden, indem Sie eine dieser (unzweideutigen) Formen benutzen.

Ausgeschriebene Form:	16 June 1994	20 November 1999
Kurzform:	16 Jun 94	20 Nov 99

(II). Sehen Sie sich diese Möglichkeiten der Zeitangabe an.

geschrieben:	9.45 am	10.13 pm
gesprochen:	nine forty-five (am)	ten thirteen (pm)
	a quarter to ten (BE)	thirteen minutes past ten (BE)
	a quarter of ten (AE)	thirteen minutes after ten (AE)
	(in the morning)	(in the evening)

Obwohl sie in der englischen Alltagssprache nicht häufig gebraucht wird, kann die „24-Stunden-Uhr" dazu benutzt werden, sich auf gedruckte Zeitpläne zu beziehen.

geschrieben:	09.00	22.13
gesprochen:	oh-nine-hundred	twenty-two thirteen

Note: „half-nine" *(im gesprochenen Englisch) bedeutet halb zehn (= nicht halb neun).*

Exercises

2.15

1 Choose the correct verb forms in this message. Then, listen and check the answers on the CD.

Wählen Sie die richtigen Verbformen in dieser Mitteilung. Hören Sie im Anschluss die Lösungen auf der CD.

Sarah,

I travel/I'm travelling this evening, so I'm writing this message to you now. It will wait/will be waiting for you at your hotel when you arrive.

There's been a change of plan! Gore & Thompson's rep can't see you in Boston – he's fallen sick. He's going to call you/calling you from Chicago tomorrow morning to arrange a new appointment.

Your flight to LA is going to depart/departs 12 noon on Thursday. Until then, please demonstrate the new model wherever possible at the other locations on our Boston mailing list.

I call/I'll call you at your hotel at 8 pm CET tomorrow. As you know, I speak/I will be speaking to Hammond on Friday. So please be ready to give an interim report on progress.

All the best
Ted

2 Laura Miles is responsible for organising presentations at a corporation based in San Diego. She has received the following communications.

Laura Miles ist für die Organisation von Präsentationen bei einer Firma in San Diego zuständig. Sie hat die folgenden Mitteilungen erhalten.

Bob Chandler, Brown Sales Consultants
Houston, 11.11

Laura
I'll be there on 11.12. Put me down for two in the afternoon. My workshop ("Intranet Sales") will take 45 minutes.

Bob

Dear Laura   Cardiff, UK

I'll be in San Diego on 11.12. I'll be happy to do a one-hour presentation for my company, Grant Laser Products, on "Developing Laser Applications".
Could I start at 4 pm?

Helen Watson

Lardale Fibre Technology

Dear Ms Miles   Manchester, 1 November

Thank you for your e-mailed invitation. As it happens, I'll be flying from Britain to California very soon. Excuse the short notice, but I'd be pleased if you could book me for a presentation at your Centre on the last day of the month. I suggest 2.30-3.30. Title: "The Lardale Method".

Sincerely

Derek Routledge

3 Using the information you have, complete Laura's Presentation Schedule in the correct order.

Vervollständigen Sie anhand der Ihnen zur Verfügung stehenden Informationen Lauras Präsentationsplan in der richtigen Reihenfolge.

PRESENTATION SCHEDULE

	TIME	DATE	PRESENTER	TOPIC
1.	10.00–11.15	10 October	Liz Dixon (Grays Compudisc)	"Using Compudisc"
2.				
3.				
4.				

Typical Mistakes

You are given the task of checking the announcement on the following page before it is printed. It contains ten spelling mistakes often made by German writers of English. Can you find them?

Sie werden mit der Aufgabe betraut, die Ankündigung auf der folgenden Seite zu prüfen, bevor sie gedruckt wird. Sie enthält zehn Rechtschreibfehler, die oft von Deutschen in geschriebenem Englisch gemacht werden. Können Sie diese finden?

Harley Business Academy
Weekend Seminar: 24–25 June

Trading on the Internet

Seminar Leader: Professor Roy Burns (University of Birmingham)

The 2-day programm will include:

Authenticating Traders on the Net
Developements in Electronic Payment/Digital Cash
The Arguements for Online Trade
Secure Ordering
Installing Customer Services
Setting up a Virtual Shopfront

Weekend Seminar fee: £120. Accomodation with breakfast for the night of 24-25 June is available in local university halls of residance at an additional cost of £20 per night. Two room catagories are available:
(a) singles
(b) doubles with seperate beds.

If you would like to take part, contact Doug Bush (Phone: 76223; Fax: 76229). The seminar is sponsored by the Harley Business Promotion Commitee, whose support we greatfully acknowlege.

ABC

Word Bank

Travelling	***Reisen***
24-hour clock	*24-Stunden Uhr*
at short notice	*kurzfristig*
boarding card	*Bordkarte*
car hire	*Autovermietung*
check in	*sich anmelden/einchecken*
connection	*Verbindung*
customs	*Zoll*
demonstrate a model	*ein Modell vorführen*

departure lounge	*Abflughalle*
diary	*Terminkalender*
domestic flight	*Inlandflug*
flight schedule	*Flugplan*
inland flight	*Inlandflug*
interim report	*Zwischenbericht*
intermediate stop	*Zwischenstop*
international flight	*internationaler Flug*
short notice	*kurzfristig*
shuttle service	*Pendelverkehr*
transfer	*umsteigen*
traveller's cheque	*Reisescheck*

Down to Business

You are Ulrike Ludwikowski, working for a pharmaceuticals company in Munich. You're due to meet two clients (Mr Bishop and Mr Broome) in England this weekend.

Sie heißen Ulrike Ludwikowski und arbeiten für ein Pharmazeutikunternehmen in München. Sie haben dieses Wochenende ein Treffen mit zwei Kunden (Mr Bishop und Mr Broome) in England verabredet.

1 Study the following fax and timetables.

Sehen Sie sich das folgende Fax sowie die Flug- und Fahrpläne auf der nächsten Seite an.

F•A•X

Dear Frau Ludwikowski 22 May

I'm looking forward to seeing you here!

As promised, I've reserved a room for you, with bath, for the nights of 24–25 and 25–26 May at the Angel Hotel in Bury St Edmunds. I understand you'll be travelling up from London. Could you possibly make it here by 9 pm? I'll be waiting in the hotel bar for you.

Have a good trip!

Raymond Broome

Air

FROM MUNICH

days	dep	arr	flt no.	stops	a/c
TO JERSEY					
12345	1125	1500	UK913/UK447	STN	143/F27
TO LONDON STANSTED					
12345	1125	1220	UK913	0	143
6	1225	1320	UK913	0	143
7	1505	1600	UK915	0	100
12345	1915	2010	UK917	0	141
7	2005	2100	UK917	0	100
TO NEWCASTLE					
12345	1125	1635	UK913/UK595	STN	143/AT4
7	1505	2010	UK915/UK597	STN	100/AT4

FROM LONDON STANSTED

days	dep	arr	flt no.	stops	a/c
TO MUNICH					
12345	0755	1045	UK912	0	143
6	0855	1145	UK912	0	143
7	1135	1425	UK914	0	100
12345	1545	1835	UK916	0	141
7	1640	1925	UK916	0	100
TO NEWCASTLE					
123456	0815	0930	UK591	0	AT4
12345	1515	1635	UK595	0	AT4
12345 7	1855	2010	UK597	0	AT4
TO PARIS (CDG)					
123456	0700	0920	UK950	0	AT7
1234567	1040	1255	UK954	0	AT7
1234567	1440	1655	UK956	0	AT7
12345 7	1815	2030	UK964	0	AT7
TO PRAGUE					
	services operated in conjunction with Czech Airlines				
12 5	1140	1425	UK3130	0	734/735
TO STAVANGER					
12345	1315	1940	UK547/UK536	ABZ	143/F50

SYMBOLS AND ABBREVIATIONS

DAYS 1 Mon, 2 Tues, 3 Wed, 4 Thurs, 5 Fri, 6 Sat, 7 Sun

STOPS 0 = Non-stop service, 1 or 2 = Intermediate landings

Rail

Ipswich to Cambridge/Ely/Peterborough

Mondays to Saturdays

		BHX		H							
London Liverpool St §	*d*	------	------	*0625*	*0625*	*0830*	*0930*	*1030*	*1130*	*1230*	*1330*
Ipswich	d	0515	0645	0806	0816	0943	1105	1212	1245	1415	*1435*
Needham Market	d	------	0655	------	0826	------	------	1222	------	------	------
Stowmarket	d	0529	0701	0818	0832	0957	1119	1228	1259	1429	1514
Elmswell	d	------	0710	------	0841	------	------	1237	------	------	1523
Thurston	d	------	0716	------	0847	------	------	1243	------	------	1529
Bury St. Edmunds	d	0550	0722	0835	0853	1014	1136	1249	1316	1447	1535
Kennett	d	0601	0733	------	0904	------	------	1300	1327	------	------
Newmarket	d	0609	0741	------	0912	------	1153	------	1335	------	1552
Dullingham	d	0615	0747	------	0918	------	------	------	1341	------	------
Cambridge	a	0633	0805	------	0936	------	1216	------	1359	------	1615
Ely	d	------	------	0901	------	1041	------	1325	------	1525	------
March	d	------	------	------	------	1059	------	1346	------	1544	------
Whittlesea	d	------	------	------	------	1109	------	1356	------	1554	------
Peterborough	a	------	------	0936	------	1121	------	1408	------	1605	------
Birmingham New St	*a*	------	------	*1149*	------	*1350*	------	*1552e*	------	*1751e*	------
Liverpool Lime St	*a*	------	------	*1429*	------	*1529*	------	*1834*	------	*2029*	------

Mondays to Saturdays

						SX BHX	SO
London Liverpool St §	*d*	*1430*	*1530*	*1700p*	*1830*	*2030*	*2030*
Ipswich	d	1613	1640	1807	1945	2200	2200
Needham Market	d	1623	1650	1817	1955	2210	2210
Stowmarket	d	1629	1656	1823	2000	2216	2216
Elmswell	d	1638	------	1832	2009	2225	2225
Thurston	d	1644	------	1838	2015	2231	2231
Bury St. Edmunds	d	1650	1713	1844	2021	2237	2236a
Kennett	d	1701	1724	1855	2032	2248	------
Newmarket	d	------	1732	------	2040	2257	------
Dullingham	d	------	1738	------	2046	2302	------
Cambridge	a	------	1756	------	2103	2320	------
Ely	d	1719	------	1913	------	------	------
March	d	1737	------	1931	------	------	------
Whittlesea	d	1747	------	1941	------	------	------
Peterborough	a	1758	------	1952	------	------	------
Birmingham New St	*a*	*2047*	------	*2256*	------	------	------
Liverpool Lime St	*a*	------	------	------	------	------	------

Sundays

London Liverpool St	*d*	------	*0830*	------	*1030*	------	------	------	*1530*	*1630*	*1930*
Ipswich	d	0850	0948	1025	1205	1308	------	1530	1648	1832	2045
Needham Market	d	0900	0958	------	1215	------	------	------	1658	------	2055
Stowmarket	d	0906	1004	1039	1221	1322	------	1544	1704	1846	2101
Elmswell	d	0915	1013	------	1230	------	------	------	1713	------	2110
Thurston	d	0921	1019	------	1236	------	------	------	1719	------	2116
Bury St. Edmunds	d	0926a	1025	1056	1242	1339	1430	1601	1725	1903	2122
Kennett	d	------	1036	------	1253	------	------	------	1736	------	2133
Newmarket	d	------	1045	------	1302	------	1448	------	1745	------	2142
Dullingham	d	------	1050	------	1307	------	------	------	1750	------	2147
Cambridge	a	------	1108	------	1325	------	1510	------	1808	------	2208
Ely	d	------	------	1125	------	1408	------	1630	------	1932	------
March	d	------	------	1143	------	1426	------	1648	------	1950	------
Whittlesea	d	------	------	------	------	------	------	------	------	------	------
Peterborough	a	------	------	1214	------	1457	------	1708	------	2009	------
Birmingham New St	*a*	------	------	*1553*	------	*1743*	------	*1953*	------	------	------
Liverpool Lime St	*a*	------	------	*1733*	------	*1929*	------	------	------	------	------

General Notes

BHX	Bank Holidays excepted.
SO	Saturdays only.
SX	Saturdays excepted.
H	Starts from Harwich International at 0740.
a	Arrival time.
d	Departure time.
e	For Birmingham change at Ely.
p	Connecting service departs 1630 on Saturdays.
§	There are other services from London.

Light italic printed timings indicate connecting services.

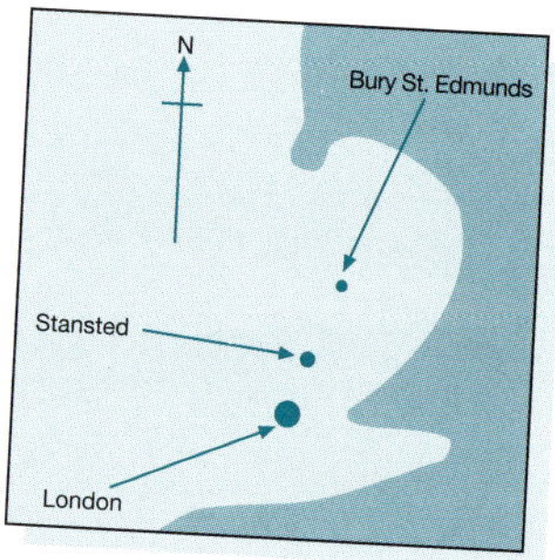

2 Now use the information you have to complete the following letter to Mr Bishop.

Benutzen Sie nun die Ihnen zur Verfügung stehenden Informationen, um den folgenden Brief an Mr Bishop zu vervollständigen.

> Dear Mr Bishop
>
> Many thanks again – offering – pick me up – Stansted Airport on Saturday the 24th. – confirm – arriving at –
>
> As you know – have to – Bury St Edmunds after our talks. This means – Liverpool Street – catch a train at –
>
> – certainly leave us enough time – discuss – settle – question of the product specifications.
>
> Looking forward – again.
>
> Sincerely
> Ulrike Ludwikowski

3 Ulrike has arrived at the hotel in Bury St Edmunds. Note down what she probably says in the following dialogue.

Ulrike ist im Hotel in Bury St Edmunds angekommen. Schreiben Sie auf, was sie wahrscheinlich im folgenden Dialog sagen wird.

Receptionist: Good evening. What can I do for you?

Ludwikowski: ______________________________

Receptionist: For two nights? Right, just let me check. Er ... how do you spell your name, please?

Ludwikowski: ______________________________

Receptionist: Ah, yes – Frau Ludwikowski. Right, your room number is 17, Frau Ludwikowski. And this is your key.

Ludwikowski: ______________________________

Receptionist: Now I'll just get someone to take your luggage. Then I'll show you to the room.

Ludwikowski: ______________________________

Receptionist: Mr Broome? Ah, yes, he's in the bar right now, I believe.

Ludwikowski: ______________________________

Receptionist: Just through that door and turn right.

Ludwikowski: ______________________________

Receptionist: Fine. Well, just come back here to Reception when you're ready. And then I'll show you to your room.

Ludwikowski: ______________________________

Listening Text 8/3

2.16

4 Listen to the discussion in full. Then practise speaking Ludwikowski's part again.

Hören Sie die Diskussion in voller Länge. Sprechen Sie dann Ludwikowskis Dialogteil noch einmal nach.

DEALING WITH VISUAL INFO

Floor plan

1 Mr Broome (who Ulrike met in Bury St Edmunds) owns a plant which produces pharmaceutical containers. Together, he and Ulrike inspect the plant – and decide that these extra facilities are needed.

Mr Broome (den Ulrike in Bury St Edmunds traf) besitzt eine Fabrik zur Produktion pharmazeutischer Behälter. Mr Broome und Ulrike besichtigen die Fabrik gemeinsam und entscheiden, dass folgende zusätzliche Einrichtungen benötigt werden.

2nd Emergency Exit Tea Room Data Base and Distribution Centre

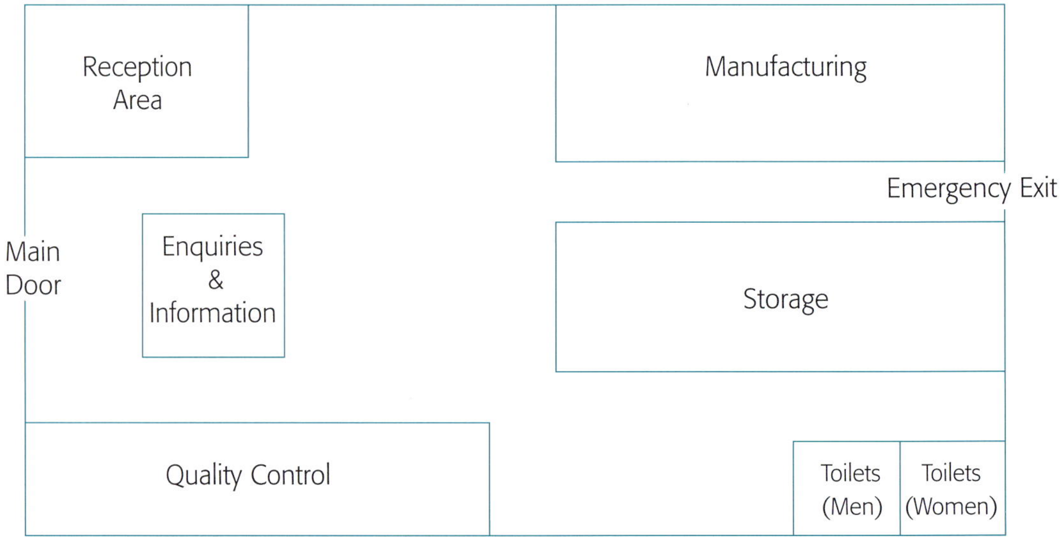

Listening Text 8/4

2.17

2 Mr Broome describes the extra facilities in a recorded message to be sent to the architect. Draw in the facilities to be added.

Mr Broome beschreibt die zusätzlichen Einrichtungen auf einem Tonband, das dem Architekt geschickt werden soll. Zeichnen Sie die zusätzlichen Einrichtungen in die Skizze ein.

The British-American Difference

Listening Text 8/5

2.18

You will hear two American speakers. They use ten American expressions with the same meanings as the British expressions below. Write the American expressions into the boxes. (You will hear them in the same order as those in the list below.)

Sie hören gleich zwei amerikanische Sprecher. Sie benutzen zehn amerikanische Ausdrücke, die gleichbedeutend mit den unten aufgelisteten britischen Ausdrücken sind. Tragen Sie die amerikanischen Ausdrücke in die Kästchen ein. (Sie hören die Ausdrücke in der gleichen Reihenfolge wie die in der unten aufgeführten Liste.)

British	**American**	**British**	**American**
1. autumn		6. toilet	
2. town centre		7. dustbins	
3. owner-occupied flat		8. chemist	
4. ground floor		9. drawing pin	
5. underground		10. motorway	

Last but not Least

Each highlighted invitation implies all of the five meanings which follow, except one. Which ones are not implied?

Jede der hervorgehobenen Einladungen impliziert alle fünf folgenden Bedeutungen, außer jeweils einer. Welche Bedeutungen sind nicht impliziert?

"What exactly are you implying?"

A

May I invite you for dinner?

❑ I'll pay.
❑ May I take you out for dinner?
❑ Please dine at my home.
❑ I'll cook.
❑ I'd like to send you an invitation.

B

Be my guest.

❑ I'll cook.
❑ Stay overnight at my house.
❑ Let's pay 50-50.
❑ I'd like you to visit my place.
❑ I'll pay.

C

Shall we have a drink?

❑ Let's go to the bar.
❑ Shall we get boozed?
❑ Please come to my house.
❑ I'll pay.
❑ You'll pay.

Making and Handling Complaints

GETTING STARTED

A certain metal goods company are having a bad day. They've received three answer-phone messages – all complaining about undelivered goods.

Die Metallwarenfirma „XY" hat heute einen schlechten Tag. Es gingen bereits drei Mitteilungen über den Anrufbeantworter ein – allesamt Beschwerden über nicht gelieferte Waren.

Listening Text 9/1

2.19

In each message, the last sentence is missing. Can you match the last sentences (below) with the speakers?

In allen Mitteilungen fehlt der letzte Satz. Können Sie die jeweils letzten Sätze (unten) den Sprechern zuordnen?

Speakers 1st speaker (Pryke) 2nd speaker (Handley) 3rd speaker (Green)

Last sentences

A "So, could you look into that for me, please?"

B "So you'd better tell me what you intend to do about it!"

C "So I suggest you look into the matter and let me know what's happened."

Listen & Repeat

2.19

1 Listen again to Listening Text 9/1. Notice how each speaker's attitude is expressed not only by words but also by the tone of voice.

Hören Sie noch einmal Hörtext 9/1. Achten Sie darauf, wie jeder Sprecher seine Haltung nicht nur durch Worte, sondern auch durch seine Betonung ausdrückt.

2 Using the tapescript for Listening Text 9/1, read aloud the three complaints, imitating as closely as possible the tone of voice used by each speaker.

Lesen Sie mit Hilfe der Transkription des Hörtextes im Anhang die drei Beschwerden laut vor. Versuchen Sie dabei, die Betonung jedes Sprechers so genau wie möglich zu imitieren.

Useful Expressions

Making & handling complaints on the phone	***Telefonisch Beschwerden vorbringen & bearbeiten***
1. Making complaints on the phone	***Telefonische Beschwerden***
Expressing a complaint	***Eine Beschwerde vorbringen***
I'm calling to complain about ...	*Ich rufe an, um mich über ... zu beschweren.*
Those ... still haven't arrived.	*Diese ... sind immer noch nicht eingetroffen.*
We're still waiting for ...	*Wir warten immer noch auf ...*
You said you'd deliver by the ...	*Sie sagten, dass Sie bis zum ... liefern würden.*
That's ten days ago!	*Das ist zehn Tage her!*
According to the contract, they should have arrived by ...	*Vertragsgemäß hätten sie bis zum ... eintreffen müssen.*
I must say – I'm very disappointed.	*Ich muss sagen, ich bin sehr enttäuscht.*
I've been counting on you to deliver on time.	*Ich habe mich auf Ihre rechtzeitige Lieferung verlassen.*
Obviously, it's your fault.	*Es ist offensichtlich Ihre Schuld.*
This is just not good enough.	*Das ist einfach nicht akzeptabel.*
(It seems to me) you didn't ...	*(Es scheint mir), Sie haben nicht ...*
should have ...	*hätten ... sollen.*
shouldn't have ...	*hätten ... nicht ... sollen.*
have been pretty careless.	*waren ziemlich fahrlässig.*
Requesting action	***Verlangen, dass etwas getan wird***
Could you look into that for me, please?	*Könnten Sie das für mich untersuchen?*
So what's the next step?	*Was ist also der nächste Schritt?*
If you ... , I'll be happy to leave it at that.	*Wenn Sie ... , lasse ich die Sache gerne auf sich beruhen.*
I'm prepared overlook this delay.	*bin ich bereit, über diese Verspätung hinwegzusehen.*
I suggest you look into the matter and let me know what's happened.	*Ich schlage vor, Sie untersuchen die Sache und lassen mich wissen, was passiert ist.*

LANGUAGE STUDY

RELATIVE CLAUSES

Ein Relativsatz ist Teil eines Satzes, der (a) ein Verb enthält und (b) normalerweise durch ein Relativpronomen, z.B. which, who, that, whose, *mit dem Rest des Satzes verbunden ist.*

Hauptsatz

The aluminium plates | which we ordered last month | still haven't come.

Relativpronomen | *Relativsatz*

Relativpronomen, die einen Relativsatz einleiten können:

who   whom   to/for/of whom   whose   to/for/of whose   which
to/for/of which   that

Diese drei Satzteil-Typen sind kürzer als vollständige Relativsätze. Daher werden sie oft im Schriftlichen benutzt – als rhetorisches Stilmittel und um Wiederholungen zu vermeiden.

Noun + V-ed: Goods produced here are exported to China. (= which are produced)

Noun + V-ing: Are there any restrictions affecting the export of CDs? (= which affect)

Noun + to + V: He was the first person to apply for the job. (= who applied)

Sehen Sie sich die Zeichensetzung in diesen Sätzen an.

a) Mr Rutter, who made the complaint, will call again later. (= *2 Kommas*)
b) The person who made the complaint will call again later. (= *0 Komma*)

In a) fügt der Relativsatz einem bereits vollständigen Satz Informationen hinzu.
In b) wäre der Satz ohne den Relativsatz unvollständig.

Exercises

1 Choose the correct expressions in this letter. Add commas where necessary.

Suchen Sie in diesem Brief die passenden Ausdrücke aus. Fügen Sie auch die notwendigen Kommas hinzu.

Dear ...

Last week, I received the 25 "Alexis" coffee machines despatched/which despatched/to despatch to us on 25 March. I immediately sent a number of them to two of our customers to order/who had ordered/ordering them. The first receiving/that received/to receive his consignment complained that the handle attachments were loose. The second customer to whom/for which/whom we had despatched five machines reports that two were damaged on arrival.

Naturally, these complaints have given us great cause for concern. What is important right now, though, is to find out the cause of the damage. Admittedly, it may have been the fault of the delivery service to contract/whose contracted/contracted to transport goods to our local customers. It must be said, though, that we have never had cause to complain about our delivery service to whom/of whom/for which I shall be speaking on Monday. I'll be getting back the machines that/of which/for which the second customer complained.

In the meantime, I would like to know your reaction to this matter. In particular, have you received other reports of problems arising/who arising/that arising from your "Alexis" coffee machines?

I look forward to receiving your early response.

Yours faithfully

2 In these sentences, add commas to the blue parts where necessary.

Setzen Sie vor und nach den blau gedruckten Teilen dieser Sätze Kommas nur dort ein, wo sie benötigt werden.

a The creditors who we have written to will be paid first.
b Mrs Reynolds whom I spoke to yesterday thinks there'll be a price reduction in May.
c Larter Metal whose share prices have been falling badly have made more staff cuts.
d The model that was on offer last month is no longer available.
e The manager who achieves the best sales figures gets the highest bonus.
f In Spain where the company has twelve outlets property values have been rising fast.

Typical Mistakes

Each of these sentences contains a mistake made by a German speaker. Can you correct them?

Jeder dieser Sätze enthält einen von einem deutschen Sprecher gemachten Fehler. Können Sie die Fehler korrigieren?

1. I suggest to charge ten dollars registration fee.
2. Visitors looking for splendid scenery here won't get disappointed.
3. Economists are discovering that what is meant by the word "chaos".
4. Everything what you've told me has been most fascinating.
5. I met the wife of Mr Reynolds yesterday.
6. "Will you be at Tuesday's meeting?" "I don't think."
7. They have absolutely no knowledges of English.
8. For two years, I worked by Schmidt & Höhne in Darmstadt.
9. They've been very slow to adapt to modern technique.
10. He's on the sales team of a great kitchen goods company.

Word Bank

Making and handling complaints	***Beschwerden vorbringen und bearbeiten***
according to the contract	*vertragsgemäß*
apologise	*entschuldigen*
apology	*Entschuldigung*
breakdown (in figures)	*Aufschlüsselung*
cancel an order	*eine Bestellung annullieren*
careless	*fahrlässig*
cause difficulty	*Schwierigkeiten verursachen*
claim a discount	*einen Rabatt fordern*
claim compensation	*Entschädigung fordern*

compensate	*entschädigen*
damage	*Schaden/Schäden*
debt collection	*Schuldeneintreibung*
debt collection agency	*Inkassobüro*
disappointed	*enttäuscht*
fault	*Schuld*
give an assurance	*versichern*
guarantee delivery	*Lieferung garantieren*
hold sb responsible for sth	*jdn für etw verantwortlich machen*
inadvertent(ly)	*versehentlich*
incur costs	*Kosten auf sich nehmen*
look into sth	*etwas untersuchen/prüfen*
mistake	*Fehler*
mistakenly	*irrtümlicherweise*
not to arrive on time	*nicht rechtzeitig ankommen*
overdue payment	*überfällige Zahlung*
overlook a delay	*über eine Verspätung hinwegsehen*
price reduction	*Preisnachlass*
prompt payment	*sofortige/umgehende Zahlung*
regret sth	*etwas bedauern*
reimburse	*erstatten*
reminder	*Mahnbrief, Zahlungserinnerung*
remit	*überweisen*
remittance	*Überweisung*
repair (of goods)	*Ausbesserung*
responsible	*verantwortlich*
run into difficulty	*Schwierigkeiten bekommen*
take legal action	*gerichtlich vorgehen*
take legal steps	*rechtliche Schritte einleiten*
terms of the contract	*Vertragsbedingungen*
undelivered	*nicht gelieferte/s/r*
urgent	*dringend*
warning	*Warnung*

Down to Business

Here is a fax which has been received by a forwarding agent.

Hier ist ein Fax, das ein Spediteur erhalten hat.

TELEFAX

4 June 19..

Dear Sirs

On 30 May, the drilling tools I had ordered were unloaded not in Valparaiso, as directed, but in Punta Arenas. I wish to complain as strongly as possible about this error.

As a result of it, I have incurred substantial costs, for which I am holding you responsible. Besides the costs for transporting the consignment from Punta Arenas to Valparaiso, I have also had to pay compensation costs to a customer for late delivery.

I am not yet able to assess the total costs I have incurred. However, I shall expect you to repay them in full. As soon as I have the exact figures, I shall send you an invoice.

In the meantime, I expect an explanation of the error.

Yours faithfully
E. Sanders
pp H.C. Warden & Co

1 The following letter is the reply. But the sentences are in the wrong order. Rearrange them into the most logical order.

Der folgende Brief ist die Antwort auf das Fax. Die Sätze befinden sich jedoch in der falschen Reihenfolge. Setzen Sie sie in der Anordnung, die Ihnen am logischsten erscheint, wieder zusammen.

Dear Mr Sanders

A We immediately contacted the local representative of the shipping company.

B We thank you for your fax of 4 June and were sorry to learn that your four cases of drilling tools were unloaded at the wrong port.

C We shall then forward it to the shipping company.

D As the shipping company are responsible, we shall claim full compensation from them on your behalf.

E He says the error probably resulted from a congestion of vessels at the port of departure.

F He has informed us that the goods, which were intended for Valparaiso, were unloaded in Punta Arenas inadvertently.

G Would you, therefore, please send your invoice (showing the breakdown of the resultant costs) to us?

We wish to express our great regret, and remain

Yours (Signature)

2 Divide the rearranged sentences into three paragraphs.

Unterteilen Sie die neu angeordneten Sätze in drei Absätze.

Useful Expressions

Making & handling complaints in writing	***Schriftlich Beschwerden vorbringen & bearbeiten***
1 Making complaints in writing	***Schriftliche Beschwerden vorbringen***
Expressing a complaint	***Eine Beschwerde vorbringen***
I was most surprised to hear/see/read that ...	*Ich war überaus überrascht zu hören/sehen/lesen, dass ...*
I wish to complain about ..	*Ich möchte mich über ... beschweren.*
The ... didn't arrive on time.	*Die ... kamen nicht rechtzeitig an.*
This was clearly the result of your error.	*Das war offensichtlich das Resultat Ihres Fehlers/Irrtums.*

I think you have handled this matter most unsatisfactorrily.	*Ich glaube, Sie haben diese Aufgabe nicht zufriedenstellend erledigt.*
I wish to protest as strongly as possible about ...	*Ich möchte schärfstens gegen ... protestieren.*
The terms of the contract are quite clear.	*Die Vertragsbedingungen sind völlig klar.*

Requesting action	***Verlangen, dass etwas getan wird***
I would like to ask you to ...	*Ich möchte Sie bitten, ... zu ...*
I am confident that you will ... so that the matter can be settled quickly.	*Ich bin zuversichtlich, dass Sie ... werden, so dass die Angelegenheit schnell geregelt werden kann.*
You will, I hope, make every effort to ...	*Ich hoffe, Sie werden alle Anstrengungen unternehmen, ... zu ...*
Please let me know what you intend to do.	*Bitte lassen Sie mich wissen, was Sie zu tun gedenken.*
I expect an explanation.	*Ich erwarte eine Erklärung.*

Expressing warning	***Warnungen aussprechen***
I would like to draw your attention to page 1 of ...	*Ich möchte Ihre Aufmerksamkeit auf die Seite 1 der/s ... lenken.*
I must insist that ...	*Ich muss darauf bestehen, dass ...*
Otherwise, I regret that I ...	*Sonst muss ich bedauerlicherweise ...*
If I do not receive ... by ... , I shall have to ...	*Wenn ich ... nicht bis ... erhalte, werde ich ... müssen.*
I am holding you responsible.	*Ich mache Sie verantwortlich.*

"The uniforms didn't arrive on time."

2. Handling complaints in writing — *Beschwerden schriftlich bearbeiten*

Apologising	***Entschuldigen***
We ...	*Wir ...*
express our regret for the confusion.	*bedauern die Verwechslung/das Durcheinander.*
must apologise for ...	*müssen uns für ... entschuldigen.*
are sorry to learn that ...	*bedauern zu erfahren, dass ...*
are sorry that, as a result of the error ... ,	*bedauern, dass wegen des Fehlers/Irrtums ...*
wish to express our great regret.	*möchten unser tiefes Bedauern ausdrücken.*
Please send us the breakdown of the costs.	*Bitte senden Sie uns die Aufschlüsselung der Kosten.*
Please accept our apologies.	*Bitte nehmen Sie unsere Entschuldigung entgegen.*

Offering explanations	***Erklärungen anbieten***
I find that we made an error ...	*Offensichtlich haben wir einen Fehler gemacht.*
The cause of the error was ...	*Die Ursache des Fehlers war/lag in ...*
The goods were unloaded in ... inadvertently.	*Die Waren wurden versehentlich in ... ausgeladen.*
The error probably resulted from ...	*Der Fehler/Irrtum resultierte wahrscheinlich aus ...*
We ...	*Wir ...*
immediately contacted ...	*nahmen sofort mit ... Verbindung auf.*
should have ...	*hätten ... sollen.*
have done everything possible to ...	*haben alles uns mögliche getan, um ...*
This has been quite outside our control.	*Dies war gänzlich außerhalb unserer Kontrolle.*

Making promises	***Versprechen abgeben***
I shall look into the matter immediately.	*Ich werde die Angelegenheit sofort prüfen.*
We shall, of course, compensate you for ...	*Wir werden Sie natürlich für ... entschädigen.*
We do assure you that ...	*Wir versichern Ihnen, dass ...*
We would like to propose ...	*Wir möchten (gerne) ... vorschlagen.*
We are willing to ...	*Wir sind bereit ... zu ...*
As soon as ... , we will ...	*Sobald ... , werden wir ...*

3 The shipping company later contacted the exporter directly, apologised and agreed to pay for the losses. So Mr Sanders sent a claim, which the shipping company agreed to pay within four weeks. Read this letter from Mr Sanders. As you read, combine the sentence parts in List A and List B to form full sentences. (The sentence parts in List A are in the right order.)

Die Reederei nahm später direkt Kontakt zum Exporteur auf, entschuldigte sich und erklärte sich einverstanden, für die Verluste aufzukommen. Daraufhin schickte Mr Sanders eine Forderung und vereinbarte mit der Reederei, dass diese innerhalb von vier Wochen zu zahlen sei. Lesen Sie diesen Brief von Mr Sanders. Kombinieren Sie während des Lesens die Satzteile in Liste A und Liste B zu vollständigen Sätzen. (Die Satzteile in Liste A befinden sich in der richtigen Reihenfolge.)

To the Manager,
CC Clearing GmbH

9 October 19..

Dear Sir

We refer to our claim for the amount of $388.50.

List A

- We would like to draw your attention to the fact that
- Furthermore,
- Would you please
- We trust that
- For your convenience,

List B

- we can look forward to receiving full payment in the near future.
- we have received no explanation for this delay.
- look into the matter immediately?
- we are sending a further copy of the claim.
- payment is now four weeks overdue.

Yours faithfully

E. Sanders

pp H.C. Warden & Co

4 Mr Sanders received no reply to his letter. So he's sending another – more firmly worded – one. Complete the words in this second letter into their full form.

Mr Sanders erhielt keine Antwort auf seinen Brief. Also schickt er einen weiteren, deutlicheren Brief. Vervollständigen Sie die Wörter in diesem zweiten Brief.

23 October 19..

To the Manager,
CC Clearing GmbH

Dear Sir

Oce agn, we mst ask yu to rfr to our clm & to our ltr of 9 Oct.

Pls nte tht pymt is now sx wks lte. As yu stl hve nt gvn us any exptn fr the dly, we mst inst on pymt in fll by 5 Nov. Othwse, we sll hve no optn bt to tke lgl actn.

Yours faithfully
E. Sanders

pp H.C. Warden & Co

Useful Expressions

Writing reminders	***Zahlungserinnerungen schreiben***
Referring to invoice/payment due	***Auf fällige Rechnungen/Zahlungen aufmerksam machen***
(Once again,) we refer to our Invoice No ... for the amount/sum of ...	*Wir verweisen (nochmals) auf unsere Rechnungsnummer ... über den Betrag/ die Summe von ...*
We must ask you to refer to our letter of ...	*Wir müssen Sie bitten, auf unseren Brief vom ... Bezug zu nehmen.*
Our statement dated ... shows a balance of ... in our favour.	*Unser Auszug vom ... zeigt einen Kontostand von ... zu unseren Gunsten.*

Referring to the overdue period	**Auf Überfälligkeit aufmerksam machen**
We would like to draw your attention to ...	*Wir möchten Ihre Aufmerksamkeit auf ... lenken.*
Please note that payment/settlement is now ... weeks late/overdue.	*Bitte nehmen Sie zur Kenntnis, dass die Zahlung/der Ausgleich jetzt ... Wochen verspätet/überfällig ist.*

Requesting action/payment	**Tätig werden/Zahlung erbitten**
We have received no explanation for this delay.	*Wir haben keine Erklärung für diese Verspätung erhalten.*

Would you please look into the matter immediately?	*Würden Sie die Angelegenheit bitte sofort prüfen?*
We trust/are sure that we can expect to receive full payment/your remittance/ prompt payment by return/very soon/ in the near future.	*Wir sind zuversichtlich/sicher, dass wir die Zahlung in voller Höhe/Ihre Überweisung/ sofortige Zahlung umgehend/baldigst/ in nächster Zukunft erwarten können.*
For your convenience, we are sending a further copy of ...	*Zu Ihrer Information schicken wir eine weitere Kopie des/r ...*

Exerting pressure	***Druck ausüben***
As you still have not given us any explanation, we must insist that you deal with this matter immediately.	*Da Sie uns noch immer keine Erklärung gegeben haben, müssen wir darauf bestehen, dass Sie sich sofort um die Sache kümmern.*
insist on/ask you to arrange for payment in full by ...	*darauf bestehen, dass Sie die Zahlung in voller Höhe bis ... zum vornehmen.*
Otherwise/If you do not/Unless you ...	*Andererseits/Sollten Sie ... nicht ... /Falls Sie nicht ...*
We shall have to take legal action to seek payment.	*Wir werden gerichtlich vorgehen müssen, um Zahlung zu erzwingen.*
We have no option but to ...	*Wir haben keine Wahl, außer ... (zu) ...*

2.20

5

Listening Text 9/2

Frau Wicke (of CC Clearing) is phoning Mr Sanders about the overdue payment. As you listen, complete this grid.

Frau Wicke (von CC Clearing) ruft Mr Sanders wegen der überfälligen Zahlung an. Vervollständigen Sie dieses Raster, während Sie zuhören.

	True or **F**alse?
1. Frau Wicke apologises before explaining everything.	☐
2. On the day before Sanders sent the first letter, the bank was instructed to make a payment.	☐
3. According to the bank's statement of account, a payment was made.	☐
4. The bank made a mistake.	☐
5. Frau Wicke ends the call with a promise.	☐
6. Sanders accepts Frau Wicke's apology.	☐

Dealing with Visual Info

Flow charts (2)

2.21

Review the progress of Mr Sanders' case in this unit and fill in the appropriate letters in the flow chart (below). The first has been done for you. You can hear a complete account of the case on CD.

Lesen Sie noch einmal den Verlauf von Mr Sanders Fall in dieser Unit und setzen Sie die passenden Buchstaben in das Flussdiagramm (unten) ein. Der erste wurde bereits für Sie eingesetzt. Sie können eine vollständige Beschreibung des Falls auf der CD hören.

A Sanders gets breakdown of costs from his customer, forwards it to the Agent.

B Mistake in shipping company's office: wrong customer is paid.

C Agent contacts shipping company, claims compensation for Sanders.

D Sanders accepts shipping company's apology.

E Shipping company contact Sanders directly, apologise, agree to pay his claim within four weeks.

F Sanders' drilling tools are unloaded at wrong port: he has to pay compensation costs to a customer for late delivery.

G Shipping company phone, apologise, explain everything.

H Shipping company discover their mistake, instruct bank to pay Sanders immediately.

I Payment four weeks overdue: Sanders complains, sends further copy of claim.

J Sanders complains to Agent.

K Shipping company receive bank's statement of account, showing a payment was made.

L Payment now six weeks overdue: Sanders sets deadline for payment, threatens legal action.

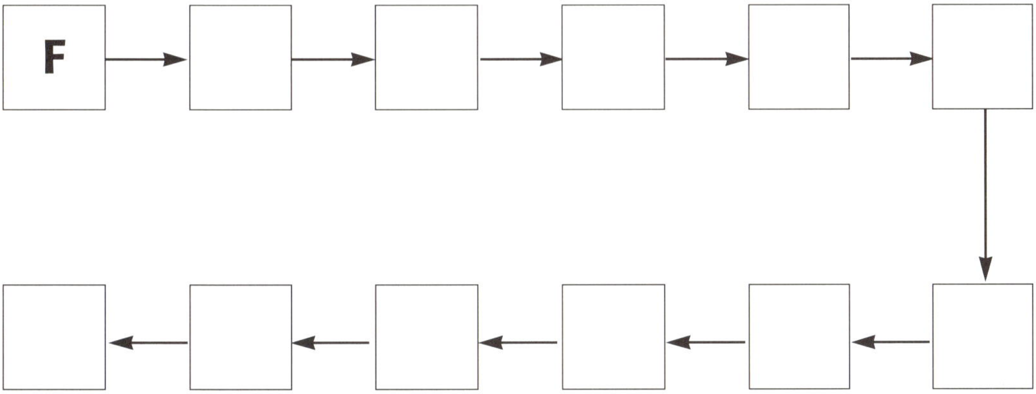

The British-American Difference

1 Look at these spelling differences between British English and American English.

Sehen Sie sich diese Unterschiede in der Schreibweise zwischen britischem und amerikanischem Englisch an.

British English		**American English**	
our	(colour, flavour)	or	(color, flavor)
re	(centre, litre)	er	(center, liter)
ll	(modelled, dialling)	l	(modeled, dialing)
ae	(Caesarean, orthopaedist)	e	(Cesarean, orthopedist)

2 Each of these eight newspaper headlines contains a word whose spelling tells you if the newspaper is British or American. Find the eight words.

Jede dieser acht Zeitungsschlagzeilen enthält ein Wort, dessen Schreibweise Ihnen verrät, ob die Zeitung britisch oder amerikanisch ist. Finden Sie die acht Wörter.

TRAVELERS MUST PAY MORE

EVERYONE'S FAVORITE WEBSITE

Archeologists Meet in Milan

Theater Director Quits

Slovakia Praises Her Neighbors

FLOOD LEVEL RISES TO 2 METRES

MORE PAY FOR ANAESTHETISTS

Flights Cancelled Due to Snow

3 Write the American words with British spellings, and vice versa.

Schreiben Sie die amerikanischen Wörter in der englischen Schreibweise und umgekehrt.

Last but not Least

These sentences contain mistakes which produce comical, unintended meanings. What did the writer mean to say with each sentence?

Diese Sätze enthalten Fehler, die komische, unbeabsichtigte Bedeutungen ergeben. Was wollte der Autor mit diesen Sätzen sagen?

THIS IS RUSSIA AND YOU'RE WELCOME TO IT!

(sign at Moscow Airport)

A hole has appeared on the Newmarket Road. Police are looking into it.

Please complain between 10 and 12 in the morning.

(hotel notice)

MORNING BARMAID REQUIRED. MALE OR FEMALE, PLEASE APPLY RED LION.

The company was landed with a huge bull after the electricity company had failed to check the meter for over three years.

WE PERMANENTLY STOCK OVER 60 CHOOSES FOR YOU TO CHEESE FROM.

New Fast Foot Restaurant to open in Edgbaston.

Valley School, Headingley. Qualified Teacher of the Dead required.

Employers also complained of schoolleavers whose aplication froms contain spelling mistakes.

There is a French widow in every bedroom.

(hotel notice)

We will be running a 3-day curse from 10 am to 3 pm.

Dealing with publicity and distribution

Getting Started

New Electronics launched GLOWY, a "long-life" light bulb, onto the British market four years ago. Now they are making plans to launch GLOWY in Germany. Herr Melchior is New Electronics' Managing Director in Germany.

Die Firma New Electronics brachte vor vier Jahren GLOWY, eine „langlebige" Glühbirne, auf den britischen Markt. Nun plant sie, GLOWY in Deutschland auf den Markt zu bringen. Herr Melchior ist der Geschäftsführer von New Electronics in Deutschland.

Listening Text 10/1

2.22

1 Herr Melchior is discussing GLOWY's prospects with two market researchers: Mr Sercombe (British) and Frau Führling (German). All three speakers have Figures 1 and 2.

Herr Melchior diskutiert mit zwei Marktforschern über GLOWYs Aussichten: Mr Sercombe (Brite) und Frau Führling (Deutsche). Allen drei Gesprächspartnern liegen die Darstellungen 1 und 2 vor.

Figure 1

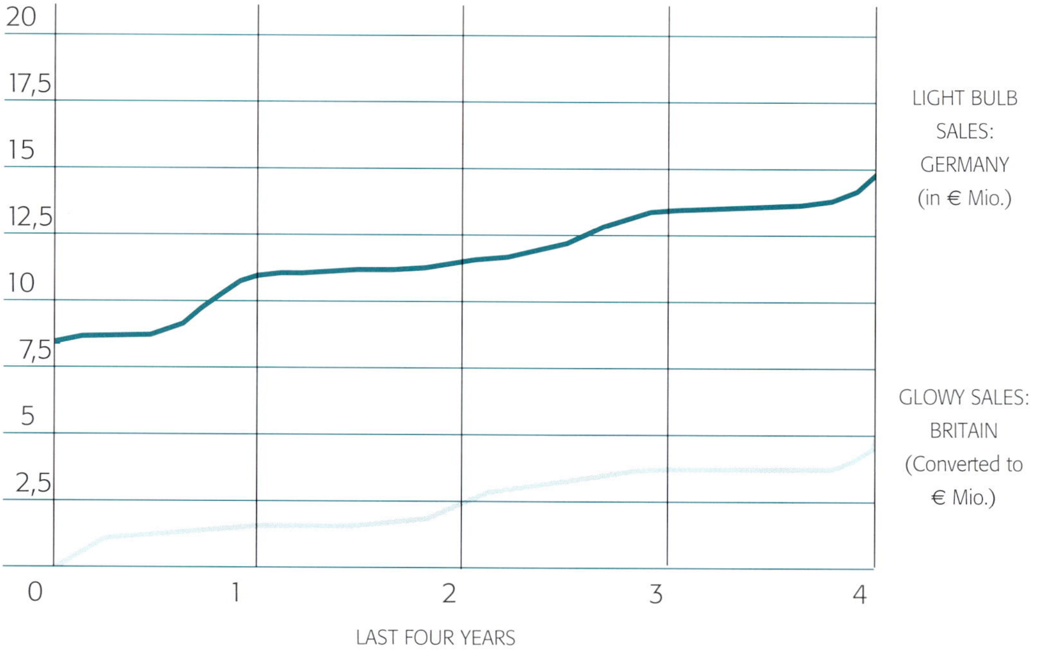

Figure 2

Turnover calculations (German version: GLOWY)

2 price versions: € 1.75 + € 2.15
2 market shares: 7% + 10% (Year's sales = € 15 million)

% of year's sales	unit price	units sales per year (approx)
7%: € 1,050,000	at € 1.75 =	600,000 units
10%: € 1,500,000	at € 1.75 =	860,000 units
7%: € 1,050,000	at € 2.15 =	490,000 units
10%: € 1,500,000	at € 2.15 =.	700,000 units

2 Which speakers refer to which figures? *Welche Gesprächspartner beziehen sich auf welche Darstellungen?*

	Sercombe	Melchior	Führling
Figure 1?			
Figure 2?			

3 List A shows six expressions. Match them with the items in List B to create six pairs. *In Liste A sind sechs Ausdrücke aufgeführt. Ordnen Sie diese den Elementen der Liste B zu, so dass Sie sechs Paare erhalten.*

LIST A

1. "As I was saying ..."
2. "We do need to know ..."
3. "Do you really think that ... ?"
4. "I'm afraid you've been misinformed."
5. "Could I come in here?"
6. "I'd like to go back to ... "

LIST B

a Interrupting *(Unterbrechen)*
b Resuming *(Fortfahren)*
c Referring back *(auf etw zurückkommen)*
d Challenging (a speaker's opinion) *(in Frage stellen)*
e Refuting *(Widerlegen)*
f Emphasising *(Betonen)*

Unit 10

Listen & Repeat

1 The following six sentences would not sound very polite in a discussion. Express each in a more acceptable way, using the word in brackets. The Useful Expressions (below) will help you.

Die folgenden sechs Sätze würden in einer Diskussion nicht sehr höflich klingen. Formulieren Sie jeden dieser Sätze auf eine höflichere Weise und benutzen Sie dabei die Wörter in Klammern. Die Useful Expressions *(unten) werden Ihnen helfen.*

Example: "I've got something to say about that!" (comment)
More acceptable: "Could I just comment on that?"

1. "I've got to break in here!" (excuse)
2. "Before you interrupted, I wanted to say it's almost lunchtime!" (about to)
3. "Let's get back to the main point, shall we?" (like to)
4. "Surely you don't think that's relevant, do you?" (really)
5. "You're dead wrong about that!" (afraid)
6. "We've got to have that information!" (do)

Listening Text 10/2

2.23

2 Listen to acceptable versions of the six sentences. Notice how each speaker's attitude is expressed not only by words but also by the tone of voice. Imitate as closely as possible the tone of voice used by each speaker.

Hören Sie die höflicheren Versionen der sechs Sätze. Achten Sie darauf, wie jeder Sprecher seine Haltung nicht nur durch Worte, sondern auch durch seine Betonung ausdrückt. Versuchen Sie, die Betonung jedes Sprechers so genau wie möglich zu imitieren.

Useful Expressions

Discussion tactics — ***Gesprächstaktik***

Interrupting	***Unterbrechen***
Could I come in here?	*Darf ich hier (einmal) einhaken?*
May I make a point on that?	*Darf ich dazu etwas sagen?*
Could I just comment on that?	*Könnte ich dazu mal etwas sagen?*
Excuse me for interrupting, but ...	*Entschuldigen Sie, dass ich unterbreche, aber ...*

Resuming	***Fortfahren***
As I was saying ...	*Wie ich schon/gerade sagte ...*
What I wanted to say was ...	*Was ich sagen wollte, war ...*
I was about to point out that ...	*Ich wollte gerade darauf hinweisen, dass ...*

Referring back	***Auf etw. zurückkommen***
I/You mentioned ...	*Ich/Sie erwähnten ...*
On the subject of ... I/you said ...	*Zum Thema ... sagte ich/sagten Sie ...*
I'd like to go back to ...	*Ich würde gerne auf ... zurückkommen.*

Challenging/questioning	***In Frage stellen***
Do you really think that ... ?	*Glauben Sie wirklich, dass ... ?*
I take your point, but surely ...	*Ich verstehe Ihr Argument, aber ... doch wohl ...*
Yes, I accept that, but on the other hand ...	*Ja, ich akzeptiere das, aber andererseits ...*
How can you explain (the difference)?	*Wie können Sie (den Unterschied) erklären?*

Refuting	***Widerlegen***
You seem to have misunderstood me. What I meant/said was ...	*Sie scheinen mich missverstanden zu haben. Was ich meinte/sagte, war ...*
I'm afraid you've been misinformed.	*Ich fürchte, Sie wurden falsch informiert.*
Perhaps I didn't explain that point clearly enough.	*Vielleicht habe ich diesen Punkt nicht deutlich genug dargelegt.*
Let me put it another way ...	*Lassen Sie es mich anders ausdrücken ...*

Emphasising	***Betonen***
(using do, does, did in statements)	
We do need to know ...	*Wir müssen (unbedingt) wissen ...*
The graph does show ...	*Das Schaubild/Die Grafik zeigt (wirklich) ...*

"You seem to have misunderstood me. What I meant was ..."

Language Study

PHRASAL VERBS

1 "Could I come in here?"
Hier sind einige weitere Verwendungen von come.

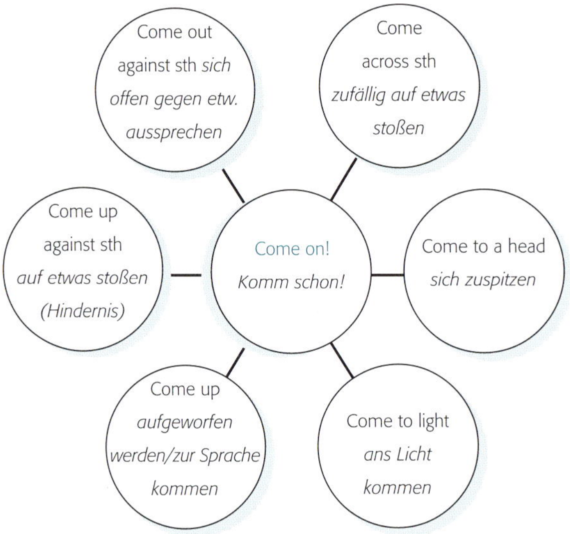

2 "We're looking at a seven to ten per cent share of the German market."
Hier sind einige Verwendungen von look.

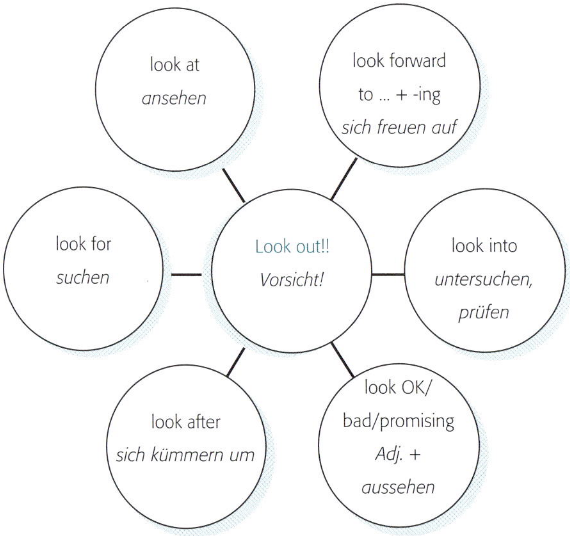

Exercise

Complete the English translations of these German sentences. Then, listen and check the answers on the CD.

Vervollständigen Sie die englischen Übersetzungen dieser deutschen Sätze. Hören Sie im Anschluss die Lösungen auf der CD.

2.24

1. *Seit dem letzten Sommer stoßen wir immer häufiger auf willkürliche Handelsbeschränkungen.* Since last summer, we've been _____________ arbitrary trade restrictions more and more.
2. *Die Veruntreuung kam mit Hilfe der neuen Wirtschaftsprüfer ans Licht.* The embezzlement _____________ with the help of the new chartered accountants.
3. *Bist du zufällig auf mein Englisch-Englisch Wörterbuch gestoßen?* Have you _____________ my English-English dictionary?
4. *Wir hoffen, dass heute keine Fragen hinsichtlich der Versicherung zur Sprache kommen.* We're hoping that no questions concerning insurance will _____________ today.
5. *Die Frage nach den Transportkosten wurde in der Besprechung aufgeworfen.* The question of transport costs _____________ at the meeting.
6. *Der Plan wird auf jeden Fall auf Widerstand der Ortsansässigen stoßen.* The plan is bound to _____________ opposition from local residents.
7. *Die Geschäftsführung hat sich offen gegen die Idee eines Werbevideos ausgesprochen.* The Management have _____________ the idea of a publicity video.
8. *Der Konflikt zwischen den beiden Managern spitzt sich zu.* The conflict between the two managers _____________.
9. *Finanzielle Unregelmäßigkeiten kamen das erste Mal während der Jahresabschlussprüfung ans Licht.* Financial irregularities first _____________ during the annual audit.
10. *Ich stieß zufällig auf Ihre Website im Internet.* I __________ your Website on the Internet.
11. *Die Krise spitzte sich mit dem Rücktritt des Vorstands zu.* The crisis _____________ with the resignation of the Board of Directors.
12. *Die Gewerkschaft sprach sich offen gegen den Vorschlag zur Arbeitsteilung aus.* The union _____________ the job-sharing proposal.
13. *Lassen Sie uns die voraussichtlichen Kosten prüfen.* Let's _____________ the likely costs.

14. *Ich brauche ungefähr zehn Tage, damit meine Leute sich diese Zahlen ansehen können.* I'll need about ten days, so my people can ____________ those figures.

15. *Wir werden einen Partner in China suchen müssen.* We'll have to ____________ a partner in China.

16. *Auf den ersten Blick sieht die Idee gut aus.* On the face of it, the idea ____________.

17. *Wir freuen uns darauf, von Ihnen zu hören.* We ____________ hearing from you.

"OK, let's look at the main aspects to be dealt with here."

!

Typical Mistakes

Each of these sentences contains a mistake made by a German speaker. Can you correct them?

Jeder dieser Sätze enthält einen von einem deutschen Sprecher gemachten Fehler. Können Sie die Fehler korrigieren?

1. He shouldn't be doing all that travelling in his age.
2. Dawsons will soon be in a position to make an analyse of the project.
3. We would appreciate to receive your reply very soon.
4. Despite of the bad weather, they should be able to finish on schedule.
5. Unless you have an own room, you won't find it easy to work.
6. The difficult situation considered, we really should have another meeting.
7. Could you use another kind of packaging, without that you charge more for delivery?
8. If we look at the figures, we'll have an idea on what to do next.
9. Her both applications have been rejected.
10. The self-service unit, so the Production Manager, will be fully operational next month.

ABC

Word Bank

Dealing with publicity & distribution	***Sich um Werbung und Vertrieb kümmern***
advertising budget	*Werbeetat*
advertising campaign	*Werbekampagne*
amount to	*sich belaufen auf*
annual turnover	*Jahresumsatz*
bring sb up to date	*jdn auf dem Laufenden halten*
brochure	*Prospekt*
business card	*Visitenkarte*
commodity sales	*Warenumsatz*
company logo	*Firmenlogo*
customer loyalty	*Kundentreue*
customer relations	*Kundenbeziehungen*
EDP-supported	*EDV-gestützt*
feasibility	*Durchführbarkeit*
gap in the market	*Marktnische*
green point	*grüner Punkt*
information bulletin	*Mitteilungsblatt*
item	*Posten*
launch	*herausbringen, auf den Markt bringen*
local branch	*Filiale*
loss-leader	*Lockartikel*
mail order	*Postversand*
market share	*Marktanteil*
marketing costs	*Marketingkosten*
net weight	*Nettogewicht*
outlay	*Auslagen*
pallet	*Palette*
poster	*Plakat*
promotion budget	*Werbeetat*
provisional	*provisorisch*
publicity campaign	*Werbekampagne*
recruit	*anwerben*
reliability	*Zuverlässigkeit*

rough calculation of costs	*Vorkalkulation*
sales rep (= representative)	*Handelsvertreter*
selling price	*Verkaufspreis*
shelf (plural: shelves)	*Regal(e)*
show a profit	*Profit verzeichnen*
special sales campaign	*Verkaufssonderaktion*
storage facilities	*Lagermöglichkeiten*
tailor-made	*maßgeschneidert*
take as a basis	*zu Grunde legen*
target group	*Zielgruppe*
time frame	*Zeitplan*
unit price	*Stückpreis*
units sold	*verkaufte Einheiten*
waste disposal costs	*Entsorgungskosten*
written offer	*schriftliches Angebot*

Down to Business

The plans to launch GLOWY in Germany are developing fast. New Electronics in London now want a progress report. As Pat Llewellin of their Market Division, your task is to write the report. To do this, complete the following five steps.

Die Pläne, GLOWY in Deutschland auf den Markt zu bringen, schreiten schnell voran. Die Londoner Niederlassung von New Electronics möchte nun einen Lagebericht. Sie sind jetzt Pat Llewellin aus der Marketing-abteilung und müssen den Bericht schreiben. Dazu sind folgende fünf Schritte notwendig.

Listening Text 10/3

2.25

1 Listen to Pat's conversation with Herr Melchior. Note down any points which you think will be useful for the progress report.

Hören Sie Pats Gespräch mit Herrn Melchior. Notieren Sie alle Punkte, die Ihrer Meinung nach für den Lagebericht nützlich sein werden.

2 Read this message from Promotional Consultants Network (= PCN). Again, note down points you think will be useful for the progress report.

Lesen Sie diese Mitteilung der Promotional Consultants Network (= PCN). *Notieren Sie wieder die Punkte, die Ihrer Meinung nach für den Lagebericht nützlich sind.*

PCN
(Promotional Consultants Network)

Message
To: P. Llewellin, New Electronics   From: J. Pearce, Consultancy Director

Pat

GLOWY: sales & promotions

Contact with points of sale – v. important.

Priorities:
- build up network of well-motivated sales reps
- send one to every branch
  (16 federal states – approx 5 reps per state needed)

To get GLOWY onto retailers' shelves, sales reps to
- visit branches; introduce GLOWY to branch managers
- take care of product presentation (= regular visits to branches (average: every 4 wks)

I hope these notes are helpful for your report!

John

3 Complete Pat's parts in the following conversation. She is speaking to the Logistics Section.

Vervollständigen Sie Pats Beiträge in dem folgenden Gespräch. Sie spricht mit der Logistikabteilung.

Pat: Rod, as you know. I'm putting this progress report together. – ask you – more information –
Rod: Fire away.
Pat: – you said – first priority – guarantee punctual delivery.
Rod: And the best methods of co-operating, yes.
Pat: So – tell – stage you're at – organising this?
Rod: Well, right now, we're getting all the trading companies to tell us if they'd require deliveries to a central store or to individual branches. Then we'll be able to decide what intermediate storage facilities we'll need.
Pat: OK– tell – concerning – forwarding agent?
Rod: Petersen Spediteur? Yes. We've contracted them to advise us on the control for our distribution system.
Pat: – EDP-supported – ?
Rod: Correct. You can also say that Petersen will be supporting us in the negotiations with the trading companies.
Pat: – promising – experience – useful –
Rod: Not only their experience – they're already well-known to the companies, so that's going to be a big advantage too.

Listening Text 10/4

2.26

4 Listen to the complete conversation. Again, note down points which you think will be useful for the progress report.

Hören Sie nun das vollständige Gespräch. Notieren Sie wieder die Punkte, die Ihrer Meinung nach für den Lagebericht nützlich sind.

5 Write the progress report, using the information you now have. This framework will help you.

Schreiben Sie den Lagebericht und benutzen Sie dabei die Ihnen zur Verfügung stehenden Informationen. Dieses Gerüst wird Ihnen behilflich sein.

GLOWY

Progress report on marketing launch in Germany **Dated: 01 March**

Negotiations

1. Herr Melchior _______________ negotiations _______________

2. For this purpose, we are producing
– _______________ offer
– _______________ sample _______________
– _______________ strategy _______________
– _______________ strategy

Sales and promotions

1. We have hired Promotional Consultants Network (= PCN)
– to recruit _______________
– to develop _______________
– to get the best _______________

2. Contact _______________ important. To get GLOWY _______________ shelves, the sales reps have to _______________.
Once GLOWY is on the shelves, the sales reps have to _______________. So it is important to build up _______________ 16 German federal states _______________.

Logistics:

1. The first priority ______________. To achieve this, we are finding out
– (from each trading company) if ______________
– what ______________ will be needed.

2. Petersen Spediteur are
– advising ______________
– supporting ______________.

Dealing with Visual Info

Cost analysis

PCN have estimated the marketing costs of GLOWY. Here are their figures.

PCN hat die Marketingkosten für GLOWY geschätzt. Hier sind ihre Zahlen.

GLOWY: Estimated Marketing Costs (per unit) — PCN: Pearce

* Transport costs:	DM 0.12 - based on DM 320 per pallet; 3500 units per pallet
* Waste disposal costs (green point):	DM 0.10 - based on 30g net packaging weight
* Promotion costs:	DM 0.28 - based on DM 15,000 outlay
Total costs (per unit):	DM 0.50

Listening Text 10/5

2.27

To get a second opinion, Herr Melchior has hired another consultant to estimate the marketing costs. Listen to Herr Melchior's discussion with him. What is the difference between the total costs (per unit) estimated by the two consultants?

Um ein zweites Gutachten zu bekommen, hat Herr Melchior einen weiteren Berater engagiert, der die Marketingkosten schätzen soll. Hören Sie Herrn Melchiors Diskussion mit ihm. Was ist der Unterschied zwischen den von den beiden Beratern geschätzten Gesamtkosten (pro Stück)?

The British-American Difference

1 **UK**

What number will you call if ...

a you've discovered a dangerous leakage of gas in the building?
b you have a question about your electricity bill?
c someone in the building is injured and needs an ambulance?
d part of the building is on fire?

2 **US**

What number will you call if you want to ...

a find out MCI's phone charges?
b have MCI connect a phone in your apartment?
c know the number of a business which can be called free of charge?
d know the number of someone in the same town?

EMERGENCY HELPLINES

999
• TELL THE OPERATOR WHICH SERVICE YOU NEED.
• GIVE YOUR TELEPHONE NUMBER.
• WHEN THE EMERGENCY SERVICE ANSWERS GIVE THE ADDRESS WHERE HELP IS NEEDED.

OR

112
THE PAN-EUROPEAN EMERGENCY NUMBER HAS BEEN PHASED IN TO GIVE A COMMON NUMBER FOR ALL E.C. CITIZENS TO TELEPHONE WHEN THEY NEED THE EMERGENCY SERVICES.

IN EMERGENCIES ALWAYS USE THE ABOVE PROCEDURE THE DETAILS BELOW ARE FOR OTHER INFORMATION REQUIREMENTS.

AMBULANCE

East Anglian Ambulance Service HQ
Hospital Lane, Hellesdon
Norwich, NR6 5NA 01603 424255
East Anglian Ambulance NHS Trust
Southern Division
Duckamere Bramford
Ipswich, IP8 4AJ 01473 749333

ELECTRICITY

Eastern Electricity
HQ, 190 London Road Rayleigh,
Essex, SS8 9EE
General Enquiries &
Emergencies 01284 763111

FIRE PREVENTION

Fire Safety Advisory Unit (Norfolk)
Fire Services HQ
Whitegate, Hethersett, NR9 3DN
..................(Answerphone) 01603 819777
Suffolk Fire Service
Parkway North, Bury St Edmunds
IP33 3BA 01284 753911

GAS

British Gas Eastern Plc
Roundtree Way, Norwich, NR7 8BR
Gas Escapes ....Area 1 01603 787022
.............................Area 2 0345 426121
.............................Area 3 0345 426123
British Gas Eastern Plc (Bury St Edmunds)
South Anglia District, Whitehall Road
Colchester, Essex, CO2 8HG
Gas Escapes 0345 426122

POLICE

London Road, Attleborough
NR17 2DW 01953 452271
Raingate Street, Bury St Edmunds
IP33 2AP 01284 774100
Stanley Rd, Diss, IP22 3BP 01379 642391
...oad
...P24 2HU 01842 754314

How to Reach the Telephone Company Serving You

DIRECTORY ASSISTANCE

To obtain local numbers, all customers:
1 + 411

To obtain numbers outside your local area, but within New Mexico:
1 + 555-1212

To obtain Toll-Free phone numbers:
1 + 800-555-1212

INSTALLATION & REPAIR OF TELEPHONE SERVICE PROVIDED BY OTHER COMPANIES

AT&T
Repair Service or Information ... 1-800-222-3000
Business Installation 1-800-222-0400
Consumer Marketing 1-800-222-0300

COMMUNICATIONS DIVERSIFIED
Repair Service or Information 982-5257
Business Installation 982-5257

GTE
Repair Service or Information 753-2226
Business Installation 753-2226
Residential Installation 753-2226

MCI
Repair Service or Information 988-5882
Business Installation 1-800-444-2222
Residential Installation 1-800-444-3333

TELEPHONE EXPRESS
Information 1-800-748-2000

Last but not Least

The English expressions below are anagrams of English two-word noun phrases you have seen earlier in the course. Their German meanings are also listed below, in the same order. Write the English phrases into the boxes given. Finally, you will have a vertical word in the python meaning *"Herstellung"*.

Die unten aufgeführten englischen Ausdrücke sind Anagramme zusammengesetzter Hauptwörter, die Sie bereits aus dem Kurs kennen. Ihre deutschen Bedeutungen sind, in der gleichen Reihenfolge, ebenfalls unten aufgeführt. Tragen Sie die englischen Ausdrücke in die Kästchen ein. Die durch die Schlange verbundenen Buchstaben ergeben das englische Wort für „Herstellung".

überfällige Zahlung – Marktforschung – Bruttogewicht – Bordkarte – Qualitätskontrolle – Konsulatsfaktura – Bilanz – Stückpreis – Betriebskosten – Sitzkapazität

NEVER TAPE MY DUO

CHEER SMART RAKE

SOS THREW GIG

NO BAD CAR GRID

QUIT CORNY ATOLL

IN VACCINE OR SOUL

LEANEST BEACH

ICE TURNIP

POST TANGO CRIES

CAGE TITANIC SPY

Die Powertestcassette enthält 10 Units, *die jeweils den* Units *in* Down to Business *entsprechen. Bevor Sie eine* Unit *auf der Testcassette bearbeiten, sollten Sie die entsprechende* Unit *im Buch durchgearbeitet haben.*

Sie hören englische Sprecher auf der Testcassette, nur die Anweisungen werden in deutscher Sprache gegeben.

1. Useful esxpressions

Sie hören fünf Useful Expressions *zum Nachsprechen. Diesen Ausdrücken sind Sie bereits in der jeweils entsprechenden* Unit *von* Down to Business *begegnet. Ihre Aufgabe besteht darin, beim Nachsprechen die Betonung und die Satzmelodie der Sprecher so gut wie möglich zu imitieren.*

2. Word Bank

Sie hören acht deutsche Ausdrücke, die Sie in Down to Business *kennen gelernt haben. Auf jeden Ausdruck folgt eine kurze Pause, in der Sie laut die entsprechende englische Übersetzung sprechen. Zur Überprüfung hören Sie im Anschluss den englischen Ausdruck mit Pausen zum Nachsprechen.*

3. Listening for Information

Sie hören einen Bericht über Geschäftssituationen, die Ihnen bereits aus der entsprechenden Unit *von* Down to Business *bekannt sind. Nach dem Zuhören sollen Sie zwei Fragen zu diesem Bericht in vollständigen Sätzen beantworten. Diese Übung wird nicht nur Ihr Hörverständnis trainieren sondern auch das „freie" Sprechen. Zur Überprüfung folgen im Anschluss immer die Antworten mit Pausen zum Nachsprechen.*

Die Powertestcassette ist ideal für unterwegs: Schieben Sie einfach die Cassette in Ihren Walkman oder Cassettenrecorder zu Hause oder im Auto und trainieren Sie damit effizient Ihr Wirtschaftsenglisch.

ARTICLES/*ARTIKEL*

Der bestimmte Artikel = the (*der/die/das*): the cheque; the account
Der unbestimmte Artikel = a/an (*ein/eine*): a cheque; an account

Hier einige Unterschiede im Gebrauch der Artikel im Englischen und im Deutschen.

Unbestimmte Artikel im Englischen

– *bei Nomen, die sich auf den Beruf, die Nationalität, Religion oder politische Gesinnung einer Person beziehen.*

He's an engineer/a student/a Catholic. *Er ist Ingenieur/Student/Katholik.*
She's an American. *Sie ist Amerikanerin.*

– *bei diesen Ausdrücken:*

to be at an end:	*am Ende sein*
to be in a hurry:	*in Eile sein*
to be in a good/bad mood:	*in guter/schlechter Stimmung sein*
it's a pity:	*es ist schade*
to have a headache/ temperature:	*Kopfschmerzen/Fieber haben*
to make a noise:	*Lärm machen*
to make it a condition/a rule:	*es zur Bedingung machen/es sich zur Regel machen*
as a rule:	*in der Regel*
as a whole:	*als Ganzes*
for a change:	*zur Abwechslung*
in a friendly manner:	*auf freundliche Art*
without a break:	*ohne Unterbrechung*
without a ticket/permit, etc:	*ohne Fahrkarte, Erlaubnis usw.*
to a high degree:	*in hohem Maße*
(not) to be in a position (to do sth):	*(nicht) in der Lage sein (etw zu tun)*

Kein Artikel im Englischen

– *bei Abstraktionen:*
It's a danger to health. *Es ist eine Gefahr für die Gesundheit.*

– *bei Materialien:*
We have to pay more for beer. *Wir müssen mehr fürs Bier bezahlen.*

– *beim Gerundium:*
Correcting the progress report took all afternoon. *Das Korrigieren des Lageberichts dauerte den ganzen Nachmittag.*

– *bei Ortsnamen:*
Could we meet at Wilhelmshöhe Station at 5.00 pm? *Können wir uns um 17.00 Uhr am Wilhelmshöher Bahnhof treffen?*
(*Ausnahme:* the High Street; the City)

– *bei Jahreszeiten, Monaten, Wochentagen, Mahlzeiten:*
in summer (*= im Sommer*), in March (*= im März*), on Tuesday (*= am Dienstag*), after supper (*= nach dem Abendessen*)

– *bei diesen Ausdrücken:*

to be in office/power/opposition:	*im Amt/an der Macht/in der Opposition sein*
to be in good shape:	*in guter Form sein*
to keep in mind:	*im Gedächtnis behalten*
to come to light:	*ans Licht kommen*
to lose courage/patience:	*den Mut/die Geduld verlieren*
to shake hands:	*die Hand geben/schütteln*
at first sight:	*auf den ersten Blick*
in practice:	*in der Praxis*
in view of:	*im Hinblick auf*
by train/car, etc:	*mit dem Zug/Auto usw.*

Bestimmter Artikel im Englischen

– *bei diesen Ausdrücken:*

in the absence/presence of:	*in Abwesenheit/Gegenwart von*
with the help of:	*mit Hilfe von*
to be out of the question:	*nicht in Frage kommen*

MODALS/*MODALVERBEN*

Modale Hilfsverben geben zusätzliche Informationen über die Absichten oder Einstellungen des Handelnden. Der Satz He takes the 8.15 train *kann mittels modaler Hilfsverben variiert werden. Einige Hilfsverben können nicht alle Zeiten bilden, so dass sie ggf. durch bedeutungsähnliche Ausdrücke ersetzt werden müssen.*

Hilfsverb	*Absicht*	*Anwendungsbeispiele*	*Ausdruck mit annähernd gleicher Bedeutung*
can	*Fähigkeit*	He can take the 8.15 train (because the meeting will be over by 7.30).	to be able to
must	*Zwang / Verpflichtung* *Vermutung*	He must take the 8.15 train (because there isn't any other). He must have taken the 8.15 train (because he's no longer at the office).	to have to
may	*Erlaubnis*	He may take the 8.15 train (normally he has to take a later one).	to be allowed
must not/ may not	*Verbot*	He must not/may not take the 8.15 train (because it doesn't stop at his station).	not to be allowed to *(Beachte: deutsch „nicht dürfen")*
need not	*keine Verpflichtung*	He need not take the 8.15 train (because he could take the 8.45 instead).	not to have to

TENSES/*ZEITEN*

Auf die Gegenwart verweisen:

Simple Present

bezieht sich auf eine Gewohnheit, ein regelmäßiges Verfahren oder eine gängige Praxis:
He hands in a progress report to the company directors each month.

In der Geschäftssprache wird es auch dazu benutzt, sich auf wirtschaftliche Prinzipien und Regeln zu beziehen:
When interest rates fall, businesses borrow more and invest more.
Prices depend on demand and supply.

Present Continuous

bezieht sich auf zeitlich begrenzte Prozesse (oder solche, die als zeitlich begrenzt behandelt werden, da man nicht sicher sein kann, ob sie langfristig oder unbefristet sind):
Signor Brigaglia is considering acting as our agent in Italy.
Now we are exporting to customers in the UK and Ireland too.
Diese Zeitform eignet sich gut zur Beschreibung wirtschaftlicher Trends oder geschäftlicher Aktivitäten von kurzer Dauer:
We're borrowing heavily at the moment, but the new computers are almost paid for.
Lawsons are working at only 80% of capacity, but business is sure to pick up later.

Auf die Vergangenheit verweisen:

Simple Past

bezieht sich auf einen bereits beendeten Prozess, und wird oft mit einem auf die Vergangenheit verweisenden Ausdruck wie in August *oder* until last year *verwendet:*

They moved into larger premises in August.
Until last year, all our contracts were with German companies.

In der Geschäftssprache werden auf die Vergangenheit verweisende Audrücke (wie die folgenden) normalerweise mit dem simple past *kombiniert:*

When we started the company	Three years ago	In 1996	After we sent the order
Soon after the committee's report	In the first quarter	Last May	On receiving your letter

Past Continuous (was/were + -ing)

Für Vorgänge, die stattfanden, als eine neue Handlung hinzukam:
When we arrived, the Chairman was already speaking.
Beschreibung einer Situation, die in der Vergangenheit liegt:
At that time, the company was still losing money.

Present Perfect (has/have + V-ed,-en)

wird benutzt, um einen Prozess zu beschreiben, der in der Vergangenheit begann und in der Gegenwart noch andauert. Es wird oft mit auf die Vergangenheit verweisenden Audrücken wie for the last 18 months oder since 1965 kombiniert:
For the last 18 months, we've specialised in packaging for fragile goods.
Since 1965, the company has hired only bilingual sales staff.

Das present perfect *wird verwendet, wenn man nicht betonen will, <u>wann</u> sondern <u>dass</u> etwas passiert ist. Es verweist auf einen bereits vergangenen Prozess, dessen Wirkung noch in der Gegenwart spürbar ist:*

We have invested a lot there, so all the equipment is state-of-the-art.
(= then) (= now)

Hier zwei Beispiele dieser „resultativen" Bedeutung des present perfect *in der Geschäftssprache:*
Chile has lifted her import restrictions on video cassettes, so we can start selling there.
Mr Watson has faxed us, so we know about the problem.

Past Perfect (had + V-ed, -en)
Für Sachverhalte, die vor einem bestimmten Zeitpunkt der Vergangenheit bereits abgeschlossen waren:
We learned that they had signed the contract three days earlier.

Auf die Zukunft verweisen:
Simple Present
um Aussagen über feste Fahr- oder Zeitpläne zu machen:
The flight arrives at 8.35.
The guarantee expires at the end of the month.

Present Continuous (be + -ing)
um sich auf einen im Voraus vereinbarten Vorgang zu beziehen, insbesondere, wenn dabei eine Zeit in der Zukunft angegeben wird:
You are coming from Birmingham on Friday morning, aren't you?
He's taking over the hardware section in the New Year.

Future Simple (will/shall)
um einen zukünftigen Sachverhalt darzulegen oder um ein Versprechen zu geben:
You will be in good time for the flight.
I'll pick you up at 9 am.

"Going to"
um Absicht auszudrücken:
I'm going to confirm all this for you by fax.
Halsteads are going to open a branch in Leipzig in the New Year.

Future Continuous (will be + -ing)
um sich auf einen Vorgang zu beziehen, dessen Eintritt im Laufe der Zeit erwartet wird:
(I expect) Davidsons will be bringing out their new Christmas catalogue soon.
(I'm sure) he'll be speaking at the Convention again this year.

Present Continuous (be + -ing?) and Future Continuous (will be + -ing?)
werden auch in Fragen benutzt, um sich höflich nach zukünftigen Plänen zu erkundigen:
Are you ordering/Will you be ordering any more supplies before Christmas?

CONDITIONAL SENTENCES/*BEDINGUNGSSÄTZE*

Bedingungssätze beinhalten eine Verknüpfung von Bedingung und Folge. Je nach Verwirklichkeitsgrad der Folge unterscheidet man verschiedene Typen. Die Bedingung kann vor der Folge stehen oder auch dahinter.

Type I: *verwirklichbare Möglichkeit* (= real possibility). *Die Folge ist möglich oder sogar sehr wahrscheinlich:*
If you give us that follow-up order by October, we will allow the 5% discount.
(present) (future)
Die if-*Bedingung (= die Möglichkeit, bis Oktober eine Nachbestellung bei uns aufzugeben) ist erfüllbar.*

Grundstrukturen:
If they order now, we'll allow a 5% discount.
We'll allow a 5% discount if they order now

Type II: *entfernte Möglichkeit* (= remote possibility). *Es ist unwahrscheinlich, dass die* if-*Bedingung erfüllt wird:*

If they proved to be OK, we would want more in the New Year.
(simple past) (would or could)
Es besteht eine sehr geringe Möglichkeit, dass die if-*Bedingung erfüllt wird.*

Grundstrukturen:
If we had enough money, we'd stage the conference ourselves.
We'd stage the conference ourselves if we had enough money.

Type III: *irreale Bedingung* (= impossible condition). *Die Bedingung kann nicht mehr verwirklicht werden:*

If they had given us a discount, we would have paid in cash.
Die if-*Bedingung (= die Möglichkeit, uns einen Rabatt zu gewähren) kann nicht erfüllt werden, da die Gelegenheit verstrichen ist.*

Andere Versionen dieses Bedingungssatz-Typus:

If the price had fallen, we [should / could / ought to / might] have placed an order immediately.

If we had received the order yesterday, we would be working on it now.
If we had paid the invoice we would have the goods now.

Grundstrukturen:
If she had tried harder, she would have got the job.
She would have got the job if she had tried harder.

ACTIVE AND PASSIVE SENTENCES/*AKTIV- UND PASSIVSÄTZE*

Aktivsätze
You must deliver the goods by the 15th.
They include packaging in the price.
Das Aktiv betont den Ausführenden der Handlung (= You/They).

Passivsätze
The goods must be delivered by the 15th.
Packaging is included in the price.
Das Passiv betont die Handlung selbst (= being delivered/included).

Passive Sätze sind unpersönlich: Sie konzentrieren sich auf die (wichtige) Handlung, nicht auf den (unwichtigen) Ausführenden der Handlung. Daher werden sie oft in der Geschäftssprache benutzt, um Verfahren, Regeln, Methoden und Taktik hervorzuheben:
Delivery has to be brought forward three months.
Letters of Credit should be used for international payments.
The office is closed at weekends.

Bildung des Passivs
Simple Present : The Johnsons are invited.
Present Continuous: The Johnsons are being invited.
Simple Past: The Johnsons were invited.
Past Continuous: The Johnsons were being invited.
Present Perfect: The Johnsons have been invited.
Past Perfect: The Johnsons had been invited.
"Will"-future: Will the Johnsons be invited?

Conditionals with "would": The Johnsons would be/would have been invited
Infinitive Passive: to be invited/to have been invited

EXPRESSIONS OF QUANTITY/*MENGENANGABEN*

1 "Some" & "any"

werden oft benutzt, um unbestimmte Mengenangaben auszudrücken.

some = *begrenzte, unbestimmte Anzahl oder Menge:*
We'd like to do some price comparisons.

any = *ganz gleich welche, irgendwelche* (= "it doesn't matter which"):
Use your dictionary to look up any words which are new to you.

some 30 years ago	*(vor etwa 30 Jahren)*
for some time now	*(seit einiger Zeit)*
at any time	*(zu jeder Zeit)*
at any price	*(um jeden Preis)*

Auch:
some *benutzt man*
– *in bejahten Sätzen:* I can give you some information about prices.
– *in Fragen, bei denen eine positive Antwort erwartet wird:* Here are the brochures – would you like some price lists too?

any *benutzt man*
– *in verneinten Sätzen:* I can't give you any information about prices.
– *in Fragen, bei denen eine negative Antwort möglich ist:* Excuse me – do you have any price lists?

2 Count nouns and mass nouns/*Zählbare und nichtzählbare Nomen*

count noun = *eine einzelne Einheit*

hat Singular- und Pluralformen:
computer(s), dollar(s), machine(s)

Mengenangaben
a lot of, a large number of, plenty of, many
(= viele)
(comparative: more – the most)
few, not many *(= wenige)*
(comparative: fewer – fewest)

mass noun = *ein kollektives Ganzes*

hat keine Pluralform:
money, knowledge, oil

a lot of, a large amount of, plenty of, much
(= viel)
(comparative: more – the most)
little, not much *(= wenig)*
(comparative: less – the least)

Auch:

a few *(ein paar)*	enough *(genug/genügend)*	a little *(etwas/ein wenig)*	some *(einige)*
a pair of *(ein Paar)*	the two *(die beiden)*	a bit of *(ein bisschen)*	
both *(beide)*	some *(einige)*	enough *(genug/genügend)*	
several *(mehrere)*	all (of) the *(alle)*	all that/this *(all jen../d.../dies..)*	

3 Numerical expressions/*Zahlwörter*

Ordinalzahlen

1st = first, 2nd = second, 3rd = third, 4th = fourth, 5th = fifth, 6th = sixth, 7th = seventh, 8th = eighth, 9th = ninth, 10th = tenth, 11th = eleventh, 12th = twelfth, 13th = thirteenth.

Ab 13th, *gilt: Wenn die Zahl mit 1, 2 oder 3 endet, wird* -first (= -1st), -second (= -2nd), -third (= -3rd) *benutzt.*

31st = thirty-first 22nd = twenty-second 133rd = one hundred and thirty-third

Wenn die Zahl nicht mit 1, 2 oder 3 endet, wird ein -th *angefügt.*

4th = fourth 35th = thirty-fifth 50th = fiftieth

der 50ste Tag = the 50th day *die 1980er* = the 1980s (the nineteen-eighties)

Multiplizieren

He's already phoned	once/twice	*(= einmal/zweimal)*	this morning.
	three times	*(= dreimal)*	
	four times, etc	*(= viermal usw.)*	

Sales have doubled/tripled/quadrupled over the last five years.
(= verdoppelt/verdreifacht/vervierfacht)

Auch:
three times as many/twice as much *(= dreimal so viele/doppelt so viel)*
four times a year *(= viermal im Jahr)*

Ausdrücke mit Artikeln

– the: half the cost *(= die halben Kosten),* twice the amount *(= die doppelte Summe),* all the goods *(= alle Waren),* both the deliveries *(= beide Lieferungen).*
– a/an: half a pound (= *ein halbes Pfund*), half an hour (= *eine halbe Stunde*), 90p a kilo *(= 90p das Kilo).*

Ausdrücke mit Präpositionen

50 metres of cable	*(= 50 Meter Kabel)*
some crates of beer	*(= einige Kisten Bier)*
20 kilos of fax paper	*(= 20 Kilo Faxpapier)*
10% of the price	*(= 10% des Preises)*
We can save up to 50%.	*(= bis zu 50%)*
The rate has fallen to 2%.	*(= auf 2%)*
The price has risen by $25.	*(= um $25)*
We take 60 orders a week on average.	*(= durchschnittlich)*
We take an average of 60 orders a week.	

Germany ranks among *(= zählt zu)* the world's leading industrial nations.
London is Britain's biggest city; Birmingham ranks second *(= an zweiter Stelle stehen).*

ORTHOGRAPHY/*RECHTSCHREIBUNG*

1 The Date/*das Datum*

amerikanisches Englisch:	month – day – year	10.12.96 (= October 12, 1996)		
britisches Englisch:	day – month – year	10.12.96 (= 10 December 1996)		

Im internationalen Schriftverkehr können Sie Verwechslungen vermeiden, indem Sie eine dieser (unzweideutigen) Formen benutzen:

Ausgeschriebene Form:	16 June 1994	20 November 1999
Kurzform:	16 Jun 94	20 Nov 99

2 The Time/*die Zeitangabe*

geschrieben:	9.45 am	10.13 pm
gesprochen:	nine forty-five (am)	ten thirteen (pm)
	a quarter to ten (BE)	thirteen minutes past ten (BE)
	a quarter of ten (AE)	thirteen minutes after ten (AE)
	(in the morning)	(in the evening)

Obwohl sie in der englischen Alltagssprache weniger üblich ist, kann die „24-Stunden-Uhr" dazu benutzt werden, sich auf gedruckte Zeitpläne zu beziehen.

geschrieben:	09.00	22.13
gesprochen:	oh-nine-hundred	twenty-two thirteen

3 Writing numbers/*Zahlen ausschreiben*

\$1,000,000	a (or: one) million dollars (= *eine Million*)
\$1,000,000,000	a (or: one) billion (= *eine Milliarde*)

Pluralformen. 20 million/billion 20 million dollars millions/billions of dollars

Bei Zahlenangaben steht im Englischen ein Punkt, wo im Deutschen ein Komma gesetzt wird (und umgekehrt):

10.8% = *10,8%*
\$998.25 = *\$998,25*
5,000,000 = *5.000.000*

4 Using capital letters/*Verwendung von Großbuchstaben*

Großbuchstaben werden bei Namen historischer Ereignisse, offiziellen Titeln und allen solchen Wörtern (einschließlich Adjektiven) benutzt, die auf Namen von Orten, Personen oder Nationalitäten basieren.

Beispiele:

the Second World War	*der zweite Weltkrieg*
the German Embassy	*die deutsche Botschaft*
in Victorian style	*im viktorianischen Stil*
the Chinese market	*der chinesische Markt*

RELATIVE CLAUSES/*RELATIVSÄTZE*

Ein Relativsatz ist Teil eines Satzes, der
(a) ein Verb enthält und
(b) normalerweise durch ein Relativpronomen mit dem Rest des Satzes verbunden ist.

Relativpronomen, die einen Relativsatz einleiten können:
who whom to/for/of whom whose to/for/of whose which to/for/of which that

Das Relativpronomen kann weggelassen werden, (i) wenn es sich dabei um das Objekt des Satzteils handelt:
I'm calling about the order you faxed this morning (= which you faxed).
oder (ii) wenn der Satzteil mit einer Präposition endet:
Are you the secretary I talked to? (= who(m) I talked to)

Zeichensetzung in Relativsätzen
Sehen Sie sich die Zeichensetzung in diesen Sätzen an:
a) Mr Rutter, who made the complaint, will call again later.
b) The person who made the complaint will call again later.

In a) fügt der Relativsatz lediglich einem bereits vollständigen Satz Informationen hinzu. = 2 Kommas
In b) wäre der Satz ohne den Relativsatz unvollständig. = 0 Kommas

Kurze Relativsätze:
Noun + V-ed:
Goods produced here are intended for the Chinese market. (= which are produced)
Noun + V-ing:
Are there any restrictions affecting the import of CDs into China? (= which affect)
Noun + to + V:
He was the first person to apply for the job. (= who applied)

Das allgemeine Relativpronomen „what":
What *kann im Sinne von „das, was" benutzt werden, wie die folgenden Beispiele zeigen:*

What is certain is that demand will fall off after Christmas.
Each year, we receive what are known as "introductory samples".
I don't know what there is to complain about.

QUESTIONS/*FRAGEN*

Fragen werden fast immer mit Hilfe von do oder eines anderen Hilfsverbs gestellt.

	Do	you	take	traveller's cheques?
	Does	Mr Andrews	speak	German?
	Did	they	pay	in cash?
	Can	I	call	you back, please?
Where	did	you	put	the file?
How much	do	we	owe	them?
How far	can	we	go?	
	Are	you		all right?

How/What-*Fragen*

How ...

How do things look right now? *Wie sehen die Dinge jetzt aus?*
How do you use this thing? *Wie benutzt man dieses Ding?*
How old is he? *Wie alt ist er?*
How are things (going)? *Wie geht es?*
How much/many? *Wie viel(e)?*
How come?/Why? *Wieso?*

What ...

What is it called?/What is its name? *Wie heißt es?*
What's the time?/What time is it? *Wie spät ist es?*
What do you say for ...? *Wie sagt man ...?*
What's the date today? *Der Wievielte ist heute?*

Note: How does it look?/What does it look like? *Wie sieht es aus?*

Schwierige Wh-*Fragen*

What ... with? (With what ... ?) *Womit?*
What can I write with? *Womit kann ich schreiben?*
What/Where ... from? (From what/where ... ?) *Woher?*
Where did this delivery come from? *Woher kam diese Lieferung?*
What ... on? (On what ... ?) *Worauf?*
What did you bet on? *Worauf haben Sie gewettet?*
What ... for? (For what purpose ... ?) *Wofür?/Wozu?*
What are these buttons for? *Wofür sind diese Knöpfe?*
Who ... belong to?/Whose ... ? (To whom ... belong?) *Wem/Wessen?*
Who does that belong to?/Whose is that? *Wem gehört das?/Wessen ist das?*
What sort/kind of ... ? *Was für (ein) ... ?*
What sort/kind of fax machine do you have? *Was für ein Faxgerät haben Sie?*
What does ... mean/stand for? (For what does ... stand?) *Was bedeutet ... ?*
What does CAD mean/stand for? *Was bedeutet CAD?*

Note:

Formell: Präposition am Anfang – nicht gebräuchlich:	With what can I write?
Informell: Präposition am Ende – gebräuchlicher:	What can I write with?

NEGATION/*VERNEINUNG*

Steht im bejahten Satz ein Hilfs- oder Modalverb, so wird bei der Verneinung not *(oder* -n't*) mit diesem Verb verbunden.*

We can meet tomorrow.	We can't meet tomorrow.

Fehlt ein Hilfsverb, so wird nach folgendem Schema verneint:

This programme works.	That one doesn't (work).
They brought samples with them.	We didn't (bring any samples).

ADJECTIVES AND ADVERBS/*ADJEKTIVE UND ADVERBIEN*

Ein Adjektiv (long, happy, political) *bezieht sich auf ein Nomen* (a long period) *oder ein Pronomen* (Their son's success made them happy).

Ein Adverb > Adjektiv + -ly
slow > slowly   happy > happily   political > politically   successful > successfully

Ausnahmen
1 good > well; difficult > with difficulty
2 adjective = adverb: hard, early, likely, straight, fast, daily/monthly/yearly, etc
3 *Endet ein Adjektiv in -ly, so wird das Adverb folgendermaßen gebildet:*
in a(n) ... way, *z.B.* orderly > in an orderly way

Ein Adverb bezieht sich auf
1 *ein Verb:* They worked steadily all day.
(*Aber:* look/taste/feel/sound/smell + *Adjektiv*: This tastes fine, looks awful, etc).
2 *ein Adjektiv:* The programme is surprisingly easy to handle.
3 ein Adverb: The company has recovered extremely quickly.
4 *eine Wortgruppe:* This was really more than we could cope with.

Steigerung von Adjektiven
Kurze Adjektive werden mit -er/-est *gesteigert, längere mit* more/most.

-er/-est	more/most
fast: She's a faster worker than he is.	impressive: Last year's results were more impressive.
long: We had to wait even longer.	comfortable: This is a more comfortable seat.
high: the highest prices	complicated: the most complicated system
big: our biggest export market	exciting: the most exciting news

Ausnahmen: good/better/best; bad/worse/worst; little/less/least; much/more/most; far/further/furthest

Steigerung von Adverbien: "more"/"most" + *Adverb.*
Prices rose more slowly than expected.   They're the most efficiently organised sales team.

GERUNDS AND INFINITIVES/*GERUNDIUM UND INFINITIV*

1 Gerundium
Eine Gerundium-Konstruktion (Verb + -ing) wird benutzt

– ***nach Verben, die in der Regel keinen Infinitiv nach sich ziehen.*** (We considered meeting in Hamburg.)
admit, adore, advise, advocate, allow, appreciate, avoid, begin, be worth, can/couldn't stand, carry on, cease, consider, contemplate, continue, cut out, debate, delay, deny, detest, discontinue, discuss, dislike, dread, encourage, enjoy, escape, fancy, favour, finish, give up, hate, imagine, intend, involve, keep (on), leave off, mention, mind, miss, oppose, permit, postpone, practice, prefer, prevent, put off, quit, recall, recollect, recommend, regard, report, require, remain, remember, resent, resist, resume, risk, start, stop, suggest, try, value, welcome

– *Verben + Präpositionen* (Let's begin by looking at the sales figures.)
accuse (sb) of, admit to, amount to, apologise for, assist in, begin by, believe in, benefit by/from, boast about/of, bother about, care about, come of/from, complain about/of, concentrate on, conclude by, confess to, consist of, count on, decide against, delight in, despair of, devote to, disapprove of, dream of/about, engage in, escape from, fail in, feel like, gamble on, get around to, hurry into, indulge in, insist on, keep from, live by, look forward to, object to, persist in, profit by, refrain from, rely on, see about, specialise in, succeed in, take up/to, talk about/of/over, think about/of, vote against, warn against, worry about

– *Adjektiven + Präpositionen* (We're used to dealing with this kind of problem.)
accustomed to, adequate for, afraid of, alarmed at, amazed at, angry at, appropriate for, ashamed of, astonished at, available for, capable of, certain of, clever/good/bad at, conscious of, correct in, crazy about, delighted at, disappointed at, engaged in, enthusiastic about, equivalent to, excited about, famous for, fond of, fortunate in, frightened of, glad about, guilty of, happy about, hopeful about, intent on, interested in, keen on, late in, necessary for, nervous about, optimistic about, pessimistic about, pleased at, preferable to, preoccupied with, proficient at, proud of, right in, ripe for, serious about, sick/tired/weary of, slow in, suitable for, used to, useful for

– *Nomen + Präpositionen* (Will you have any difficulty in convincing the directors?)
advantage of, alternative to, aversion to, basis for, belief in, blame for, capability of, chance of, choice between, compromise between, danger of, a great deal of, death by, delight in, difference between, difficulty in, dislike for/of, excuse for, experience in, facility for, fear of, fondness for, habit of, hesitation in, hope of, impression of, intention of, interest in, love for, means of, method of, necessity for, need for, objection to, occasion for, opportunity of, place for, plan for, pleasure in/of, (there's no) point in, possibility of, preference for, privilege of, reason for, reputation for/of, satisfaction in, surprise at, talent/aptitude/flair/genius for, taste for, tendency towards, trouble in, (with a) view to, way of

2 Infinitiv
Eine Infinitiv-Konstruktion wird benutzt

– *nach gewissen Verben* (Will you manage to finish on time?)
agree, aim, ask, beg, begin, care, cease, choose, claim, continue, decide, demand, desire, dislike, dread, endeavour, expect, fail, forget, get (= be allowed), go, hate, hope, intend, learn, like, manage, mean, neglect, offer, plan, prefer, promise, prove, refuse, remember, seem, start, stop, tend, threaten, try, want, wish

– *Verben + Objekt* (They expect us to pay by the 30th.)
advise, allow, ask, beg, cause, command, desire, encourage, expect, force, get (= persuade), invite, like, love, order, persuade, prefer, promise, remind, teach, tell, urge, want, warn, wish

– *Verben* + for + *Subjekt des Infinitivsatzes* (I waited for him to call back.)
ask, arrange, wait, prepare

– *Nomen* (permission to go ahead)
chance, opportunity, ability, permission, plan, right, wish

– *Adjektiven* (likely to succeed)
able, afraid, keen, happy, glad, certain, likely, sure, pleased, interested, possible, difficult

Nach folgenden Verben können entweder das Gerundium oder der Infinitiv stehen
begin continue hate intend like love prefer start
They began diversifying/to diversify last year.
We prefer meeting/to meet on Tuesdays.

Nach folgenden Verben können entweder das Gerundium oder der Infinitiv stehen, wobei die Bedeutung jedoch jeweils eine andere ist:

to remember + -ing: *sich erinnern, etw getan zu haben*
to remember to + *Infinitiv*: *daran denken, etw zu tun (= nicht vergessen, etw zu tun)*
to regret + -ing: bereuen, *etw getan zu haben*
to regret to + *Infinitiv*: *bereuen, etw tun zu müssen*
to forget + -ing: *vergessen, etw getan zu haben*
to forget to + *Infinitiv*: *vergessen, etw zu tun*
to stop + -ing: *aufhören, etw zu tun*
to stop to + *Infinitiv*: *aufhören, um etw anderes zu tun*
to try + -ing: *etw probieren*
to try to + *Infinitiv*: *sich bemühen, etw zu tun*
to go on (= continue) + -ing: *etw weiterhin tun*
to go on to + *Infinitiv*: *etw (Neues) als nächstes tun*

PRONOUNS/*PRONOMEN*

Satzgegenstand

I (*ich*)	we (*wir*)
you (*du/Sie*)	you (*ihr/Sie*)
he/she/it (*er/sie/es*)	they (*sie*)

We'll arrive earlier than Derek. Are you coming too? She should take the money.

Ergänzung (Akkusativ/Dativ)

me (*mich/mir*)	us (*uns*)
you (*dich/dir/Sie/Ihnen*)	you (*euch/Sie/Ihnen*)
him (*ihn/ihm*)	
her (*sie/ihr*)	them (*sie/ihnen*)
it (*es/ihm/ihn/ihr/sie*)	

Derek will arrive later than us. "Who's coming?" "Me!" Sue should take the money, not him.

Possessivpronomen

vor einem Nomen:

my (*mein/e*)	our (*unser/e*)
your (*dein/e*)	your (*euer/eure/ Ihr/e*)
his (*sein/e*)	
her (*ihr/e*)	their (*ihr/e*)
its (*sein/e ihr/e*)	

alleinstehend:

mine (*meine/r/s*)	ours (*unsere/r/s*)
yours (*ihre/r/s/ Ihre/r/s*)	yours (*eure/r/s/ Ihre/r/s*)
his (*seine/r/s*)	
hers (*ihre/r/s*)	theirs (*ihre/r/s*)
its (*seine/r/s/ ihr/e*)	

Our market is smaller than theirs. My train leaves at 8.10 – I think yours leaves at 8.25.

Reflexivpronomen

myself (*ich/mich selbst*)	ourselves (*wir/uns selbst*)
yourself (*du/dich/ Sie/sich selbst*)	yourselves (*ihr/euch/ Sie/sich selbst*)
himself (*er/sich selbst*)	
herself (*sie/sich selbst*)	themselves (*sie/sich selbst*)
itself (*es/sich selbst*)	

May I introduce myself? They'll choose the software themselves. The factory itself is quite small.

Demonstrativpronomen

this (*diese/r/s*) these (*diese*) that (*jene/r/s*) those (*jene*)

We've just been discussing this advert. These forms are better designed than those.

Listening Texts

UNIT 1

LISTENING TEXT 1/1

Brigaglia: Good morning – Herr Siebert?
Siebert: Yes, and you must be Signor Brigaglia?
Brigaglia: Yes, indeed.
Siebert: Nice to meet you. Glad you could come. Did you have a good trip?
Brigaglia: Oh, yes, thank you. And I've had some time to look around the Fair for a while.
Siebert: Well, please take a seat, Signor Brigaglia. Would you like a cup of coffee before we begin?
Brigaglia: No, thanks. Maybe later.
Siebert: Right, well, make yourself at home and I'll be with you rightaway.
Brigaglia: Fine.

LISTENING TEXT 1/2

Siebert: Ah, Signor Brigaglia, I'd like you to meet Herr Preetz, our sales manager. Herr Preetz, this is Signor Brigaglia from Turin.
Preetz: How do you do.
Brigaglia: Nice to meet you.
Siebert: And may I introduce Frau Kewitz, who handles our European marketing? Frau Kewitz, Signor Brigaglia. As you know, Signor Brigaglia is considering acting as our agent in Italy.
Kewitz: Hello, Signor Brigaglia.
Brigaglia: Pleased to meet you.
Siebert: And you know Herr Vogt, don't you? You met in Turin ...
Vogt: Yes, in August. Nice to see you again, Signor Brigaglia.
Brigaglia: Hello again, Herr Vogt. I'm glad to see you got out of that restaurant alive.
Vogt: Ah, yes – Festival Night – that was quite a crowd, wasn't it? ...

LISTENING TEXT 1/3

Well, Signor Brigaglia, let me give you a run-down on Siebert, so you know what kind of operation we are. We're a small company in the industrial packaging field. We employ 55 skilled and semi-skilled production workers. And we have 10 to 15 full-time and part-time office staff, depending on the level of orders.

The company has three Sections, all located at our industrial site in Dortmund. The biggest is my Section – namely, Production. It includes Quality Control. We've invested a lot there, so all the equipment is state-of-the-art. Then there's Sales and Marketing – that's Herr Preetz' and Frau Graf's part of the operation. And, finally, there's Storage, Despatch and Transport. Herr Vogt is in charge of that Section. They moved into larger premises in August, due to the increase in orders.

All decisions about planning and finance are made collectively by the Section leaders and myself. We have a policy meeting every week. On top of that, I hand in a progress report to the company directors each month.

For the last 18 months, we've specialised in packaging for fragile goods, like electrical equipment and glassware. And this is now the most profitable part of our business. Until last year, all our contracts were with German companies. But now we're exporting to customers in the UK and Ireland too. We're very much hoping our European marketing drive will bring an influx of new orders – possibly by late August, early September. And this is where you come in, Signor Brigaglia ...

LISTENING TEXT 1/4

Brian: Joyce, I thought you'd like to see this. I spotted it on the Internet this morning.
Joyce: I see.
Brian: We are looking for a partner in China, aren't we?
Joyce: Well, we certainly will be. It's important to finalise these European contracts first.
Brian: But after that ... ?
Joyce: After that ... Well, we can start putting out feelers right now. Er – do you know anything about this company, Brian?
Brian: Well, I only saw the ad this morning. So I faxed them to see what they'd come up with.
Joyce: Good.
Brian: And – do you know – they phoned me immediately – from China – so they could answer our questions!
Joyce: Heavens. They're really on the ball, aren't they?
Brian: That's what I thought. But I told them it'll be enough for now if they fax us some information about their operation.
Joyce: Right.
Brian: And I said we'll do the same from this end. Is that OK?
Joyce: Fine. OK, Brian. I'm interested. Keep me informed, would you?
Brian: Will do.
Joyce: And if we open up a provisional contract with them, I'll include it in this month's report.
Brian: OK – that would go down well with the directors!

LISTENING TEXT 1/5

Hello, this is Guangzhou Lam Soon Homecare Products. At the moment, we're unable to take your call personally. But if you leave a message after the signal, we'll call you back as soon as we can.

UNIT 2

LISTENING TEXT 2/1

Everett: Yes, we like the look of your tools, Herr Horn, especially the lightweight design.
Horn: So, would you like to place a trial order, Mr Everett?
Everett: Well, I'll have to call my manager first, but we'll probably order five today ...
Horn: Excellent.
Everett: ... and we may well make a follow-up order for five more later.
Horn: As you know, Mr Everett, you'll definitely get a 5% discount for your first order.
Everett: Yes.
Horn: So couldn't you persuade your manager to make a firm order for all ten right away?
Everett: There's little chance he'll agree to that, Herr Horn.
Horn: Perhaps we could come to some arrangement here, Mr Everett. If you ordered five now, and five more very soon, we could allow that discount on both orders.
Everett: Can you keep that offer open for a further six months, Herr Horn?
Horn: Well, I'm willing to meet you halfway on this. If you give us that follow-up order by – let's say the first of October, we'll allow the 5% discount.
Everett: Fine.

Horn: Can we agree on that then? We'll keep the discount open on all goods ordered by the first of October.
Everett: Well, hold on – there's a strong possibility that we'll want some of those abrasives too.
Horn: Oh yes?
Everett: But we're bound to hold off on that till we've had our six-monthly review.
Horn: I see. Is that likely to be a large order, Mr Everett?
Everett: It may be just ten units to start with. If they proved to be OK, we'd want more in the New Year. But, of course, I can't promise anything ...
Horn: I understand.
Everett: ... but may I tell my people that you'd allow the discount on those units too?
Horn: For the initial units, yes. Yes, we can agree to that, Mr Everett.
Everett: Good.
Horn: But we'd have to insist on the catalogue price for any orders made after the first of October. We are working to a very tight profit margin, you know.
Everett: Of course. Well, Herr Horn, it's a pleasure to do business with you.
Horn: The pleasure's mine, Mr Everett. I'm glad we see eye-to-eye on this.
Everett: I'll call my manager now, and maybe I could see you later in the day and ...
Horn: Why don't we meet for a drink at the bar? You're staying the night here, aren't you?
Everett: Good idea. How about – what? – 7.30?
Horn: 7.30. Right. See you then.

LISTENING TEXT 2/2

Debeauvais: ... well, I think we've made headway this morning, Herr Rüffin. So, to sum up, you'd want our premises for six months.
Rüffin: Yes, for six months at first, Monsieur Debeauvais. Then we'd like to review our options and decide whether we want to continue.
Debeauvais: All right, so we're agreed – we won't charge you rent on condition that you loan us the equipment we need for remodelling our plant in Lyon.
Rüffin: Agreed.
Debeauvais: And you know there's a strong probability that the work will take longer than six months – possibly even eight.
Rüffin: Right. Provided you stick to the size and quantity of tools we agreed on earlier, Monsieur Debeauvais, it'll be OK for you to use them up to a maximum of ten months ...
Debeauvais: That would be really very helpful ...
Rüffin: ... on condition, of course, that we have all the equipment returned in working order.
Debeauvais: Of course. We can agree on that. Er ... now let me see – may we discuss the matter of operating costs?
Rüffin: Yes, I wanted to bring that up too.
Debeauvais: Now your six-month lease will be rent-free, and you'll pay your own fax and phone bills, as we agreed. But there are operating costs to be paid too – electricity, cleaning, maintenance, property insurance. And security – we have a guard on duty round the clock, seven days a week, you know.
Rüffin: So, could you give me an estimate, Monsieur Debeauvais? How much would our share of the operating costs be – per month?
Debeauvais: Well, rather than talk about costs, I think we can come to an arrangement on this, Herr Rüffin. Look, here's our proposal: we would pay the rent and the operating costs for the whole building if you provided some technical assistance with those power tools of yours.
Rüffin: Technical assistance?
Debeauvais: Yes, for a couple of days down in Lyon to help us install the equipment.
Rüffin: Hm ... Well, I think we'd be willing to meet you halfway on that, Monsieur Debeauvais. We'll help you install the equipment on those terms ...
Debeauvais: Good.

Rüffin: ... but we'll have to insist on full labour charges for that installation work. You see, we have a backlog of orders to complete at home. In fact, all our technical staff have been working overtime for three months or more ...

LISTENING TEXT 2/3

Debeauvais: ... so you're quite sure about this, Herr Rüffin? Wouldn't you prefer to have the premises, say, for five months?
Rüffin: Quite sure, Monsieur Debeauvais. We've decided, after all, that four months is enough to begin with.
Debeauvais: Starting on the first of March.
Rüffin: Starting on the first of March.
Debeauvais: Right, I've made a note of that. Now this business with the technician ...
Rüffin: Yes, as I said, Monsieur Debeauvais, one man's enough for that job, I can assure you. There's really no need for two.
Debeauvais: And we'll have him for three full days, you say.
Rüffin: Yes, starting on the 3rd of March. Two days for installation, one day for testing out.
Debeauvais: OK, I've got that. And those are the only changes from your side?
Rüffin: Yes, Monsieur Debeauvais. Apart from those points, we're ready to sign. Anything from your side?
Debeauvais: There's just one point we're unhappy about. It's the clause concerning your equipment.
Rüffin: Oh yes?
Debeauvais: As things stand, we undertake (reading) 'to pay the costs of repair for any damage caused to the equipment during the period of loan'.
Rüffin: Well, yes, Monsieur Debeauvais. We do need that security. Er, what do you have in mind?
Debeauvais: Well, I've discussed this with my colleagues here, and we'd like to suggest a new wording – and I really don't think you'll have any objections to this. What about rephrasing it like this – (reading) 'to repair or replace any equipment damaged during the period of loan'? Would that be acceptable?
Rüffin: (reading) 'Repair or replace any equipment damaged during the period of loan.' Yes ... yes, I'm sure that would be acceptable to us, Monsieur Debeauvais.
Debeauvais: Can we take it as agreed then, Herr Rüffin?
Rüffin: Certainly. Let's write that in.
Debeauvais: Right. Now the next step, I suggest, is to draw up the new contract for checking. Then ...

UNIT 3

LISTENING TEXT 3/1

Horn: ... Let me put you in the picture. We've got around a 30% share of the German market. And now we're aiming to expand into other EU countries.
Hellenic Marketing Services: I see.
Horn: ... and we've learned that orders for interior construction work are on the increase in Greece. There's been a steady eight per cent rise over the last two years.
Hellenic Marketing Services: So you think the market here might be worth exploring.
Horn: Exactly. Now, you've got the English version of our catalogue. So you know which products we're highlighting. The aim would be to introduce them to potential customers in Greece.
Hellenic Marketing Services: And you'd like to get an agent to promote the products here?
Horn: Well, that's our aim in the middle-term. But the first thing is: we want to commission a market research study – to see whether, in fact, we ought to get into this market at all.
Hellenic Marketing Services: We'd be happy to help you with that, Herr Horn.
Horn: OK. We want to know the size of the market, and the likely demand for the products. Will people actually want them? And what about future demand?

	This construction boom, for example – is it going to continue? Or will it fade next month, or the month after?
Hellenic Marketing Services:	Naturally, we can't make any promises about how things will go, Herr Horn. But we can certainly do a thorough report for you. We'll assess the competition, for example, and tell you who your main rivals are.
Horn:	Right, that's something we definitely want to know.
Hellenic Marketing Services:	We'd be delighted to do a research report for you along those lines, Herr Horn. But I do need some more details. I've got your catalogue and price list. But they're rather thin on technical information ...
Horn:	Ah, the product specifications. I'll fax them today.
Hellenic Marketing Services:	And if you could give us the terms of delivery for customers in Greece ...
Horn:	Yes, I thought you'd mention that. I'll fax those too. What about samples? Do you need samples?
Hellenic Marketing Services:	Of the products, you mean? No. If you could just send me those delivery terms and the technical information ... Then I'll look at it all and come back to you directly with a proposal. Would that be satisfactory?
Horn:	Just one question – how long will it take, do you think?
Hellenic Marketing Services:	If you commission a market research report from us this week, Herr Horn, I can guarantee we'll have it in your hands by the end of the month.

LISTENING TEXT 3/2

OK, let me fill you in. We're dealers in small electronic office goods. The prospects are good in this line of business. Orders have been on the increase for some months now. Our aim in the long-term is to be the major US distributor in this field.

Now, we like the look of your printer. It's user-friendly – it could be attractive in the market for office goods here. We'll have to do some market research to find out the likely demand for that type of product. And we'll have to look at the question of product suitability. Exactly which people can we expect to buy it? What rival products are on the market?

Furthermore, we must also look at the question of technical standards. In particular, we have to look into the US federal requirements on safety.

In the meantime, we need some more details from you – about pricing. We want to know your prices, including delivery, for all possible versions, with and without barcode facility; with and without self-adhesive labels; and both widths.

I can't make any promises. But we're definitely interested in a marketing arrangement. With the right price, we think we can sell your product here in the States. The big question is: can you make the price competitive? Please let me know.

LISTENING TEXT 3/3

Barbara? Gerry Wilson of Chicago here. Look, my company has looked at the results of our research on your label printer. And I can tell you we're certainly interested in a sole distributorship, under which we'd sell it in the US. Before we go deeper into that, though, I've got a couple of requests. First, would you tell us how quickly you could deliver a bulk order? That's something we definitely want to know.

Next thing – we have a sample of the model with the barcode facility. But, for testing purposes, we'd very much like to have one without that facility? Could you do that for us, please? Thanks a lot.

UNIT 4

LISTENING TEXT 4/1

Angela:	Right, Stefan, so that's the final list, is it? How many have we got?
Stefan:	Exactly 15. Basically a mixture of English-speaking company reps and ministry officials. We had a fax yesterday to say they'll all be at the hotel for the meeting.
Angela:	On the morning of the 24th.
Stefan:	Yes. So we're agreed then: I'll do the first half – with the slides – explaining the production process. Then you'll take over after the refreshments break.

Angela: Yes, I went through the OHP transparencies this morning. I'm all prepared for my side of it.
Stefan: OK – a straight-through presentation, then. Questions and discussion at the end.
Angela: Agreed.
Stefan: And you'll make the arrangements with the hotel, will you?
Angela: I'll fax them this morning.

LISTENING TEXT 4/2

Good morning, ladies and gentlemen. (Can you all hear me?) Thank you for coming. My name's Stefan Braun, and this is my colleague Angela Parfitt. On behalf of our company, I'd like to welcome you to our presentation. I hope you had a pleasant journey, and that you find everything to your satisfaction.

Just a couple of points before we begin. First, you should all have a personal name card and a blue presentation folder. Does anyone not have one? All right, next thing – may I remind you that lunch will be served in the restaurant at one o'clock? And, before that, we'll have a break for tea or coffee at about 10.30. Should you need any help, please see Angela or myself.
I hope you have an enjoyable and rewarding morning. There'll be an opportunity for a general question-and-answer session at the end of the presentation. But do feel free to raise questions at any time. Are there any questions right now? No?
Then let's get started. I'd like to begin ...

LISTENING TEXT 4/3

Wiseman: Hello, Trevor Wiseman here.
Fuchs: Ah, Mr Wiseman. Good morning. Hanne Fuchs here. I'm calling from Munich.
Wiseman: Ah, Frau Fuchs, hello. It's about the conference, isn't it?
Fuchs: Yes, indeed. We got your message, Mr Wiseman. And I'm happy to say we can fit you in.
Wiseman: Ah, splendid. And how about the hotel?
Fuchs: Yes, that's OK too. One of the participants had to drop out, so you'll take over his hotel reservation.
Wiseman: Right. Good. Er ... where are we staying this year?
Fuchs: At the Pankhurst Lodge Hotel. It's next to the Conference Centre.
Wiseman: Oh yes, I know the Pankhurst. We used it the year before last, I think. Will many of us be staying overnight?
Fuchs: 12, Mr Wiseman. 12 out of 15.
Wiseman: And will we be using the hotel bar for the get-together after the conference?
Fuchs: No, we've got the Club Bar at the Conference Centre this year.
Wiseman: OK. Right, thank you – and see you on Friday morning, Frau Fuchs.
Fuchs: Yes, looking forward to seeing you. Goodbye, Mr Wiseman.
Wiseman: Bye for now.

LISTENING TEXT 4/4

Good morning, ladies and gentlemen. (Can you all hear me?) My name's Hanne Fuchs and I'd like to welcome you to the conference. I hope you all had a pleasant journey and that you find everything to your satisfaction. Just a couple of points before we begin. First, should you need any help, please see my colleague Jack Prewer. You'll find him at the main entrance. Next, you should all have a folder and a name tag. Does anyone not have these? Everyone has a folder and a name tag? Yes? All right. Now, we'll have a coffee break at about 11 am and lunch will be served in the restaurant at 1.00 pm. Are there any questions?

LISTENING TEXT 4/5

Crystal Videoconferencing: ... so, for setting-up your videoconference, we'd charge you what we call a Room Fee.
Fuchs: How much is that?

Crystal Videoconferencing: Well, that depends. Normally the Room Fee is 38 pounds per 15 minutes. But – let's see – your end of the videoconference would be London, right?
Fuchs: Yes.
Crystal Videoconferencing: Right, and we have a videoconferencing centre in London. And the other end would be Chicago, you say?
Fuchs: That's right.
Crystal Videoconferencing: OK, we have a centre in Chicago too. Now, the point is, if you used Crystal Videoconferencing centres at both ends, that Room Fee would be reduced by 40%.
Fuchs: Oh, that's good news!
Crystal Videoconferencing: Yes. Oh, and I should point out that we do require a minimum hire of one hour.
Fuchs: Right. So – what other costs would we have?.
Crystal Videoconferencing: Well, we also charge a Communication Fee of 25 pounds per 15 minutes.
Fuchs: Right.
Crystal Videoconferencing: And, finally, there's a Scheduling Fee. That's a straight 50 pounds per videoconference.
Fuchs: 50 pounds.
Crystal Videoconferencing: Yes. Oh – and if you wanted to stage your videoconference at very short notice, well, we'd also charge a Reservation Fee of 50 pounds.
Fuchs: Ah – what do you mean by 'short notice' here?
Crystal Videoconferencing: Well, if we had to set it up within the next four days.
Fuchs: I see. OK. Right. I think I've got all that ...
Crystal Videoconferencing: I'll be happy to fax all this to you, Frau Fuchs.
Fuchs: Yes. Yes, would you do that, please?
Crystal Videoconferencing: Right away, Frau Fuchs. I'll also fax you more information on our facilities. Then perhaps I could call you ...

LISTENING TEXT 4/6

Managing Director: ... so we actually spent the same on last year's conference and this year's?
Hanne: Yes, practically the same amount. Almost to the penny.
Managing Director: But didn't we save a lot on meals this year? We had a special deal, didn't we?
Hanne: Oh, yes – from that new catering service. And, as a result, we spent – let's see – we spent 11 per cent less this time.
Managing Director: And the hotel costs were only one per cent more, you say?
Hanne: That's right. And all the miscellaneous items – you know, fax and phone, materials, postage – those items are also down from 18 to 10 per cent this year.
Managing Director: So, why wasn't the conference actually cheaper to stage this time? It was the travel costs, I suppose.
Hanne: Right. They were just 22 per cent last year. This time they're up to 40 per cent.
Managing Director: I see. Well. Looks like we should try and economise in that area next year.

UNIT 5

LISTENING TEXT 5/1

Erika: ... and for the two orders that came in today – for the A2 designs. That's 150 kg of A2s we need by next week. How many A2s do we have in stock?
Raylene: None. Well, practically none – that Stuttgart order last week almost cleaned us out.
Erika: OK, so we'll order 150 kg of A2s. Tell them it's urgent, will you?
Raylene: Will do.
Erika: And let's bring in an extra 300 kg, so we'll have plenty in stock.
Raylene: They're not urgent, though.
Erika: That's right. And we also need to stock up on A5s, don't we?

Raylene: Yeah, we're down to the last dozen A5s. And they sold well last year.
Erika: So we'd better order 300 kg.
Raylene: Yeah, they'll take at least six weeks. But we can manage with what we've got till then.

LISTENING TEXT 5/2

Raylene: ... and we'd like a consignment by air right away. Would you be able to send 150 kilos of A2s immediately?
Anwar: A2s. Certainly. We have a big stock of A2s.
Raylene: Good. But I'd like to make the order on the condition that the goods are delivered by the 15th. Could you give me a guarantee on that, please?
Anwar: Oh, we'll certainly get them to you by then. I'll arrange the shipment and prepare the documentation immediately.
Raylene: Right. Can you tell me what the total cost of that shipment would be?
Anwar: Yes, I can give you a close estimate. Let's see. A2 ...
Raylene: Your list price is $11.75 per kilo. So the cost of the goods will be $1762.50. We've figured that out.
Anwar: $1762.50. OK, add freight charges. 150 kilos at $4.20 per kilo. That's $630. Allow, say, $80 for documentation, packing, handling and clearance, tax. Then there's insurance. Let's see. 2% of the value of the goods ...
Raylene: Right.
Anwar: ... Two per cent of $1762.50 is exactly $35.25.
Raylene: So, what's the bottom line?
Anwar: OK, you're talking about a final total of exactly $2507.75.
Raylene: Right. I'll fax you that order right now. And we're agreed – delivery by the 15th, OK?
Anwar: Leave it to me. And thank you.

LISTENING TEXT 5/3

1. two hundred and seventy dollars and eight-five cents
   or: two hundred seventy eight-five
2. fifteen pounds and thirty-five p
   or: fifteen pounds thirty-five
3. three thousand one hundred and fifty dollars
   or: thirty one hundred and fifty dollars
4. sixty-five point eight per cent
5. eighty-five point eight five per cent
6. twenty point oh five per cent
7. twelve million dollars

LISTENING TEXT 5/4

Keith: Jill, about this memo from Head Office ...
Jill: Yes, I'm just working on that. Look, Keith – have you seen this survey the Hauliers Association have just put out?
Keith: Yes, I have. And it confirms our own findings, doesn't it? Road transport costs are rising because of congestion.
Jill: Yes – too many vehicles using the roads ...
Keith: ... meaning slower, longer journeys and higher costs for fuel and wages.
Jill: Yeah. We've already seen this in the deterioration in prompt deliveries to our retail outlets.
Keith: Yes, down from 97 to 90 per cent in six months.
Jill: So, what about rail transport?
Keith: No. No, that's still no good for us. Our cost analysis shows rail would still be 15 to 20 per cent more expensive. It's OK for long journeys – over 400 kilometres, say.
Jill: But our average delivery is around 200 kilometres, right?

Keith: That's right. And there's another important point. Our refrigerated goods – well, we just wouldn't be able to supervise them as we can on the road ...
Jill: ... where we have phone contact with the drivers.
Keith: Exactly. And if there were any delay – well, it'd be hard to get access to the goods. Now that's a serious matter when you want to keep them at controlled temperatures. And frankly, there's also a danger of loss or damage to goods in transit.
Jill: So – what do we recommend, then?
Keith: Well, the answer is to increase the stocks in the retail outlets.
Jill: Hm. You know, Head Office aren't going to like that idea. They take the view that money tied up in stocks is dead money!
Keith: Yes, and they're dead right. Ideally, we'd continue to deliver stocks on a just-in-time basis. But with transport costs rising, that's getting harder to do.
Jill: So – we recommend increasing the stocks in the retail outlets?
Keith: Yes, and at the same time, we should recommend tighter packaging and squeezing more onto the delivery vehicles. For a company like ours, that makes more sense, economically, than using rail.

LISTENING TEXT 5/5

Partner: Right, I've got the original timetable in front of me. So what changes have you made?
Organiser: OK, will you fill them in as I read them to you?
Partner: Yes, go ahead.
Organiser: OK. When we worked out the original timetable, we expected to have the demonstration at our offices. But we're going to have twice as many participants as we thought. So Olaf came up with the idea of switching it to the Dorint Hotel, across the road.
Partner: Ah, so I'd better change 'TransExpress, Main Office' to 'Dorint Hotel'.
Organiser: Exactly. And we'll have lunch at the Dorint too.
Partner: Ah, so I should change 'Odysseus Restaurant' to 'Dorint Hotel'?
Organiser: Right. Now, when the participants have finished lunch, they'll go straight into the hands-on session. But that will be an open-ended session.
Partner: I see. So it won't end at 15.30?
Organiser: That's right. So, for the hands-on session, would you change '14.00–15.30' to 'from 14.00', please?
Partner: OK. I've done that.
Organiser: That means the participants will be free to stay as long as they like, testing our software.
Partner: Good.
Organiser: Right. The shuttle service will run from 15.30. Actually, we might start it even later in the afternoon. But we're holding off that decision for the time being. You see, we want to keep participants there as long as possible. On the other hand, we mustn't mess up their travel arrangements!

UNIT 6

LISTENING TEXT 6/1

Hello, Mr Khan. This is Pia Rank, calling from Germany. I've just received the invoice you faxed for the tennis shoes – thanks very much. There's just one question. The ATP model at fifty-five dollars apiece. We agreed that you'd let us have those ATPs at fifty dollars apiece. That makes the amount for ATPs exactly twenty-five hundred dollars. So we have to deduct two hundred and fifty from the total. Let's see – twenty-five thousand two hundred and sixty minus two hundred and fifty. That comes to twenty-five thousand and ten. Could you check those figures, please? And send me a corrected invoice? Thank you very much.

LISTENING TEXT 6/2

five hundred dollars minus nine dollars fifty
twenty-pounds plus eleven pounds ten
thirty divided by three makes ten

six times fifty-five dollars
fifty-five dollars multiplied by six
ten per cent of fifty-five dollars
twenty units at fifty-five dollars apiece

LISTENING TEXT 6/3

Rank:	Pia Rank speaking. Can I help you?
Thompson:	Hello, Ms Rank. This is Jeff Thompson of Boyd, Brown in Hamburg.
Rank:	Ah, Mr Thompson. You're calling about the New Zealand delivery again, are you?
Thompson:	Yes, as you know, there was that engine failure with the original vessel just after loading up in Wellington ...
Rank:	Yes, so the goods were transferred ...
Thompson:	Transferred to another vessel. Yes, the MS Sherwood. Well, the Sherwood docked in here this morning.
Rank:	Ah.
Thompson:	... and you'll be happy to know we have all your boxes safe and sound, Ms Rank. Eight kilos apiece ...
Rank:	Right.
Thompson:	... and – well, I'm just very sorry indeed that we've had this delay, Ms Rank. It was completely outside our control. But as soon as we heard ...

LISTENING TEXT 6/4

Secretary:	Hello, Sport-Rank. Can I help you?
Taraki:	Hello, yes, Taraki speaking. Wansaka Communications. I'm calling from Tokyo. Could I speak to Ms Rank, please?
Secretary:	I'm afraid Ms Rank's in Britain for a couple of days, Mr Taraki. Perhaps I can help you.
Taraki:	Well, I really need to speak to Ms Rank.
Secretary:	Well, let me give you a number in England where you'll certainly be able to reach her.
Taraki:	Ah, that would be very helpful.
Secretary:	Right, Mr Taraki. The country code for Britain is forty-four. And the number is one two eight four. Then: seven double-five six four eight.
Taraki:	OK. So, that's the code for Britain – followed by: one two eight four seven double-five six four eight.
Secretary:	Right. And the extension number is thirty-four.
Taraki:	Thirty-four. Fine – thank you. Er – there's one more thing you might do for me, please. Could you possibly send me copies of your Spring and Winter catalogues from last year? We'd like to do some price comparisons.
Secretary:	By all means.
Taraki:	But not to the company address, please. I'll be at home for several days, you see. Would you send them direct to me, please, at four three seven Azamino ...
Secretary:	That's four three seven – er, would you spell that word, please?
Taraki:	Azamino? That's A – Z – A – M – I ...
Secretary:	Er– hold on ... A – Z – A – M ... M for Mary, right?
Taraki:	That's right. Then I – N – O.
Secretary:	I – N – O.
Taraki:	That's it. Then, next line – Aoba-Ku. That's A – O – B – A – dash – K – U.
Secretary:	A - O - P....?
Taraki:	No – not P. B! B for Benjamin.
Secretary:	Ah. So that's A – O – B – A – dash – K – U.
Taraki:	Right. Then next line: Yokohama double-two-five.
Secretary:	Yo – ko – ha – ma. That's Y – O – K – A – H ...
Taraki:	No, no – Y – O – K – O – O for Oliver ...

Secretary: Ah.
Taraki: Then: H – A – M – that's M for Mary – then A. Then double-two-five. Next line: Japan.
Secretary: Japan. Right, Mr Taraki. I'll airmail those catalogues to you today.
Taraki: Thank you.
Secretary: And do let me know if you run into any difficulty getting through to Ms Rank.
Taraki: OK. You've been very helpful. Thanks a lot.
Secretary: Don't mention it. Goodbye for now, Mr Taraki.
Taraki: Goodbye.

LISTENING TEXT 6/5

Phone company: ... so, as I understand it, you've got a number of mobile phones already. And now you want some more, to be installed in your cars.
Ms Rank: That's right.
Phone company: And as your team travels a lot, I suppose they'll want to roam.
Ms Rank: Sorry, I'm not familiar with that expression.
Phone company: Ah, 'to roam' means to use your phone in foreign networks when you're travelling abroad. And the model we've got right here gives you that. And it has all the facilities you'll need – fax calls, recall-voice messaging ...
Ms Rank: Recall-voice messaging. Could you explain that, please?
Phone company: That means that received messages are recorded even when the phone is switched off. Another big advantage is its call confidentiality.
Ms Rank: Sorry, I didn't catch that – call ...?
Phone company: Call confidentiality. That means: no one can listen in on your conversations.
Ms Rank: I see. Well, that seems to be what we need.
Phone company: Er – you'll be needing three phones, you said?
Ms Rank: Yes, two mainly for business ...
Phone company: Does that include Saturdays?
Ms Rank: Oh, certainly. We do a lot of road work Saturdays. It's the only day we can get hold of a lot of our customers.
Phone company: I see.
Ms Rank: And the other – well, that'll be for occasional use. Mainly for receiving calls in the evening, actually.

LISTENING TEXT 6/6

Electronic communications have developed fast – very fast indeed. And this, in turn, has caused big changes in the ways English is used internationally. Let's just consider the fact that much of the English that's used internationally is used between computers. It's been estimated that around ten per cent of the information stored on the world's computers is stored in English. And, as everyone can see, English is the dominant language used on the Internet.

As a further result of electronic communications, more and more people now have two languages. First, there's their native language, which they use at home and with friends and in the street and in other social situations. And then there's their second language. This is the one used for formal communications – telephoning, doing business, writing letters and faxes, things like that. And, regardless of what first language people may have, that second language has to be English.

This has produced some curious results. For example, it means that English is now being used by more people as a second language than as a first language. This situation has never existed before with any language.

Another curious result is that, with the rapid growth of the Internet and fax technology – well, there are now many English users around the world who can write the language colloquially, but can't actually speak it! So, what can we make of all these changes? Well, one general effect we see is that electronic communications are widening the use of English as a global language.

LISTENING TEXT 6/7

... and business organisations which grow big run into a big problem. They find they become less agile and less competitive than smaller companies. What results does this have? Well, the first one is: those big companies try to regain their competitive edge by breaking themselves into smaller companies and units. They shrink their headquarters. Or they cut out whole layers of management, right? Then – in their new, smaller form – they try to focus on their 'core competences' – that is, the things they alone can do better than anyone else.

OK, so that's how big companies get downsized. They might well expand again later. But that's what causes them to downsize.

Now what results flow from this? Well, these downsized companies – they start outsourcing. That's what we call it – outsourcing. That is, the companies contract out a lot of the work they used to do themselves. Work like catering and office-cleaning. Work like building maintenance and security. This is outsourcing – and it leads to an increase in the number of small consultancies offering specialist services, such as office security. As a result of outsourcing, there's an increase, too, in large service companies working in a large area. For example, a labour supply company might open up many more bases, and provide casual daily labour for hundreds of employers.
Now, any company which is outsourcing – well, it loses a measure of its independence and control by giving these to other people. If the computer system fails, for instance, the company doesn't have its own technician any more. And so it might have to wait a long time before its computer consultant comes over and puts it right. And of course, this waiting can do a lot of damage to the company's business.

OK. There's one more result of downsizing we should look at. Downsizing leads – more and more – to employers and employees agreeing on short-term contracts. It leads more and more people to expect that – well, that they're going to have a lot of different employers and a lot of different jobs during their working life. They don't expect a lifelong career with a single employer. So workers feel they've got to keep their skills up-to-date, so they can always be ready to hunt for a new job.

UNIT 7

LISTENING TEXT 7/1

Joyce: Brian, there are a few details in these accounts I'd like to clarify. For example, what about these Hallways figures?
Brian: Ah, we're having some difficulty with Hallways. They normally pay within 30 days.
Joyce: That's what I thought.
Brian: But now they're asking for three months' credit.
Joyce: Three months! Hm – do they have any payments outstanding?
Brian: Just this one – but we only issued the invoice last Tuesday.
Joyce: And will they be paying this one within 30 days?
Brian: Yes, that's what we agreed.
Joyce: Right. Well, look into this, would you, Brian? And find out as discreetly as you can why they want three months' credit now.

LISTENING TEXT 7/2

Grosskopf: ... have to get all the details right. So – let's just run through it again, Mrs Russell ... You'll open a letter of credit in our favour ...
Russell: Yes, irrevocable – for US $3,500 exactly.
Grosskopf: And by airmail, right?
Russell: That's right ... er, our database should be up-to-date, Herr Grosskopf. Your bank is still the Dresdner Bank in Hamburg, isn't it?

Grosskopf: It is.
Russell: OK. So, you'll be despatching the goods to Houston as soon as you can?
Grosskopf: Twelve cases of electronic printers. Yes, we're speaking to our shipping agent right now, Mrs Russell.
Russell: Fine. CIF Houston, then. And all the documents to be presented within 14 days of sending the goods.
Grosskopf: Yes. That's full sets of Bills of Lading, marked Freight Paid ...
Russell: ... and marked: Notify Argus Office Supplies, Houston.
Grosskopf: Yes. And Import Licence and Insurance Certificate to be included.
Russell: Excellent. Well, Herr Grosskopf, I think we've settled everything. Unless you can think of anything else which ...

LISTENING TEXT 7/3

Grosskopf: Mrs Russell? It's about the Letter of Credit. There are still a few details I'd like to clarify.
Russell: Go ahead.
Grosskopf: First, when will the Letter of Credit expire?
Russell: The 30th of November. That's what we agreed
Grosskopf: Right. And who'll be responsible for paying the bank charges?
Russell: Well, we'll be covering those – as we usually do.
Grosskopf: OK. I just wanted to confirm that. Now, concerning the insurance, we're providing an "all risks" cover. That's what we agreed, right?
Russell: That's right, Herr Grosskopf.
Grosskopf: OK. Well, that's it, Mrs Russell. Thanks very much. We'll advise you as soon as the goods have been shipped.
Russell: Thank you, Herr Grosskopf. Goodbye.

UNIT 8

LISTENING TEXT 8/1

Wardingley: Rollerpress Products. Good morning.
Schubert: Hello, Mrs Wardingley?
Wardingley: Speaking.
Schubert: Olaf Schubert here. I'm calling from Frankfurt.
Wardingley: Ah, Herr Schubert. I was just about to call you.
Schubert: Yes, I was wondering ...
Wardingley: ... about our meeting on Friday.
Schubert: Exactly.
Wardingley: Yes. Look, I've made the arrangements. You're coming from Birmingham on Friday morning, aren't you?
Schubert: Yes, on the twelve-oh-one – that's the one minute past twelve from Birmingham.
Wardingley: Right. Then I suggest we meet you ... by 'we', I mean Mr Brown and myself – we'll meet you at the Station Hotel Restaurant ...
Schubert: That's actually in the railway station, is it?
Wardingley: Yes, in the main hall. Then, later, we could go to our base to look at the designs. How's that? Would that arrangement be convenient for you?
Schubert: Yes, that's fine. Provided I can get that seventeen-fifty flight back to Frankfurt.
Wardingley: Oh, sure. You'll be in good time. I'll take you to the airport myself.
Schubert: Good. Thank you.
Wardingley: Right. I'll confirm all this for you by fax, Herr Schubert. And we'll see you next Friday in Manchester.
Schubert: Looking forward to it, Mrs Wardingley.
Wardingley: We are too, Herr Schubert. Bye for now.
Schubert: Goodbye – and thank you.

LISTENING TEXT 8/2

Speaker A: I'll meet you at the station on Tuesday morning, You're coming on the eleven fourteen, aren't you?
Speaker B: Yes, I am. Er ... how will I recognise you?
Speaker A: I'll be wearing a blue coat and carrying a copy of 'The Economist'.
Speaker B: Then I'll certainly be able to find you. Then we'll go on to the Design Centre?
Speaker A: Yes, I've made the arrangements for your visit there.
Speaker B: Thanks very much.
Speaker A: Then, afterwards, I'll take you back to the station myself.
Speaker B: In good time for the three thirty-four to Leeds, I hope?
Speaker A: Oh, certainly. Would that arrangement be convenient for you?
Speaker B: Yes, indeed. That sounds fine.

LISTENING TEXT 8/3

Receptionist: Good evening. What can I do for you?
Ludwikowski: My name's Ludwikowski. I have a reservation. A single room with bath, for two nights.
Receptionist: For two nights? Right, just let me check. Er ... how do you spell your name, please?
Ludwikowski: L - U - D - W - I - K - O - W - S - K - I. Ludwikowski.
Receptionist: Ah, yes – Frau Ludwikowski. Right, your room number is 17, Frau Ludwikowski. And this is your key.
Ludwikowski: Thank you.
Receptionist: Now I'll just get someone to take your luggage. Then I'll show you to the room.
Ludwikowski: Thanks – but, just now, I'm expecting to meet a Mr Broome in the bar.
Receptionist: Mr Broome? Ah, yes, he's in the bar right now, I believe.
Ludwikowski: Ah, where is it exactly?
Receptionist: Just through that door and turn right.
Ludwikowski: Right. I think I'd better go there now.
Receptionist: Fine. Well, just come back here to Reception when you're ready. And then I'll show you to your room.
Ludwikowski: Right. Thanks. See you later.

LISTENING TEXT 8/4

Now, we've decided one Emergency Exit really isn't enough for safety purposes. We do need another – and it should be located immediately next to the Manufacturing Area. Next, we need a Tea Room. This should be next to – and equal in area to – the Men's Toilet. Finally, we'll have to install a Data Base and Distribution Centre. This'll be attached to – and be the same size as – Enquiries and Information, OK? It's got to be located between Enquiries and Information and the Storage Area.

LISTENING TEXT 8/5

Dianne: Pan Cargo. Dianne Wilson speaking.
Gerry: Hiya. It's me!
Dianne: Gerry! God! I haven't heard from you since ... oh ... last fall? Where are you calling from?
Gerry: Downtown. I got a condo on El Camino. First floor. God, it's noisy!
Dianne: Yes, I can hear the subway over the phone – or is that coming from your bathroom? Say, what're you up to these days? You still selling trash cans?
Gerry: No, no. Those days are gone. I work in a drugstore on Park Hill now. Look, why don't we meet over coffee?
Dianne: Sure ...
Gerry: Ouch!
Dianne: What happened?
Gerry: Damn – sat on a thumbtack. OK. So ... how about ... What time is it now?
Dianne: Ten after four. Bit late for today. How about tomorrow? Around four?

Gerry: Let's make it five. The freeway's pretty clogged up during the rush hour.
Dianne: OK. See you then. Looking forward to seeing you again, Gerry.
Gerry: Me too, Bye for now, Di.
Dianne: Bye.

UNIT 9

LISTENING TEXT 9/1

1st speaker: H & P Boarding of Huddersfield here. My name's Pryke. Look, I've been waiting all day for an order I made – order number 668. Double-glazing frames, OK? Right, you gave me your assurance they'd be here yesterday. And I've got a customer waiting. So I've been counting on you to deliver on time. But those frames still haven't arrived! This is just not good enough! Now, if I don't get those goods today, I'm going to cancel that order and look for another supplier.

2nd speaker: Hello, Marriott Construction here. Richard Handley speaking. Er ... I'm afraid those aluminium plates we ordered last month still haven't come. Er ... so we're still waiting for them! According to the contract, they should have arrived last week – by the 18th, to be exact. And, er – well, it's getting tight here as we're very low on stock. Now, as you know, if goods arrive up to seven days late, we can claim a 10% discount. Well, if you can make sure they reach us, say, by tomorrow night, well, I'll be happy to leave it at that.

3rd speaker: Burlington House here. This is Norah Green. Look, those trolleys haven't arrived. And you guaranteed delivery by the 18th. That's six days ago! I must say – I'm very disappointed. Now, if you can get those goods to me right away, I'm prepared overlook this delay. Otherwise, I'll just have to return them to you when they do arrive. Without payment, of course. I very much hope it won't come to that. You've managed to keep to deadlines in the past, and I've been satisfied with the business I've done with you.

LISTENING TEXT 9/2

Wicke: Hello, Mr Sanders?
Sanders: Speaking.
Wicke: Erika Wicke of CC Clearing here. In Hamburg.
Sanders: Ah, Frau Wicke. You're calling about our letter, I take it?
Wicke: Yes, concerning the overdue payment. Look, I really have to apologise for a very unfortunate mistake, Mr Sanders.
Sanders: Oh, yes?
Wicke: Yes, you see, we did instruct our bank to pay you. On the 8th of October, in fact. The day before we got your first reminder.
Sanders: Well, I can assure you we haven't received payment, Frau Wicke. Otherwise, we ...
Wicke: Yes, I know. Er – let me explain. You see, we got your first letter after we'd instructed our bank. We didn't answer your letter because we just assumed that you got the payment. It had gone through, you see. It appeared as a payment on the statement of account from our bank. So – well, we left it at that.
Sanders: So – why haven't we been credited?
Wicke: Well, the moment we got your reminder today, I contacted the bank to find out what went wrong. And I'm most embarrassed to say there was a mistake in our office. We made out the payment to the wrong customer – one with a similar name to your company's. Walden – W - A - L - D - E - N. Instead of Warden.
Sanders: I see.
Wicke: Yes, I've only just discovered this. And, well – you'll be happy to know that I've instructed the bank to make sure you're paid immediately.
Sanders: Well, I'm very pleased to hear it, Frau Wicke.
Wicke: And please accept our apologies, Mr Sanders. We do regret this very much.
Sanders: Well, assuming everything goes through smoothly this time, Frau Wicke, I'll be happy to leave it at that.

LISTENING TEXT 10/1

Sercombe: The graph does suggest GLOWY has a real potential on the German market. To begin with, light bulb sales have been rising steadily in Germany. And last year – as you see – they reached 15 million euro for the first time. And you can also see GLOWY's climb on the British market. Now, in Britain, the product properties 'durable' and 'long-life' were used to advertise GLOWY – this was important in filling a gap in that market. You'll be aiming for the same gap in the German market – and, well, we calculate that a seven to ten per cent share of that market is a realistic aim. For the first year, that is ...

Melchior: Excuse me for interrupting, Mr Sercombe, but do you have figures for the current year?

Sercombe: Er – no. No, I'm afraid we won't have those till the spending survey results are published in March, Herr Melchior.

Melchior: I see.

Sercombe: Now, as I was saying, we're looking at a seven to ten per cent share of the German market. And our research suggests a price spread of one euro seventy five to two euro fifteen for GLOWY in Germany. So we've taken both those prices as a basis – one-seventy five and two fifteen. Comparison with similar products does make one-seventy five seem a realistic price. We'll have to do more research on this, but our study of the German market does suggest GLOWY could be a winner.

Melchior: May I make a point on that? These calculations of yours are based on anticipated turnover – the number of units to be sold, right?

Sercombe: Right.

Melchior: But you're not assuming that number depends just on the selling price, are you? I mean, when people decide what to buy, they're not only influenced by price.

Führling: Well, could I come in here? You're absolutely right, of course, Herr Melchior. People also consider the quality of a product. They can be influenced by its novelty appeal. And they're heavily influenced by advertising. And, really, this is one reason why we have a wide price range in the calculations. You see, we need to know how much you intend to spend on advertising. And we need to know about your intended advertising strategy.

Sercombe: Exactly. And I was about to point out that, for our calculations, we assumed an advertising budget of zero point seventy-five million euro in the first year. But you'll have to let us know ...

Melchior: Could I just comment on that? Zero point seventy-five million euro is pretty high ...

Sercombe: Well, of course, high advertising costs are unavoidable in that first year. Their effects can be expected later ...

Melchior: You seem to have misunderstood me, Mr Sercombe. What I meant was: zero point seventy-five million euro is high, but we have, in fact, decided to allocate exactly that amount as our advertising budget for the first 18 months.

Sercombe: Ah, OK ... Right, I've made a note of that, Herr Melchior. Er – I'd like to go back to this question of figures. We need to know about advertising strategy, OK. But we also need more information about profit margins. For our calculations, we assumed profit margins of 25% for retailers and 25% for wholesalers ...

Melchior: Ah, yes, these will have to be decided in the negotiations with the trading companies.

Sercombe: Yes, I accept that, but on the other hand, we do need more information on that before we can narrow down our price calculation.

LISTENING TEXT 10/2

1. Excuse me for interrupting.
2. I was about to point out that it's almost lunchtime.
3. I'd like to go back to the main point.
4. Do you really think that's relevant?
5. I'm afraid you've been misinformed.
6. We do need that information.

LISTENING TEXT 10/3

Llewellin: Herr Melchior, I'm just preparing this report for London office. Could I ask you to bring me up to date with developments from your side, please?
Melchior: Right, I'm due to lead the negotiations with the German trading companies ...
Llewellin: On the third of April.
Melchior: On the third of next month, yes. And right now my people are preparing a written offer for them, together with a sample of GLOWY under a German package label.
Llewellin: I take it you'll need all that on the table during the negotiations.
Melchior: Most certainly. And I'll also be describing our British advertising strategy. That's to say – the one we used to introduce GLOWY onto the British market.
Llewellin: But you'll also be talking about the advertising campaign for GLOWY in Germany, won't you?
Melchior: Oh, not just talking about it. I've got to put forward a very impressive and convincing strategy. That's what our promotion people are working on right now.
Llewellin: PCN, you mean.
Melchior: PCN. Yes. PCN have also got the job of recruiting and training the sales reps, and making sure that we get the best places on the shelves.
Llewellin: How can they manage to do that?
Melchior: Well, as a first step, they have to find out from every branch who actually receives the goods; and who actually fills those shelves!

LISTENING TEXT 10/4

Pat: Rod, as you know, I'm putting this progress report together. And I'd like to ask you for more information, please.
Rod: Fire away.
Pat: Well, you said your first priority is to guarantee punctual delivery.
Rod: And the best methods of co-operating, yes.
Pat: So – can you tell me what stage you're at in organising this?
Rod: Well, right now, we're getting all the trading companies to tell us if they'd require deliveries to a central store or to individual branches. Then we'll be able to decide what intermediate storage facilities we'll need.
Pat: OK. And what can you tell me concerning that forwarding agent?
Rod: Petersen Spediteur? Yes. We've contracted them to advise us on the control for our distribution system.
Pat: That'll be EDP-supported, right?
Rod: Correct. You can also say that Petersen will be supporting us in the negotiations with the trading companies.
Pat: Ah, that sounds promising. I mean, their experience should be useful to us.
Rod: Not only their experience – they're already well-known to the companies, so that's going to be a big advantage too.

LISTENING TEXT 10/5

Consultant: ... so I've got those estimates for you, Herr Melchior. On a per-unit basis, as you requested.
Melchior: So you can give me the breakdown?
Consultant: With pleasure. First, transport. Now, we based our calculations on an offer of one hundred and seventy five euro a pallet. That's just an estimate, of course ...
Melchior: Yes, I'm afraid we can't give you the exact delivery quantities before the end of the month.
Consultant: Very well. We've also assumed a total of thirty-two hundred units per pallet.
Melchior: Yes. Yes, that should be close enough.
Consultant: All right. So, based on these provisional figures, we calculate transport costs at five cents.
Melchior: Per unit.
Consultant: Per unit. Then, there's the cost of waste disposal, under the green point system.
Melchior: Right.

Consultant: So – waste disposal. Cost per unit – well, here again, we had to work on an assumption.
Melchior: The packaging weight, you mean?
Consultant: That's right. You'd have to give us the exact packaging weight before we can give you a closer estimate, Herr Melchior. But, we assumed a packaging weight of 30 grams. And that would give us a per-unit waste disposal cost of five cents.
Melchior: OK. So – what about the promotion costs?
Consultant: Well, here, we based the calculation on an outlay of 7 thousand 5 hundred euros ...
Melchior: OK.
Consultant: And on that basis, per-unit promotion costs work out at 15 cents.
Melchior: 15, you say.
Consultant: Right. Which means, according to our calculations, the total marketing costs – per unit – allowing for adjustments when we get more information from you ...

Listening Review

3.1

ARRANGING AN APPOINTMENT

Gerald: Hello, Gerald Seymour speaking.
Karen: Gerald? It's Karen here – Karen Griffiths.
Gerald: Karen! Hullo! I was wondering when I'd hear from you again. Where are you calling from?
Karen: Home, actually. I live in Hamburg now.
Gerald: Hamburg! Heavens – you do get around.You're still with Reinhard's, are you?
Karen: Yes, they invited me to move to Hamburg when they opened a new agency here. I said yes immediately. It means more responsibility –
Gerald: And more salary too?
Karen: Oh, certainly.
Gerald: Good for you!
Karen: Yes. And, Gerald, the reason I'm calling so suddenly ...
Gerald: Aha, we're going to do business, are we?
Karen: Well, I hope so. The point is: I'll be in London next month. For that conference on European Business Law.
Gerald: Really? Me too!
Karen: Yes, I know. I've just received the advance list of speakers. And I see you're offering a workshop on the Friday afternoon.
Gerald: That's right.
Karen: Well, I'd like to suggest we meet. You see, I have a couple of ideas which you might be interested in ...
Gerald: ... and you'd like to discuss them.
Karen: Right.
Gerald: Sounds fine. I'd love to. Um – let's see – when will you actually be arriving in London?
Karen: On the Friday morning. I can't get away any earlier, I'm afraid.
Gerald: OK, my workshop runs from two to three-thirty – er, will you be coming to that?
Karen: No. I can't, I'm afraid, Gerald. I'm going to Jill Reynolds' talk on insurance law that afternoon. Look, I wonder – would you be free on Saturday morning?

Gerald: Well, I do have a pretty tight schedule, I'm afraid, Karen. Saturday's right out – unless we meet in the evening.

Karen: Well, yes, the evening would be fine. I didn't like to suggest it, in case you wanted to get away from business talk after your long day!

Gerald: I'm always ready for business talk, Karen! OK, Saturday evening it is, then! Shall we say – what? – seven-thirty?

Karen: Seven-thirty will be fine.

Gerald: Good. Right, let's meet at the Jug of Wine. That's a little restaurant on the top floor of Crown Centre ...

Karen: Crown Centre – where the conference takes place, you mean.

Gerald: Exactly.

Karen: The Jug of Wine. OK, Gerald, I've got that. Seven-thirty. Oh, just one more thing – let me give you my fax and phone number ...

Gerald: Right.

Karen: ... so you can contact me if anything comes up. The phone number is 040 - 41 31 1957.

Gerald: 040 - 41 31 1957.

Karen: And the fax number's the same except for the final seven. Just change that last seven to a nine, and you've got the fax number.

Gerald: OK, got that, Karen. And I'm looking forward to seeing you again.

Karen: Me too! And, Gerald, I do think you'll be interested in these proposals of mine – so bring your notebook, will you?

Gerald: Will do. Right – see you on Saturday the 7th, Karen.

Karen: Right you are, Gerald. Goodbye for now. Bye!

3.2

STARTING YOUR OWN BUSINESS

Speaker at a conference: So you want to start your own business. You may even have a new product or service that noone has ever thought of before. But a good idea alone is no guarantee of success. To really make that product or service sell, you have to find out who'll want to buy it, how you'll market it, what price you can charge, and whether you can expect enough profit to earn a living. And you'll also have to decide what form your business will have. It's very important to get legal and financial advice before you decide on the best form of business for your product or service.

Sole trading, for instance. To become a sole trader, all you need is to declare that you're working for yourself. So you have the freeedom to do things the way you choose. In lots of ways, this kind of business is quite easy to manage. But, of course, you'll be totally responsible for every aspect of the business. And, if things go wrong – well, not only will your business assets be at risk, but your personal possessions too. So we do advise that you get legal and financial advice before getting started.

Alternatively, you could start a partnership. This means two or more people running a business together. A partnership is relatively easy to get started – but, again, you should take legal advice on how to do it. A partnership agreement has to be written, for example. This states exactly how the business will be organised. It states who has to put what into the business, who does what work, how your profits are to be shared, and what would happen if you decided to end the partnership. After the business part nership begins, each partner is personally responsible for the debts of the business. So trust between the partners is very necessary and important. Because if your partner builds up debts and fails to tell you about them, you are as responsible for them as your partner is!

Another possibility is to form a limited company. Legally speaking, a limited company is different from its owners. So you wouldn't normally be responsible for its debts. But, of course, the company does have legal and financial obligations. And there are very exact rules and regulations controlling the activities of a limited company. So, again, if you want to start a limited company, you really do have to get financial and legal advice first.

3.3

VIDEOCONFERENCING

Videoconference technician: So, this is your first videoconference, Mrs James?
Mrs James: Yes. And, frankly, I'd be very grateful for any tips you could give me. You know, for getting it right.
Videoconference technician: With pleasure. Well, the first thing is: make sure you're suitably dressed. Don't wear clothes with large areas of black or dark blue or red or white.
Mrs James: Why not?
Videoconference technician: Well, these colours actually prevent viewers giving you their full attention, you know?
Mrs James: I see. Right – what colours should I wear?
Videoconference technician: Oh – light blue, light green, pink. You know, lighter colours.
Mrs James: I see.
Videoconference technician: And another thing: make sure you've got all your notes in order before you begin. If you happen to be unprepared – well, it's far more obvious on screen than when you're face to face with someone.
Mrs James: Oh, I'll be prepared – believe me. I've been preparing all week!
Videoconference technician: Right. Now, you said you'll be using some graphics, Mrs James.
Mrs James: That's right.
Videoconference technician: Very well. My advice is: check them all, and make sure you haven't packed too much text into them. The most important thing is that the text is readable. You know, too much text in graphics makes life pretty hard for the viewers.
Mrs James: Oh, I'm sure you're right. But how much is too much? I mean, I do have to add some information to those diagrams.
Videoconference technician: Mrs James, I suggest a maximum of eight lines of text per graphic. More than that is too much.

3.4

SENDING MONEY ABROAD

Bank official: Nowadays, money can be sent round the world instantly, at the push of a button. But this high-tech method can be expensive. So often a slower, traditional method is both cheaper and adequate. For example, you could send an international money order – known as an IMO. One big advantage of an IMO is that it can be completed by the bank immediately – there's no need for you to order it in advance. IMOs are ideal for low-value payments which are not especially urgent. For example, to pay for goods ordered by mail. Depending on the destination of the IMO, the payment can be made within a few days. Another important advantage of an IMO is that it's a relatively safe method of payment. That is, if it's lost, stolen or no longer needed, it's quite easy to have it replaced or refunded by the bank.

3.5

ANSWERPHONE MESSAGE

Answerphone speaker: Hello, this is Westminster Business Training Institute. You have called us outside our normal working hours of 9am to 6pm, Monday to Friday, so I'm afraid we're not here to take your call right now. But if you'd care to leave a message and your name and number, we'll call you back as soon as we can. Please speak after the signal.

RECORDED MESSAGE

Hello. Er – this is James Porter. Um – I've just seen your advert – for your – er – your Business Technology courses. Um – yes. I'd like some information, please. Er – especially the Multimedia Production seminar. Especially about that. Er – I'll be here tomorrow – er – after four-thirty. Er – yes, if you could call me after four-thirty – yes, I'd be very – er– oh! my phone number. My phone number is 885 882. Er – right, thank you. Er – goodbye for now.

3.6

COMPANY REPORT

Company Director: Our market share is still higher than most of our competitors'. We've got about 20 per cent in the region right now, and we're hoping to increase that to 25 per cent next year. Our sales force has many years of experience and market know-how, and they're continuing to develop business for us.

We have a large amount of stocks across all our branches. And, since the beginning of the year, we've been operating a 24-hour delivery service. This means we're now able to provide a local, direct service in all parts of the region. And I'm happy to say we've had a lot of customers expressing sastisfaction with this new service. So, all in all, prospects look good.

3.7

FAULTY GOODS

Mrs Handley: ... so I decided I'd better call you right away. It's about these complaints we've been getting. Complaints about goods sold in your area. Now, I don't need to tell you how very worrying this is, John.

John: Oh, I can assure you we're very worried too, Mrs Handley.

Mrs Handley: Yes, but do you have any explanation?

John: Well, Claire and I are working on this right now. We're looking very hard at the sales profile – trying to find out if there are any areas of similarity, and whether the goods were provided by one supplier. We're also trying to find out if a faulty batch was supplied.

Mrs Handley: Well, you'd better let me have a report on this soon. Very soon indeed.

John: I'll fax it to you as soon as we've got to the bottom of this, Mrs Handley.

Mrs Handley: I'd be extremely grateful. The sooner the better. And, while we're on the subject, I want to speak to you about that Stuttgart matter ...

3.8

HOTEL RESERVATION

Receptionist: Bristol Hotel. Good morning

Heinemann: Good morning. Paul Heinemann speaking. Could you tell me if you have a double room for the weekend after next?

Receptionist: The weekend after next. Er – which nights exactly? You mean Saturday and Sunday nights?

Heinemann: No, sorry. I mean from Friday to Saturday and Saturday to Sunday.

Receptionist: Ah, so you'd arrive on the 24th ...

Heinemann: ... departing on the 26th, yes.

Receptionist: 24th to the 26th. Let me see. Yes ... yes ... We have a double room available for those two nights. With WC. Or we have a double room with WC and shower, if you prefer.

Heinemann: Right. Could you tell me the prices, please?

Receptionist: A double with WC, no shower – that would be a hundred and thirty pounds. That includes VAT. With WC and shower – that's a hundred and forty pounds. Also inclusive of VAT.

Heinemann: A hundred and forty. Right. Yes ... I'd like to reserve the double with shower, please.

Receptionist: For the nights of the 24th to the 26th.

Heinemann: Right.

Receptionist: And may I have your name again, please?

Heinemann: Heinemann. Paul Heinemann. Actually, I stayed at your hotel this time last year. For the Trades Fair, you know. As I remember, you require a deposit ...

Receptionist: Well, in this case, Mr Heinemann, provided I can check your name on our file here, a deposit won't be necessary. Er – is that H - E - I - N - E - M - A - N?

Heinemann: Double-N. Heinemann with double-N.

Receptionist: Right ... I'm just checking that ... ah, there it is. Mr Paul Heinemann. From Stuttgart, right?

Heinemann: That's it.

Receptionist: And is your fax number the same as last year, Mr Heinemann? Yes, same fax and phone numbers.

Receptionist: Right.

Heinemann: So – would you send me a confirmation of the booking, please?

Receptionist: With pleasure. I'll fax it right away.

Heinemann: Thank you very much.

Receptionist: Thank you, Mr Heinemann. Goodbye.
Heinemann: Goodbye.

TRANSLATING 3.9

... for instance, communications like letters and faxes. When these are written in a foreign language – well, it's often enough if the receiver understands just the broad sense and meaning. But contracts and legal documents and any documentation dealing with import or export procedures – well, these need to be understood in detail. Because, failure to understand them can have serious consequences.

MARKETING IN CHINA 3.10

Speaker A: So you've made some progress on the China project?
Speaker B: Yes, quite a lot, actually. I've been checking the Internet, and I have a list of about twenty mailing lists in China. And I've found quite a number of firms offering direct marketing services for companies who want to sell in China.
Speaker A: Well done.
Speaker B: Now, we'll look at the cost of advertising in Chinese newspapers – as we agreed. But I'm beginning to think that direct mailing might be the most effective strategy for us.
Speaker A: Direct mailing? To potential clients in China, you mean? Wouldn't that be expensive?
Speaker B: No, maybe not. This is the point. You see, it costs just a few pfennigs to mail a letter inside China.
Speaker A: I see. Hm. Well, that certainly seems worth looking into.
Speaker B: That's right. Now, I'm going to that promotion seminar in Birmingham tomorrow. It'll be focussing on market surveys in three major Chinese cities – Hong Kong, Shenzhen and Shanghai. I'll find out what I can there, and bring back as much info as I can. Then we'll talk about it again on Wednesday, OK?

A COMPLAINT 3.11

Norah Geller: Euroglass. Good afternoon.
Mr Jenkins: Jenkins Photographics here. Is that Mrs Geller?
Norah Geller: Yes, Norah Geller speaking. Is that you, Mr Jenkins?
Mr Jenkins: Yes, Mrs Geller – and I have a question about that instruments consignment.
Norah Geller: Ah, yes. No difficulty, I hope?
Mr Jenkins: Well, I've just got your invoice – and there's no reference to the five per cent discount we agreed on! Has there been an error?
Norah Geller: Oh, I'm sorry if there has been, Mr Jenkins. You certainly get a discount on that order.
Mr Jenkins: Right.
Norah Geller: Leave it with me. I'll look into the matter and let you know.
Mr Jenkins: Yes – by letter, if you please. And there's another thing – the goods still haven't arrived! You said you'd deliver by the 15th of March. That's 10 days ago!
Norah Geller: Yes – again, we do apologise. As I told you last week, the rail strike has caused a lot of difficulty ...
Mr Jenkins: Look, the terms of the contract are quite clear. If I don't get those goods by the end of next week, I'm afraid I'll have to cancel the order.
Norah Geller: We're certainly doing all we can ...
Mr Jenkins: As I said, I can give you till the end of next week. If you haven't delivered by then, I'll certainly look for another supplier. And that's that. Goodbye, Mrs Geller.
Norah Geller: Er ... very well. Goodbye, Mr Jenkins!

ARRANGING A MEETING 3.12

Speaker A: ... so that's how it stands now. We've adapted the model to your specifications. And we'd very much like to demonstrate it to you now.
Speaker B: Good.

Speaker A: And since you might wish to include this model in next year's catalogue, we suggest we have that meeting as soon as possible.

Speaker B: Agreed.

Speaker A: Mr Macey will be coming with me again. He's in charge of our scheduling and accounts, as you know.

Speaker B: Fine. And I'll arrange for our Herr Fröhlich to take part again.

Speaker A: Excellent. Now Mr Macey and I could fly to Hamburg – well, on any day, really. Oh, er – would you be willing to share our travel and hotel costs again, on a 50-50 basis?

Speaker B: Oh, certainly.

Speaker A: Thank you. Now, I think we can assume the meeting will take about two hours, as it did last time. And assuming we agree on the new model, we should use part of the time to discuss production scheduling and costs.

Speaker B: Right.

Speaker A: So, it's really a matter, now, of fixing a suitable time and date. As I said, we can make it at almost any time. So perhaps you could suggest ...

3.13

AT THE SEMINAR

Introductory speaker: ... so you have to ask yourself: is your company 100% capable of making the product or offering the service? In other words, what are the limits on the company's capability?

Then there's the question of demand and competition. The key questions here are: how different is your product or service from others on the market? Which parts of the market are attractive? What difficulties or dangers can be expected from the market? You also need to look at the size of the market. Will people want to buy your product or your service? How many people are likely to buy it? Will the demand be steady or is it likely to fade after a short time? Who are your competitors? We'll be looking at questions like these in today's section of the seminar.

Then there's the question of finance. How much will you need to cover your start-up and running costs – for example, for employees and equipment? What about consultancy costs? We'll also look at the possibility of sharing consultancy costs with other companies. We'll look at the cost of premises, and the question of whether to rent or buy. Then we'll discuss how to assess the difference between costs and income – in order to assess your profit margin. We'll be discussing all these aspects tomorrow, together with the topics of working capital, bank overdrafts, how to process payments and the very important matter of cash flow. That is: how much can you expect to earn week-to-week – and how soon?

Right. On the third and final morning of the seminar, we'll look at the technical side of running a new business. That means dealing with questions of transport, import restrictions, technical standards and distribution. Then, on the last afternoon, we'll have Mr Davies of Highgate Promotions with us to deal with the very important question of advertising and publicity. And for those of you who will be staying for the Wednesday evening session, we'll deal with the intercultural and international aspects of marketing.

Well, that's the timetable. As you see, we've added a couple of points to the printed version you have. But we think you'll certainly find these three days most rewarding ...

3.14

ADVERTISING IN THE TRADE

Promotion agent: So you want to advertise your service within the trade – that is, to other companies and distributors, and not to the public.

Trader: That's right. We're really not sure how to do this, and that's why we called on you.

Promotion agent: Good. With our experience in advertising and publicity, we're certainly able to help. Let me see, now, you've just been advertising in trade magazines up to now, right?

Trader: That's right. And we took part in last year's trade fairs in Dortmund and London. But that's all. We'd certainly like to look at other possbilities of making our goods known.

Promotion agent: Right. And you say you have a mailing list of the potential clients you want to reach.
Trader: Yes, about 150 companies with e-mail and fax. And there're about thirty more we can contact only by post.
Promotion agent: All right. Now there's a variety of ways you can send out your logo and your publicity literature to potential clients – oh, information leaflets, product catalogues, labels and stickers, business cards, brochures. And much of this could be done on the Internet, of course. But with your type of product, we seriously recommend a publicity video.
Trader: A video.
Promotion agent: Yes. This is something we can help you with. But, really, with your particular service, there would be real advantages to producing a video. For instance, there's the ...

BOOKING FLIGHTS

3.15

Travel Agent: Can I help you?
Customer: Yes. I have to fly to Munich on the 17th. Could you book me onto a flight, please?
Travel Agent: With pleasure. On the 17th. So, what time of day would you like to leave?
Customer: Well, I need to be there in time for a three o'clock meeting.
Travel Agent: Three o'clock.Very well. There's a daily Lufthansa flight arriving Munich at 14.15. That's a quarter past two. Would that be all right?
Customer: Quarter past two. That's perfect. Are there still seats on that flight? Business class?
Travel Agent: For one person?
Customer: Yes, one person. Non-smoking, if possible.
Travel Agent: Right, yes, I can do that. Shall I reserve that for you, sir?
Customer: Yes, and I'll buy the ticket now.
Travel Agent: Thank you. And would you like to reserve a return flight?
Customer: No, actually, I have to go direct to Chicago from there. So could you book me onto a flight from Munich to Chicago the next day, please?
Travel Agent: Thursday the 18th?
Customer: Right. Preferably around 10 in the morning.

PHONING ABOUT A JOB

3.16

Sandra Carter: Carter's Book Mall.
Mr Brightwell: Hullo, my name's Brightwell. I'm calling about your advert in today's 'Borough Advertiser'.
Sandra Carter: Ah, yes, I can help you with that. I'm the Manager. Sandra Carter's my name.
Mr Brightwell: Well, Mrs Carter, I'd like to say that I'm very interested in the position. I do feel I have the qualifications you asked for. But – well, I have a couple of questions. Er – you mentioned references. Er – could you give me an idea of how many you'd need?
Sandra Carter: Well, two or three would be adequate. I'd be satisfied with just two, if they're very satisfactory. Er – may I ask you a question, before we go any further?
Mr Brightwell: By all means.
Sandra Carter: The fact is: we're looking for someone with relevant experience in the book trade, as I said in the advert. Do you mind telling me what experience you have?
Mr Brightwell: Well, for the last two and a half years, I've been retail manager of a business with a fairly large turnover. We deal mainly in books and magazines. We run several other lines at the same time, though – stationery, toys, video cassettes. And before that, when I was a student, I worked at weekends and during the holidays for a private dealer who specialised in good-quality second-hand books.
Sandra Carter: Well, that's what I call relevant experience. I think it would be worthwhile if we met and had a talk – er, Mr ... er ... Brightwell, did you say?
Mr Brightwell: Yes. Well, I'm very pleased to hear that. But – well, there's just one other question, Mrs Carter. It's the matter of the salary. Your advert says 'excellent income'. Now, I wonder if you're in a position to give me a little more information on that ...

3.17

RECEIVING A VISITOR

Frau Fertsch: Hullo, my name's Fertsch. I'm looking for a Mr James.
Roland James: Ah, Frau Fertsch, how do you do! I'm Roland James. Welcome to Vinten Electrics.
Frau Fertsch: Oh, you're Mr James. Nice to meet you.
Roland James: I hope you haven't been waiting long, Frau Fertsch.
Frau Fertsch: No, I've just arrived. Mr Reynolds said I'd find you here right away.
Roland James: Yes, normally there are several of us here. But I'm the only one on duty today. All the other staff are on a half-day training course in town. So this gives me a chance to show you around the place without any interruptions.
Frau Fertsch: Fine.
Roland James: So, you're going to be with us for three weeks?
Frau Fertsch: Yes, on the work exchange scheme.
Roland James: And you've just arrived from – Dortmund, is it?
Frau Fertsch: Düsseldorf, actually. Our head office is in Dortmund. But I work at our Düsseldorf branch.
Roland James: Ah, yes. Of course, most of our contact is with your people in Dortmund. I was there just last month, actually.
Frau Fertsch: Ah, Dortmund isn't a particularly beautiful city, I'm afraid.
Roland James: Oh, I don't know. I certainly enjoyed my time there. Look, would you like a cup of coffee or a short break before I show you around? You must be pretty tired after the flight.
Frau Fertsch: No, really. I'd like to see the place right way – if you have the time, that is!
Roland James: Oh, my pleasure, Frau Fertsch! Right – er – let's start with the Reception Area.

3.18

BUSINESS CARDS

Sales rep: Now this type of business card has a thin plastic coating, as you see.
Customer: Mm. Very nice.
Sales rep: Yes, the coating gives it a longer life, of course. And, at the same time, it's rather more attractive than the traditional business card, isn't it? Now, with this layout, we can print your personal name and company name, and your fax, phone and e-mail information. All in quite large print, as you see.
Customer: Right.
Sales rep: Alternatively, we can offer you this smaller-print version here. The same information appears in two types of script – English and Japanese, for example – like this one.
Customer: Hm. And what would this type cost me?
Sales rep: Well, here's our list price for a set of two hundred. And we'd be happy to offer you a discount if you ordered ten or more sets.

3.19

JOINT VENTURES

Business consultant: A joint venture is the most common way for a German company to enter the market in this country. A joint venture is a partnership with a company in this country, where the German company invests at least a quarter of the capital. Both companies may invest in the form of cash, buildings, factory premises, equipment, industrial properties, materials, technical expertise or land use.

The first step in starting a joint venture is to find a suitable partner company. In theory, this is a simple process. In practice, questions of contract have to be settled. This means agreeing on terms of investment and co-operation, the sharing of profits, the sharing of risks and losses, the method of management and the ownership of properties. All these conditions have to be agreed by both companies before the joint venture can really get started. Officially, negotiations begin with a Letter of Intent. This letter states that both companies are interested in starting a joint venture together and it states the basis for future discussions.

3.20

A DELAYED FLIGHT

Barry: Hullo? Joan?
Joan: Hullo, is that you, Barry?

Barry: Yes, I'm calling from Gatwick.

Joan: You're still in London!

Barry: Yes, it's been terrible! There's a lot of fog here, you see, and it means practically every flight has been delayed.

Joan: Oh, dear. Well, we'd better do some rescheduling. When do you expect to be in Düsseldorf, then?

Barry: Well, I'm looking at the departures board now, and I see that my flight has been rescheduled for 12.35.

Joan: 12.35! Oh, heavens – that means you won't be here till this afternoon!

Barry: Unfortunately, you're right.

Joan: So – what do you think I should do about Herr Frank?

Barry: Well, I know it's very inconvenient for everyone. But could you possibly contact Herr Frank right away, and explain the situation? And ask him if he's able to stay on till later in the day?

Joan: I'll certainly do that, but –

Barry: And suggest to him, would you, that he could meet Olaf in the meantime. And Olaf can give him a run-down on the Research and Development side of the company.

Joan: Yes, all right.

Barry: And if Herr Frank's agreeable, then tell Olaf to drop what he's doing and come over and deal with Herr Frank. As soon as possible.

Joan: Yes ... yes, all right, Barry. I'll do it immediately.

Barry: And call me back right away when that's done, will, you? You've got my mobile phone number.

Joan: Will do, Barry. Er, just tell me your estimated time of arrival in Düsseldorf, will you? Then I can tell Herr Frank how long it will be before you arrive ...

CHANGING THE ORDER

3.21

Mr Lee: Lee Textiles (Singapore) here. Hullo.

Frau Petersen: Hello, Mr Lee. Kirsten Petersen here, of Petersen & Braun, Hamburg.

Mr Lee: Oh, Hullo, Frau Petersen. What can I do for you?

Frau Petersen: I'm phoning about our order, Mr Lee. We've been trying to fax you. But we can't get through.

Mr Lee: Ah, yes, I'm sorry. Our fax has been out of order since yesterday. We're doing all we can to get it fixed ...

Frau Petersen: Well, it's all right. We can settle this matter by phone. The fact is: we want to change that order we sent.

Mr Lee: I've got it in front of me now. The one you faxed – let's see – on, on Monday?

Frau Petersen: That's the one. For 400 shirts. By sea.

Mr Lee: Right.

Frau Petersen: You haven't despatched them yet, have you?

Mr Lee: No. And, due to our fax problem, we haven't been able to send you a confirmation of order yet. But we'll do it as soon as ...

Frau Petersen: No, no, the point is: we've just heard from one of our customers. And we now want some of those shirts urgently – so we can deliver to him as soon as possible.

Mr Lee: Ah, I see.

Frau Petersen: So we'd like to change our order. Can you send 150 of those shirts by air freight, please? And the remaining 250 by sea.

Mr Lee: 150 by air. The rest by sea. No problem, Frau Petersen. You can leave it to me.

Frau Petersen: And will you accept this as our order? As you know, we'd do this by fax normally, but ...

Mr Lee: Fine, fine. I'll fax you the confirmation as soon as we're back to normal. In the meantime, I'll get those 150 shirts despatched. Right away, in fact. That's 150 'Beach Style 2000', right?

Frau Petersen: Right. With the usual terms of delivery and payment for air freight goods, right?

Mr Lee: Fine. As I said, you can leave it to me, Frau Petersen. And, again, I'm sorry about the problem with the fax.

Frau Petersen: Not at all, Mr Lee. Thanks a lot – and goodbye for now.
Mr Lee: Goodbye, Frau Petersen.

3.22

A BUSINESS ARRANGEMENT

Agent: ... so we're looking for a high-class hotel in your country which we could do business with. And my impression is that your hotel is ideal.
Hotel Manager: I'm happy to hear that. And we're certainly interested in your proposal.
Agent: Fine. So the idea is: we secure reservations for you from customers in Germany –
Hotel Manager: Right.
Agent: – and, as most of those customers will be businesses and companies, they'll want facilities for meetings and conferences and presentations of various kinds.
Hotel Manager: I can promise you we have very suitable facilities.
Agent: I'm sure you're right. And the financial terms are clear, I hope? We secure the customers for you, and in return we ask for a ten per cent commission on the final price you charge those customers.
Hotel Manager: Agreed.
Agent: And you can guarantee a reply by fax within one hour for any enquiry we make, at any time, concerning vacancies, price and availability of your rooms and facilities?
Hotel Manager: Certainly. Our fax and reception staff operate 24 hours a day.
Agent: Splendid. Now could we just run through this checklist, to make sure you have the facilities our customers will be looking for?
Hotel Manager: By all means.
Agent: First: do you provide self-dial telephones and fax facilities for your guests?
Hotel Manager: Yes, all room guests have a direct external line. And there are fax and Internet services in our business centre.
Agent: Excellent. Now, what about conference facilities – like overhead projectors, video recorders, CD and cassette recorders and photocopying?
Hotel Manager: Oh, we offer the full range. No difficulties there.
Agent: Good. And do you have a restaurant?
Hotel Manager: A first-class restaurant and bar, yes. And a fitness room, too, if you'd like to mention that in your publicity.
Agent: Good. Yes. we certainly will. Now, finally, what about access to the railway station and airport? Could you – ?
Hotel Manager: Oh, we run a shuttle service to the airport and the station whenever we host a conference. So, again, no difficulties there.

3.23

THE COMPANY TECHNOLOGY

Managing Director: ... and we have outlets around the country, all supplying materials for interior design. We offer our customers a very personal service ...
Visitor: Yes, I can see that.
Managing Director: ... and, really, we can only do this if we continue to develop the business. We depend on our technology for this. We place very great importance on computer data. This way, we can make substantial analyses and make exact forecasts of customers' needs. We also use the computer system to keep records of our customers and records of suppliers and of stock. John Lawley supervises the day-to-day transactions which we carry out around the country. Er ... you've met John, haven't you?
Visitor: Yes, we met at the reception yesterday.
Managing Director: Right. And I use our management information system here, for financial planning and analysis. Now, our customers purchase goods from our retail outlets. But many of them. you know, need help in selecting suitable materials. And they need guidance in calculating the quantities they need.
Visitor: And this is where your personal service comes in, is it?

Managing Director: Exactly. When a customer needs help in assessing quantity, one of our reps calls at the customer's premises to carry out detailed measurements. All the details are taken on the premises and recorded on a portable computer. Then we download that data, enter it into the system, and add in the costings – depending on the customer's choice of material, of course. Our computer here automatically produces a cost estimate and gives details of quantity and price.

ENGLISH – THE LANGUAGE OF INTERNATIONAL BUSINESS

3.24

Public speaker: ... and if you look at the languages used in European business, you can easily see the importance of English. A survey has shown that, of all German companies who use foreign languages, 93 per cent of them use English. Of French companies who use foreign languages, 81 per cent use English. In Spain, the figure is 58 per cent, and so on. Furthermore, with the development of the European Union, it's becoming more and more necessary for business people to speak at least one foreign language. In the Netherlands, it's been estimated that 91 per cent of business executives speak a foreign language. In Denmark, it's 90 per cent – and 87 per cent in Finland. In Germany, the percentage is somewhat lower – just 67 per cent. But the point is that, in most cases, that foreign language is English.

BUSINESS DEVELOPMENT CENTRE

3.25

Business Development Centre: Well, Mr Murdie, let me describe our work here. Then you can decide which of our services you might be interested in.

Mr Murdie: Good idea.

Business Development Centre: So. As a Business Development Centre, our primary aim is to support small- and medium-sized businesses in the region. We offer various services to help them develop and grow.

Mr Murdie: I see.

Business Development Centre: We're open mainly to owners and managers. They – you – can visit us or make enquiries by e-mail or phone. We've got a well-equipped business training and conference room, along with computer-aided tutorial rooms. We have a mailing list service, and fax, copying and typing services. And we have excellent access to databases.

Mr Murdie: Very good.

Business Development Centre: Let me tell you about our start-up service. This includes introductions to professions and specialists, and guidance and help with profit and cash flow forecasting. And, particularly for start-up clients, we can offer marketing advice and assistance too.

Mr Murdie: Well, that's very impressive. Er – but to tell you the truth, my company's particular interest is in overseas contacts.

Business Development Centre: Ah, well, you'll probably be interested in our service in foreign company enquiries and foreign company credit checks Oh, and this coming Friday, we're doing a seminar on 'overseas trade missions'.

SPELLING OVER THE PHONE

3.26

Speaker A: .. and a package we sent to you has been returned to us. It seems we didn't use the right spelling for your address. We took it from your handwritten fax, but – well – I'm afraid the address isn't very clear.

Speaker B: Oh?

Speaker A: That street name. Is it – 'Bet-a-lorry-strasse'? 'Bets-a ... '?

Speaker B: 'Pestalozzistrasse'. That's P -

Speaker A: P? P for Peter?

Speaker B: Yes.

Speaker A: Damn. Well, that's our first mistake. We used a B in the street name ...

Speaker B: Oh, dear.

Speaker A: Right, go ahead, please. P - E - T - Z ...
Speaker B: No. P - E - then S for Sugar, T for Tommy, A for Andrew ...
Speaker A: Ah, P - E - S - T - A - L ...
Speaker B: Right. Then O for Oliver, then double-Z - I.
Speaker A: Double-Z - I.
Speaker B: Yes, then 'Strasse' – all one word. 'Pestalozzistrasse'.
Speaker A: OK, got that, thank you. Now, next – in the next line. That looks to me like ...

3.27

CONFIRMING THE APPOINTMENT

Receptionist: Sparmarkt Windrose.
Mr Boyd: Hullo. Phillip Boyd speaking. I'd like to speak to Herr Graf, please.
Receptionist: Ah, Mr Boyd. I'm afraid Herr Graf isn't in just now. Can I help you, or take a message?
Mr Boyd: Yes. Would you tell him, please, that I'll meet him on Thursday the 12th?
Receptionist: Thursday the 12th. Er – any particular time?
Mr Boyd: Well, yes, at nine in the morning. But Herr Graf knows about that. You see, the last time we spoke, he offered me a choice of dates. And I'm just phoning now to say which one suits me best.
Receptionist: Oh, I see. So Thursday the 12th, Mr Boyd. I'll tell Herr Graf as soon as gets in. Do you want him to phone you back?
Mr Boyd: No, not necesary, thank you. Just give him my best wishes, please.
Receptionist: I'll do that.
Mr Boyd: Thank you – and goodbye for now.
Receptionist: Goodbye, Mr Boyd.

3.28

ARRANGING TO MEET AGAIN

Mr Harding: Well, Mrs Chambers, I think we'll have to meet again, won't we?
Mrs Chambers: To go through these claims. Yes – and pretty soon, I'd say.
Mr Harding: How soon could you make it?
Mrs Chambers: I'm flexible. Any day, really. But I prefer afternoons.
Mr Harding: Well, how about Thursday afternoon?
Mrs Chambers: Thursday. Yes, that'll be convenient.
Mr Harding: Right. Say, two o'clock? We'll need – what? – three hours, would you say?
Mrs Chambers: Could we start at two-thirty? Then I'd be able to take the ten past two train from my place.
Mr Harding: OK, two-thirty it is, Mrs Chambers. You've got my number, haven't you?
Mrs Chambers: I certainly have. Right, see you next week, Mr Harding.

3.29

EXCHANGE RATES

Speaker A: Right, I've got the bank statements here. And you have the exchange rates, right?
Speaker B: Yes, freshly printed.
Speaker A: OK. Er – what's the rate for the dollar?
Speaker B: The US dollar. One pound sterling buys – er, one dollar fifty-nine cents today.
Speaker A: One fifty-nine. And the yen?
Speaker B: Japanese yen ... one ninety-nine forty-four.
Speaker A: Hm, that's way up on yesterday's rate. Why's that?
Speaker B: Oh, it's the result of the Japanese Finance Minister's speech yesterday. The yen has strengthened across all the major currencies, apparently.
Speaker A: Ah. So, what's the rate for the Hong Kong dollar now?
Speaker B: Er – twelve dollars twenty-one cents to the pound. Practically no change.
Speaker A: What about the Rand. Is that still falling?
Speaker B: Er – let's see. South African Rand – here. Six eighty-seven. No. That's steady again. Six eighty-seven. No real weakening there.

THE COSTS OF NEW PREMISES

3.30

Business consultant: An office in this city will cost you about one thousand US dollars per month, for about a hundred and fifty square metres. This would be for the space itself, without furniture or equipment. A deposit of three hundred US dollars per phone line will be necessary. Internet service costs about sixty US dollars per 80 hours of use.

Apartments range from a thousand US dollars per month to about five thousand. The actual figure depends largely on quality and on the exact location. Nowadays, the northern suburban area is cheaper than other areas of the city.

INTRODUCING

3.31

Company representative: I'd like you to meet Hartmut Link, our accounts manager. Hartmut, this is Mr Rayner from Hull. And may I introduce Frau Grünewald, who's also in our finance section? Frau Grünewald, Mr Rayner, our guest from Hull. And this is Herr Dechert. Herr Dechert, I think you met Mr Rayner at the conference in Dortmund, didn't you? Herr Dechert is in charge of the production side here.

DEALING WITH A VISITOR

3.32

Bittkowski: Hullo. I wonder if you could help me? Where could I find Mrs Baldwin, please?

Receptionist: Ah, do you have an appointment, please?

Bittkowski: Yes, my name's Bittkowski. I'm from Henkel und Söhne in Dresden. And I'm supposed to be meeting Mrs Baldwin at 9.30.

Receptionist: If you'll just take a seat, Herr Bittkowski, I'll call Mrs Baldwin now and tell her you're here.

Bittkowski: Thank you.

INVITATION TO DINNER

3.33

Mrs Baldwin: Look, come and meet me for lunch? Be my guest.

Bittkowski: Well, that would be very nice

Mrs Baldwin: Then we could go through your brochures together afterwards.

Bittkowski: Fine. So – where do you suggest?

Mrs Baldwin: How about the Mövenpick Restaurant, say, in an hour?

ON THE MOVE

3.34

Airline official: Good morning. Passports and tickets, please. Is this all your luggage, madam?

Traveller: Yes, just one suitcase.

Airline official: Would you like a seat in the Smoking or No smoking section?

Traveller: Smoking, please. And an aisle seat, if it's possible.

Airline official: Yes, that's easy – you're one of the first passengers to check in. So, this is your boarding card. And that's your seat number.

Traveller: Thank you very much.

Airline official: Board at Gate B2 – in about one and a half hours.

Traveller: Thanks. And is the flight due to leave on time?

Airline official: Yes, it's due to depart on time at 11.50.

ARRANGEMENTS FOR THE TALKS

3.35

Speaker A: Let's see. The talks are supposed to start at 2.30.

Speaker B: Right.

Speaker A: And my flight comes in about an hour earlier.

Speaker B: Yes. At 1.10. I'll be there to meet you at the airport.

Speaker A: Good. So, we meet the Thompson and Lyle representatives at the hotel ...

Speaker B: ... At the Angel.

Speaker A: And my presentation should start around 4.30.

Speaker B: Yes. Is there anything you need – besides the flip chart and overhead projector?

Speaker A: No, that's all, thanks. You've taken care of the conference room at the Angel, have you?

Speaker B: I have.
Speaker A: And you've scheduled a break after two hours.
Speaker B: Right. Just before your presentation.

3.36

CHECKING TRAVEL ARRANGEMENTS

Traveller: Good morning. I'm taking the morning flight to Düsseldorf. Could you just confirm that it arrives at 13.15? As shown in last year's timetable?
Airline official: Yes, ma'am. Arrival 13.15.
Traveller: Right. And will there be a shuttle service to the main railway station?
Airline official: Oh, there's a frequent train service between the airport and the station. No need to worry about that, ma'am.
Traveller: Oh, good. And you're sure that service is running now.
Airline official: Yes, ma'am. It runs all year round.

3.37

SAYING GOODBYE

Speaker A: Well, thank you for coming. It was nice seeing you again.
Speaker B: Oh, I've enjoyed it – and we've made some progress, haven't we?
Speaker A: Indeed we have. There are still a few points to sort out. But I'll be in contact with you about those after I've spoken with Mr Duell.
Speaker B: Fine.
Speaker A: So, have a good journey. And we'll meet again in Leipzig.
Speaker B: OK. And give my regards to Mr Duell.
Speaker A: I certainly will – as soon as he gets back from America.
Speaker B: Right, see you again, then. Goodbye.
Speaker A: Goodbye.

3.38

BEFORE THE MEETING

Colleague: Mr Churchyard, could we run through a couple of points before the meeting begins?
Mr Churchyard: Certainly.
Colleague: Well, first thing. Without going into detail, could you tell me how much staff numbers have increased over the last two years?
Mr Churchyard: Oh, I can tell you exactly. We have five more full-time staff, making a total of twenty.
Colleague: OK. Now, if we could clear up a couple of points before the meeting – as you know, I'm very concerned about the salary increases.
Mr Churchyard: Yes, indeed.
Colleague: So could we briefly discuss this matter now? Before we talk about staffing levels at the meeting? That would make sense.
Mr Churchyard: Fine by me.
Colleague: Right. The company's prediction is that four new jobs will be created during the next year. All full-time. And salaries are expected to rise by eight per cent. Now, frankly, I'm a bit worried by this.

3.39

UPDATE

Speaker A: As you know, I've just got back from Scandinavia. So could you give me a short update on sales?
Speaker B: Well, we're doing well with the Exotica and Diamond models. And we've just had a large order from that new company in Essen.
Speaker A: Good. And has anything been done about the transport problem?
Speaker B: Yes. It seems very likely that we'll be using Petersen Spediteur in future. They've offered much better terms.
Speaker A: Good – and have we terminated the contract with Speedlink?
Speaker B: Yes, it runs out at the end of the month.

PROGRESS REPORT

3.40

Committee Chairperson: One piece of information before we start, ladies and gentlemen. Pete Morris has just faxed us from America about the Albuquerque deal. He says delivery has been delayed by two months. I'd say this won't create too much of a problem for us, as sales will be slack here in October. And we won't have too much storage space available. OK? Next, you should all have a file in front of you containing the June figures. You all have one? OK, well, I think we can begin. Doug, would you l ike to ... ?

ORDERING BY PHONE

3.41

Mr Cull: T.H. Nice & Company here. I'm calling from London. We've looked at the sample you sent us ...
Seller: Ah, yes?
Mr Cull: ... and we're in a position now to place an order with you.
Seller: Ah, excellent. T.H. Nice & Company, you say?
Mr Cull: Yes. And we'd like to order five steel cabinets. Catalogue number 187.
Seller: That's five of 187.
Mr Cull: That's it.
Seller: And may I have your name, please?
Mr Cull: My name's Cull. C - U - double-L. And if you'll accept this as my order, you can send the confirmation direct to me, please.
Mr Cull: Certainly, Mr Cull. Thank you very much. Now concerning the delivery and payment ...

DISCUSSING NUMBERS

3.42

Seller: ... and if you order another batch within three months, we can grant you a discount of five per cent. You'd save up to seventy pounds.
Customer: Yes, but how fast can you deliver? I mean ...
Seller: Oh, we can normally deliver within five days. By special delivery, much less. That's from our German base in Bremen.
Customer: And would that cost extra?
Seller: Yes, for special deliveries, we do charge an extra eight pounds fifty per case.
Customer: So, when would it actually arrive – by special delivery, I mean?
Seller: Well, we'll have it in Regensburg in twenty-four hours.
Customer: Right. So, purchase price. Plus special delivery. What's the bottom line going to be? For two cases?

HANDING OUT A BROCHURE

3.43

Seller: Right, let me give you our brochure. It illustrates our whole range. Let me just show you – the particular goods you're interested in are on pages 18 to 20.
Customer: Thank you, but I'll need at least a week to discuss with my colleagues what we need.
Seller: Take your time. And if you'd like to have any of these products on a trial basis ...
Customer: Yes, we'd certainly be interested in that. But I can't tell you anything definite yet, I'm afraid.
Seller: All right. Our terms of delivery and payment are all listed here, on page 3.
Customer: OK.
Seller: And you'll be in touch with me before the end of the month, you said.

DISCUSSING SALES TRENDS

3.44

Speaker A: Have you seen these figures? They're really worrying.
Speaker B: Well, we always expect a fall in sales at the end of the season.
Speaker A: Yes, but look – these figures are very bad, compared with last year's.
Speaker B: Yes, well, it's partly the recession, of course.
Speaker A: You think there's any chance of things picking up before Christmas?
Speaker B: Oh, I'm pretty sure they will. Actually, I'd say prospects are good. Have you looked at the advance orders?

3.45

LEAVING A MESSAGE

Laura Hunter: Lyle & Roland. Good morning.

Horst Neuner: Good morning. Horst Neuner here. May I speak to Mrs Laura Hunter, please?

Laura Hunter: Laura Hunter speaking.

Horst Neuner: Ah, Mrs Hunter. Our Frau Biermann is away at the moment. But she asked me to let you know that your report looks very satisfactory.

Laura Hunter: Oh good. She's read it already, has she?

Horst Neuner: Yes, she has. And I should also tell you that she'll contact you again on Friday at the very latest.

Laura Hunter: Right. Thank you. Anything about the talks with Lothar and Schubert?

Horst Neuner: No. Frau Biermann didn't tell me anything about that. I could ask her when she gets back.

Laura Hunter: No, don't bother. That'll be all right.

Horst Neuner: Right. Thank you, and goodbye for now, Mrs Hunter.

Laura Hunter: Goodbye, and thank you.

3.46

DISCUSSING THE FIGURES

Speaker A: OK, electronic toys are doing well. Our sales have risen by twelve per cent in the last fifteen months.

Speaker B: That's an increase in turnover of around $6,000.

Speaker A: Right, so the electronic toys are doing fine. But this report – it's disturbing. Parents spent 20% less on toys and games last Christmas ...

Speaker B: Compared with the previous Christmas. Yes.

Speaker A: You know, this brings us right back to advertising. If we raised our advertising budget by – I don't know ..

Speaker B: Well, let's say we raised it by two hundred dollars a month.

Speaker A: OK, two hundred dollars a month – it'll be just a matter ot time before we get it all back through increased sales.

3.47

MAKING ARRANGEMENTS

Roy: Well, I think that's all we can do for the moment, Diane.

Diane: Right. So when can we meet again?

Roy: I'll need – let's see – I'll need about five days, so my colleagues can analyse these figures.

Diane: So, next week then?

Roy: Yes, I'm sure we'll be ready in a week.

Diane: OK, then, Roy. I suggest we make a provisional agreement to meet again in a week – same time, same place.

Roy: That's on the 28th.

Diane: Yes. Is the 28th all right for you?

Roy: Yeah, But I'll have to confirm it with you later, Diane.

Diane: OK, then: 2 o'clock, on the 28, here at the Suffolk.

Roy: Right you are.

UNIT 1

Getting started

New appointments

Name	Day	Time
Brigaglia	Friday	10-12
Robertshaw	Saturday	12-13

Language study

1. expired 2. always brings
3. are rising (also possible: have risen (present perfect))
4. take part (also possible: have taken part (present perfect))
5. heard from 6. hire 7. have appointed 8. are now building

Typical Mistakes

1. The bank has agreed to lend us DM10,000.
2. It was probably/possibly a mistake to sign the contract so quickly.
3. The news is good – all the consignments have arrived on time.
4. What's your opinion about the Schubert proposal?
5. Most people aren't interested in this brand.
6. Could we discuss (or: talk about) this order from Harvey & Black?
7. Perhaps you could tell us something about next season's designs.
8. Herr Reinhardt can't come just at the moment – he's on the telephone.
9. What do you call *Lagerung* in English? (or: How do you say *Lagerung* in English? or: What is *Lagerung* in English?)
10. What does "premises" mean in this contract?

Down to Business

1

a False: They "will be" looking for a partner in China.
b False: He did not see the advert before this morning, and he faxed them immediately.
c True: "They phoned me immediately – from China."
d True: "I told them it'll be enough for now if they kindly fax us some information about their operation ... I said we'll do the same from this end."

2

a (5) b (2) c (1) d (3) e (4)

3

Having seen your advert on the Internet, we would like to know if you would be interested in a partnership with us. Allow us to introduce ourselves.

We are a small, relatively new company, producing and distributing chemical detergents. Below the Management level, we have a total of 68 staff, including 40 skilled production workers.

We specialize in detergents for use on industrial machinery. We have state-of-the-art equipment for this. The export of industrial detergents is the most profitable part of our business. We are currently exporting to customers in six European countries and in Japan. We are very keen to market our goods in China too.

Do you wish to market your goods in Europe? If you see any possibility of a partnership, please send us similar information about your company.

4

Brian's message: Mr Ren Yunping? This is Brian Cull of Rayner Detergents speaking. Sorry I haven't got through to you personally. I'm calling to give you some information about our company structure. Well, apart from the Management, the company has three sections. The biggest is Production, which includes Storage. That's Miss Joyce Brown's part of the operation and it has 40 skilled staff. The smallest section is Sales & Finance, which has just ten staff. I'm in charge of that. Finally, there's Research & Development. The Head of that section is Mr George Landbrooke. He's in charge of 18 staff there. OK, that's all for now. You've got our phone and fax number. And we're very much looking forward to hearing from you again.

Dealing with visual info:

(1)(d) (2)(b) (3)(f) (4)(a) (5)(c) (6)(e) (7)(g)

The British-American Difference

NOTICE BOARD

Trade Union Notice

CCL has announced it is going to cut a fifth of its workforce within the next two years. We strongly oppose this plan and call for a general meeting at 19.00 hr, Friday, July 11 to discuss further steps. We regret the short notice but strongly encourage those members whose holiday starts on July 12th also to join the meeting. Further topics on the agenda will include the future of the company's equal opportunities programme and the envisaged rise in National Insurance contributions.

W. Kelsterman

Speaker

Last but not least

9-12: Excellent! 3-8: Not bad. 0-2: You'd better take care!

UNIT 2

Getting started

1.d 2.c 3.a 4.e 5.b

Language study

1

1. probable 2. probable 3. certain 4. improbable. 5. probable 6. certain 7. only possible

2

1. b If we spent a lot more on advertising, we'd (or: we would) be able to sell that new model.
2. b If salaries were increased before Christmas, all the staff would stay with the company.
3. a If we can afford it, we'll (or: we will) get a laser copier.
4. a If they advertise now, they'll (or: they will) find a new designer by August.

Typical Mistakes

1. She often goes to the Far East.
2. Can you explain to me the reason for the mistake?
3. We don't want to invest any more this year. Our directors don't either.
4. We'll probably hire about a hundred and thirty part-timers in the summer season.
5. Owing to the unfavourable economic situation, we had to cut our sales staff.
6. Look, we need that information by next week – can you manage that?
7. At the moment, these mowers are selling at $44.50 a piece.
8. Thank you for calling – I'll send you the goods immediately.
9. I look forward to hearing from you.

Down to Business

1

a not correct – it is only possible that H&R will continue to rent
b not correct – the statement is probable, but not certain c correct d correct e correct
f not correct – rather than discuss costs, he suggests "an arrangement" instead
g correct h correct

2

a Let's first look at the question of costs.
b Can you keep that offer open for two weeks?
c Perhaps we could come to some arrangement.
d We can agree to that.
e I'm willing to meet you halfway on this.
f We are working to a tight profit margin, you know.
g May I invite you to meet me for lunch?
h I suggest we meet at L'Escargot at 12.30.

3

Dear Monsieur Debeauvais

It was a pleasure to meet you again last week, and to do business with you.

As promised, I am sending a summary of what we agreed. This summary should be helpful to you when drawing up the contract.

You will give us the Paris premises rent-free for six months, after which time we will decide whether we want to continue. During those six months, we will pay the fax and phone bills, but not the operating costs.

In return, we will loan, for ten months maximum, the equipment you need for remodelling your Lyon plant, on condition that the tools used
(a) are of the size and quantity we agreed on;
(b) are returned in working order.
We will provide technical assistance with our power tools for two days in Lyon to help install the equipment. For your part, you will pay full labour charges for this installation work.

Provided you find all this in order, would you please go ahead and draw up the contract, as agreed? If we keep to the time-frame of two weeks for this, we will be able to sign by the end of the month.

Yours sincerely
B. Rüffin
for Horn & Rüffin GmbH

5

(Obligations of SARL Labatte/Debeauvais)
"between 1 March and 31 August" changes to
"between 1 March and 30 June"

"to pay the costs of repair for any damage caused to the equipment ... " changes to
"to repair or replace any equipment damaged during the period of loan."

(Obligations of Horn & Rüffin GmbH)
"to provide two technicians ... on 3 and 4 March of the current year" changes to
"to provide one technician ... on 3, 4 and 5 March of the current year"

Dealing with visual info

1

3. 4. 6. 1. 5. 2.

3

First of all, when a customer requires a specially designed tool, the order is processed by Sales Section. Next, Production Section have the task of planning the tool. After this, Management acquire the materials needed, according to the production plan. Some of the materials may be in stock; others have to be purchased. Then, when the materials are ready, Production Section proceed with manufacture of the tool. Following this, Sales Section despatch the finished tool to the customer. Finally, they pass a copy of the despatch note to Management, who are responsible for bookkeeping.

The British-American Difference

British English	German	American English
spare-time	*Freizeit*	leisure-time
sales receipt	*Kassenbon*	proof-of-purchase
pay the whole bill	*für alle zahlen*	pick up the tab
VAT	*Mehrwertsteuer*	sales tax
Underground	*U-Bahn*	subway
full stop	*Punkt*	period
ordinary shares	*Stammaktien*	common stock
preference shares	*Vorzugsaktien*	preferred stock
anticlockwise	*gegen dem Uhrzeigersinn*	counterclockwise
rubber	*Radiergummi*	eraser
do it again	*wiederholen*	do it over

Last but not least

Letter to Mr Watson (= bad news): 5. 3. 8. 2.
Letter to Ms Churchyard (= good news): 7. 1. 6. 4.

UNIT 3

Getting started

1

The three mistakes:
– H&R want an agent in Greece, not a licensee.
– They will not send product samples.
– Hellenic Marketing Services already have the price list.

2

1. 3. 6. 5. 2. 4.

Language study

1

(1)	As a result	Consequently
(2)	On the other hand	By contrast
(3)	Furthermore	Moreover
(4)	On the whole	In general
(5)	In the meantime	Meanwhile

2

1. What kind of communications system do you have?
2. What do you use the laptops for?
3. What's this program called?
4. Whose property is this?
5. What does CAD stand for?
6. Who do you allow the 5% discount to? (or, more formal: To whom do you allow the 5% discount?)
7. How do you produce the quotations?
8. What's the date next Wednesday?
9. How come you have no fax equipment here?
10. How do things look (or: How are things looking) for the future?

Typical Mistakes

1. Profits have risen by eight per cent over the past six months.
2. The directors will be meeting on the first Wednesday of the month, as usual.
3. We've received this information from a good client of ours.
4. The export figures aren't particularly impressive this year.
5. So we'll see each other (or: meet) at the Trades Fair on Friday at 10, right?
6. "Did you have lunch on the journey?" "Yes, I did."
7. The CD market grew very rapidly during that time.
8. In the past, the company was based at Erfurt. (or: The company used to be based ...)
9. They told us (or: said) that they would contact us today.
10. These prices are no longer current (or: valid, or: up-to-date) – we need the new catalogue.

Down to Business
2 & 3
Listening Text 3/2 gives the full version of Gerry's words.

4

Dear Gerry
Thanks for your answerphone message yesterday. We are very interested in your proposal.
I can confirm that we could deliver a bulk order in ten days by air.
As requested, we are despatching to you immediately, by air, a sample of STAR LABEL PRINTER without the barcode facility. We hope that you will find it satisfactory.
I am also enclosing further technical information about the product.
Please let me know if I can be of any more help. Looking forward to hearing from you.
With best wishes
Barbara Steube

6
a The cost   b Ideas   c Our tools   d Info + materials   e Help with registering your homepage

Dealing with visual info
2
All the statements are true, except:
4. The smokers chart shows that Denmark has a higher percentage than Italy (= more smokers per 100 people). But it doesn't show which of the two states has more smokers in total.
7. The wine and beer charts don't show percentages (of people) but totals (of litres).

3

(1) all (or: each)	(2) Four	(3) Luxembourg	(4) 100 (or: cent of the)
(5) third	(6) France	(7) beer	(8) second-highest
(9) second-lowest	(10) average Italian	(11) ten litres	(12) Greece

The British-American Difference

British English

Dear Mr Kaye
As requested, we are sending you a brief statement on the stock control audit of Lukas & Sons (hereafter referred to as Lukas). The audit was carried out six weeks after Lukas' clearance sale from February to March.
Lukas Inc. specialises in making made-to-measure shopping trolleys for shopping centres as well as lifts. According to the annual accounts, the business was booming for the first six months of last year but suddenly collapsed in mid-August. As sales had not picked up again after five months, Lukas decided to have a clearance sale and try to sell the production plant for US$ 2,600,000 o.n.o.
The stock-taking was carried out by means of readings of the counters attached to the production equipment. These were checked against the accounts. Our assessment concerning the stock-taking did not give rise to any queries.
With best wishes
H. Preetz (Accountant)

American English

Dear Mr Kaye
As requested, we are sending you a brief statement on the inventory control audit of Lukas & Sons (hereafter referred to as Lukas). The audit was carried out six weeks after Lukas' close-out sale from February thru March.
Lukas Inc. specializes in fabricating custom-made shopping carts for malls as well as elevators. According to the annual accounts, the business was booming for the first six months of last year but suddenly collapsed in mid-August. As sales had not picked up again after five months, Lukas decided to have a close-out sale and try to sell the production plant for US$ 2,600,000 o.b.o.
The inventory was carried out by means of readings of the counters attached to the production equipment. These were checked against the accounts. Our assessment concerning the inventory did not give rise to any queries.
With best wishes
H. Preetz (Accountant)

Last but not least

The Company

Strengths

1 Produces top-class lightweight electronic printers
2 Good reputation in the trade.

Weaknesses

1 Unable to produce custom-made printers.
2 Limited production capacity (max 50 units per week).
3 12% of technical work has to be sub-contracted.

The Market

Opportunities

1 Our printers are suitable for offices + home-based deskwork.

2 Home-based deskwork is expanding in Europe (30% increase in two years).
3 Large potential market (Europe + US).

Threats
1 Possible recession next year would badly damage sales drive.
2 We lack a US distributor.
3 Main competitor (ElektroPro) could introduce rival printer model in the spring.
4 Printer may fail US safety standards.

UNIT 4

Getting started
Angela's fax:
Thank you for your information faxed yesterday, concerning our meeting at the Cairnhill on the 24th.
I would like to reserve a meeting room from 9.00 am to 1.00 pm for 15 persons at Y50.00 per person.
Would you please arrange the room in advance, according to your Classroom seating style?
I look forward to your confirmation.

Note:
– Stefan needs a slide projector, Angela an OHP. The "Y50.00 per person" offer includes both; the "Y40.00 per person" does not.
– The "Classroom" seating arrangement is probably best:
(a) Angela's and Stefan's presentation will be frontal;
(b) Participants won't have to communicate with each other, but simply need a clear view of the speakers and the screen.

Language study

1. c	2. b	3. a	4. d	5. f
6. e	7. i	8 j	9. g	10. h

Typical Mistakes
1. London is the best example of an international city that I can think of.
2. He's studying with great concentration for his exam.
3. I'll visit you if (ever) I'm in Chicago.
4. Have you had any previous experience in this line of work?
5. You have to be careful how you deal with him – he's very sensitive.
6. Would you take Herr Bracht to the station, please?
7. Finally, we'd better discuss the question of bank loans.
8. If the production staff worked overtime, those orders could go out on Wednesday.
9. "Do you think we"ll get a repeat order from Reynolds?" "I hope so!"
10. We really can't expect much (or: any) profit in the first six months.

Down to Business
1

Jack Prewer:	No action (Maybe he'll need to change guest list & name tags – but these can wait till Friday.)
Trevor Wiseman:	Phone (His message says "Please phone".)
Christine Wardingley:	Send fax (Christine's request – "I would like to ask you again to remit this as soon as possible" – is quite pressing!)
Michael Hurst:	No action

4
a2. b3. c4. d1.

7

Crystal Videoconferencing:	Scale of Fees
Room Fee:	£38 per 15 minutes (Reduced by 40% if Crystal Videoconferencing's centres are used at both ends)
Communication Fee:	£25 per 15 minutes
Scheduling Fee:	£50 per videoconference
Reservation Fee:	(payable if videoconference is to be set up within four days): £50.
Minimum hire period:	one hour

Dealing with visual info

2

(1) meals	(2) 11	(3) hotel	(4) 18
(5) 10 per cent	(6) travel	(7) 22	(8) 40 per cent.

You can hear the full discussion on Listening Text 4/6

The British-American Difference

a 1 Ltd 2 Managing Director
b 1 Inc 2 Realtor (or: Real Estate Agent)
c 1 holding company 2 Ltd 3 Chartered Accountant 4 company 5 wholesalers
d 1 Silent partner or Sleeping partner (Either version – British or American – would be correct here, since the company is Dutch.)

Last but not least

A 4. e B 2. b C 5. a D 3. g E 6. c F 7. d G 1. f

UNIT 5

Getting started

	Quantities to be ordered (in kg)	
	A2	A5
by air	150	–
by sea	300	300

Language study

KEEP COSTS DOWN!
For ordering, these guidelines should be followed:

1. Make sure your customers are supplied from stock whenever possible.
2. Air freight consignments of more than 200 kg should not be ordered.
3. Only carriers who deliver direct to Frankfurt may be contracted. Costs for warehousing, wharfage and inland transport are to be avoided this way.
4. All large deliveries must be ordered by sea.
5. The additional costs can often be reduced. For example, a Tax Certificate and Certificate of Origin are not always needed. And, often, cheaper packing for hard-wearing cotton goods can be ordered.

Typical Mistakes

1. It's typical <u>of</u> them to send in their order at the last moment.
2. <u>Most businesses</u> close at Christmas.
3. Output fell as a result of obsolete machinery and <u>crowded</u> conditions.
4. It's <u>worth spending</u> more on training programmes.

5. The Internet gives us more market information than the newspapers.
6. We're in danger of being left with unpaid bills.
7. The two of them will be going to the conference.
8. According to the contract, we have the right to withdraw after three months.
9. The accounts office deals with bad debts on an individual basis.
10. You have only heard one person's opinion. (or: You have heard only one person's opinion.)

Down to Business

1

(Completing the notes)

(a) congestion	(b) fuel + wages	(c) 97% to 90%
(d) cost analysis	(e) 15–20%	(f) get access
(g) loss or damage	(h) packaging	(i) delivery

2

The recent Hauliers Association survey confirms our findings. First, there has been an increase in road transport costs due to congestion. Second, too many vehicles have resulted in slower, longer journeys as well as higher fuel and wages costs. Consequently, prompt deliveries to our retail outlets have fallen from 97% to 90% in the last six months.

But we still do not recommend rail transport. Our cost analysis shows that rail would be 15 to 20% more expensive than road. Furthermore, if we used rail, we would not be able to supervise the transport of refrigerated goods. It would be hard to get access to them during delays. There is also a danger of loss or damage in transit.

Therefore, we recommend, instead, increasing the stocks in the retail outlets. In addition, we recommend tighter packaging and squeezing more onto the delivery vehicles.

The British-American Difference

German	**UK**	**US**
Eisenbahn	railway	railroad
Straßenbahn	tram	streetcar
Einzelfahrschein	single ticket	one-way ticket
Saisonkarte	season ticket	commuter ticket
Kreisverkehr	roundabout	traffic circle
Taxi	taxi	cab
Autobahn	motorway	freeway
Lastwagen	lorry	truck
Güterzug	goods train	freight train
Parkplatz	car park	parking lot
Benzin	petrol	gas *oder* gasoline
Lastzug	articulated lorry	truck-trailer
Kofferkuli	luggage trolley	baggage cart
Hin- und Rückfahrt	return journey	round trip

The British-American Difference

German	UK	US
Postleitzahl	post code	ZIP code
Nachnahme	cash on delivery (COD)	collect on delivery (c.o.d.)
(Post) verschicken	to post	to mail
Briefträger	postman	mailman
Briefkasten	postbox	mailbox
postlagernd	poste restante	General Delivery
Ferngespräch	trunk call	long-distance call
gebührenfreie Telefonnummer	0800 or 0500 number	800 number
R-Gespräch führen	to reverse the charges	to call collect
Stand (Messe)	stand	booth
Werbezettel	publicity leaflet	broadside
ausfüllen (Formular)	to fill in	to fill out
Schwarzes Brett	notice board	bulletin board

Last but not least

1 (1)(b) (2)(f) (3)(e) (4)(a) (5)(d) (6)(c)

2 Correct order: 3 1 4 6 5 2

UNIT 7

Getting started

1 + 2

1.h 2.a 3.b (+ extra sentence a) 4.l 5.d
6.e 7.f 8.g 9.i 10.c
11.k (+ extra sentence b) 12.j (+ extra sentence c)

3

Correct order: 1 4 5 2 7 3 6 8 9 (= Listening Text 7/1)

Language study

1

1. would have got
2. would have had to pay
3. had not broken even
4. had kept
5. could have taken
6. had known

2

1. would have known
2. had thought
3. could have avoided
4. we'd used
5. we'd probably be selling
6. had used

Typical Mistakes

the day before yesterday	*vorgestern*
three days ago	*vorvorgestern*
a week ago today	*heute vor einer Woche/ heute vor acht Tagen*
two weeks ago	*vor zwei Wochen*
a fortnight ago yesterday	*gestern vor zwei Wochen*
two days later	*der übernachste Tag*
the day after tomorrow	*übermorgen*
tomorrow week	*morgen in acht Tagen*
in a fortnight	*in vierzehn Tagen*

Down to Business
1 + 4

APPLICATION FOR A DOCUMENTARY LETTER OF CREDIT

* Delete as necessary
Please open an *IRREVOCABLE / ~~REVOCABLE~~ Letter of Credit
☒ By Airmail ❑ By Teletransmission

Beneficiary's Bankers: Dresdner Bank, Hamburg

Name and Address of Applicant	Name and Address of Beneficiary
Argus Office Supplies 14338 Katy Boulevard Houston Texas 75001 USA	Grosskopf Printers GmbH Goethestr. 14-16 22559 Hamburg Germany

Commission / Charges ☒ All our a/c ❑ All beneficiary's a/c

Amount ☒ For
❑ Up to US$3,500
❑ About

Credit to expire on 30 November 20.. in the beneficiary's country

Documents to be presented within 14 days of shipment.

Transportation from: HAMBURG
to: HOUSTON
Terms & relevant place: *CIF, ~~C&F, FOB~~, etc HOUSTON

Documents required:
Full set Bills of Lading to order marked *Freight paid / ~~Freight payable at destination~~ and *Notify ARGUS OFFICE SUPPLIES, HOUSTON
Insurance Certificate. Risks as follows: ALL RISKS
Other documents: IMPORT LICENSE

Quantity and description of goods
12 cases of electronic printers

Special instructions:
None

2
For the complete version of the conversation, see Listening Text 7/3.

Dealing with visual info

1. :-# My lips are sealed!
2. :-(I'm frowning.
3. :-& I'm tongue-tied.
4. I-O I'm yawning.
5. :-D I'm laughing.
6. :-O Wow!

The British-American Difference

German	UK	US
laufendes Konto	current account	checking account
fakturieren	invoicing	billing
Vergütung	compensation	remuneration
Teilzahlung	part payment	partial payment

Steuerfreibetrag	tax allowance	tax exemption
Abschlagszahlung	interim payment	progress payment
Sparkonto	deposit account	savings account
Bankrott gehen	go into liquidation	go bankrupt
Rechnung (im Restaurant)	bill (in a restaurant)	check (in a restaurant)
Geldschein	note	bill (Banknote)

Last but not least

1

Missing nationalities:
a Frenchman/Frenchwoman; the Dutch; the Danes; a Briton; a Spaniard

Missing currencies:

Germany:	Deutsche Mark or German Mark or D-Mark (DM)
Italy:	Lira (L)
Rep of Ireland:	Irish Pound or Punt (IR£ or £)
Greece:	Drachma (Dr)
Portugal:	Escudo (Esc)
Spain:	Peseta (Pta)
Austria:	Schilling (Sch or ASch)

2 & 3

1. a + extra sentence C 2. e 3. f + extra sentence A
4. d + extra sentence B 5. b 6. g + extra sentence D 7. c

UNIT 8

Getting started

2

(a) 4093	(b) Birmingham	(c) Aston Olympic Hotel	(d) 09.00
(e) Birmingham	(f) Manchester	(g) Station Hotel	(h) 17.50
(i) Manchester	(j) 4075	(k) Frankfurt	

3.

1 9 4 8 2 6 3 5 7 (= Listening Text 8/2)

Language study

1

I'm travelling this evening, so I'm writing this message to you now. It will be waiting for you at your hotel when you arrive.

There's been a change of plan! Gore & Thompson's rep can't see you in Boston – he's fallen sick. He's going to call you from Chicago tomorrow morning to arrange a new appointment.

Your flight to LA departs 12 noon on Thursday. Until then, please demonstrate the new model wherever possible at the other locations on our Boston mailing list.

I'll call you at your hotel at 8 pm CET tomorrow. As you know, I will be speaking to Hammond on Friday. So please be ready to give an interim report on progress.

3

Presentation Schedule

Time	Date	Presenter	Topic
1. 10.00-11.15	10 October	Liz Dixon (Grays Compudisc)	"Using Compudisc"
2. 14.00-14.45	12 November	Bob Chandler (Brown Sales Consultants)	"Intranet Sales"
3. 14.30-15.30	30 November	Derek Routledge (Lardale Fibre Technology)	"The Lardale Method"
4. 16.00-17.00	11 December	Helen Watson (Grant Laser Products)	"Developing Laser Applications"

Typical Mistakes

Spelling mistakes	> Corrections		
developements	> developments	programm	> BE programme; AE program
accomodation	> accommodation	arguements	> arguments
catagories	> categories	residance	> residence
greatfully	> gratefully	seperate	> separate
acknowlege	> acknowledge	commitee	> committee

Down to Business

2

The full text of Ludwikowski's letter:

Many thanks again for offering to pick me up at Stansted Airport on Saturday the 24th. This is to confirm that I'll be arriving at 1320 (or: 1.20 pm).
As you know, I have to move on to Bury St Edmunds after our talks. This means I would like to get to Liverpool Street in time to catch a train at 1830 (or: 6.30 pm).
This will certainly leave us enough time to discuss and settle the question of the product specifications.
Looking forward to meeting you again.

Note:
As Ludwikowski flies Munich to Stansted on a Saturday, only one scheduled flight is possible – departing 1225, arriving 1320.
She wants the last train from Liverpool Street which reaches Bury St Edmunds by 9 pm (see Broome's fax). Thus: depart Liverpool Street 1830, arrive Bury St Edmunds at 2021.

Dealing with visual info

2

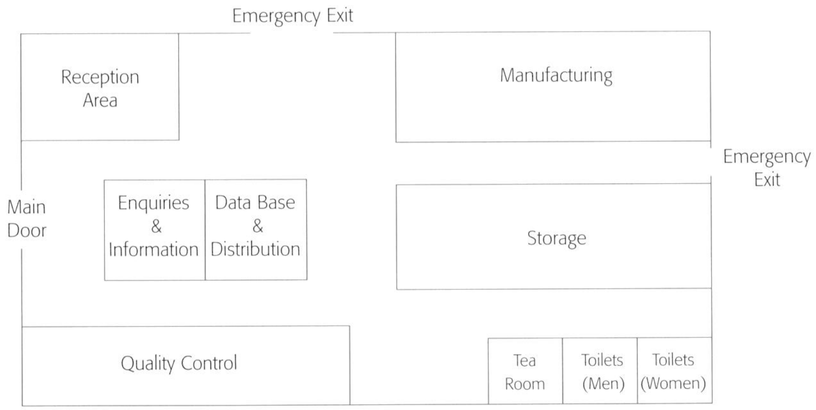

The British-American Difference

British: American

1. autumn: fall
2. town centre: downtown
3. owner-occupied flat: condo
4. ground floor. first floor
5. underground: subway
6. toilet: bathroom
7. dustbins: trash cans
8. chemist: drugstore
9. drawing pin: thumbtack
10. motorway: freeway

Last but not least

1.

Not possible: A: I'd like to send you an invitation. B: Let's pay 50–50. C: You'll pay.

UNIT 9

Getting started

1st speaker (Pryke): B (= very strong)
2nd speaker (Handley): A (= mild)
3rd speaker (Green): C (= strong)

Language study

1

Dear ...

Last week, I received the 25 "Alexis" coffee machines despatched to us on 25 March. I immediately sent a number of them to two of our customers who had ordered them. The first to receive his consignment complained that the handle attachments were loose. The second customer, to whom we had despatched five machines, reports that two were damaged on arrival. (2 commas added)

Naturally, these complaints have given us great cause for concern. What is important right now, though, is to find out the cause of the damage. Admittedly, it may have been the fault of the delivery service contracted to transport goods to our local customers. It must be said, though, that we have never had cause to complain about our delivery service, to whom I shall be speaking on Monday. I'll be getting back the machines of which the second customer complained. (1 comma added)

In the meantime, I would like to know your reaction to this matter. In particular, have you received other reports of problems arising from your "Alexis" coffee machines?

I look forward to receiving your early response.

Yours faithfully

2

(a) 0 comma; (b) 2 commas; (c) 2 commas; (d) 0 comma; (e) 0 comma; (f) 2 commas

Typical Mistakes

1. I suggest charging (or: suggest we charge) ten dollars registration fee.
2. Visitors looking for splendid scenery here won't be disappointed.
3. Economists are discovering what is meant by the word "chaos".
4. Everything (that) you've told me has been most fascinating.
5. I met Mr Reynolds' wife yesterday.
6. "Will you be at Tuesday's meeting?" "I don't think so".
7. They have absolutely no knowledge of English.
8. For two years, I worked with (or: at or: for) Schmidt & Höhne in Darmstadt.
9. They've been very slow to adapt to modern technology.
10. He's on the sales team of a big (or: large) kitchen goods company.

Down to Business

1 + 2

Correct order:

Paragraph 1: B Paragraph 2: AFE Paragraph 3: DGC

The fax, in full, reads like this:

> 5 June
>
> Dear Mr Sanders
> We thank you for your fax of 4 June and were sorry to learn that your four cases of drilling tools were unloaded at the wrong port.
> We immediately contacted the local representative of the shipping company. He has informed us that the goods, which were intended for Valparaiso, were unloaded in Punta Arenas inadvertently. He says the error probably resulted from a congestion of vessels at the port of departure.
> As the shipping company are responsible, we shall claim full compensation from them on your behalf.
> Would you, therefore, please send your invoice (showing the breakdown of the resultant costs) to us?
> We shall then forward it to the shipping company.
> We wish to express our great regret, and remain

3

> Dear Sir
> We refer to our claim for the amount of $388.50.
> We would like to draw your attention to the fact that payment is now four weeks overdue.
> Furthermore, we have received no explanation for this delay. Would you please look into the matter immediately?
> We trust that we can look forward to receiving full payment in the near future.
> For your convenience, we are sending a further copy of the claim.
> Yours faithfully

4

Once again, we must ask you to refer to our claim and to our letter of 9 October.
Please note that payment is now six weeks late. As you still have not given us any explanation for the delay, we must insist on payment in full by 5 November. Otherwise, we shall have no option but to take legal action.

5

1. True ("Look, I really have to apologise ...")
2. True ("We did instruct our bank to pay you. On the 8th of October, in fact")
3. True ("It appeared as a payment on the statement of account")
4. False ("There was a mistake in our office")
5. False ("We regret this very much" – an apology)
6. True ("I'll be happy to leave it at that")

Dealing with visual info

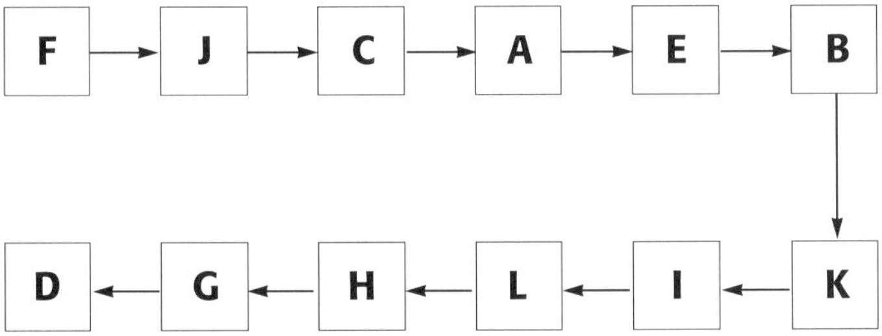

The British-American Difference

2 & 3

British English (BE)	
Flights Cancelled Due to Snow	(AE: canceled)
More Pay for Anaesthetists	(AE: Anesthetists)
Flood Level Rises to 2 Metres	(AE: Meters)
American English (AE)	
Archeologists Meet in Milan	(BE: Archaeologists)
Theater Director Quits	(BE: Theatre)
Travelers Must Pay More	(BE: Travellers)
Slovakia Praises Her Neighbors	(BE: Neighbours)
Everyone's Favorite Website	(BE: Favourite)

Last but not least

Here are some acceptable versions of the sentences:
"Welcome to Russia!"
"Morning bar assistant required. Male or female, Please apply Red Lion."
"We permanently stock over 60 cheeses for you to choose from."
"Valley School, Headingley. Qualified Teacher of the Deaf required."
"There is a French window in every bedroom."
"A hole has appeared on the Newmarket Road. Police are investigating it."
"If you would like to complain, please do so between 10 and 12 in the morning."
"The company was landed with a huge bill after ... "
"New Fast Food Restaurant to open in Edgbaston."
"Employers also complained of schoolleavers whose application forms contain spelling mistakes."
"We will be running a 3-day course from 10 am to 3 pm."

UNIT 10

Getting started

2 Figure 1: only Sercombe; Figure 2: all three speakers.

3 1.b 2.f 3.d 4.e 5.a 6.c

Language study

1. coming up against
2. came to light
3. come across
4. come up
5. came up
6. come up against
7. come out against
8. is coming to a head
9. came to light
10. came across
11. came to a head
12. came out against
13. look into
14. look at
15. look for
16. looks good
17. look forward to

Typical Mistakes

1. He shouldn't be doing all that travelling <u>at</u> his age.
2. Dawsons will soon be in a position to make an <u>analysis</u> of the project.
3. We would appreciate <u>receiving</u> your reply very soon.
4. <u>Despite</u> (or: <u>In spite of</u>) the bad weather, they should be able to finish on schedule.
5. Unless you have <u>your own room</u> (or: <u>a room of your own</u>), you won't find it easy to work.
6. <u>Considering the difficult situation</u>, we really should have another meeting.
7. Could you use another kind of packaging, <u>without charging</u> more for delivery?
8. If we look at the figures, we'll have an <u>idea about</u> (or: <u>of</u>) <u>what to do next.</u>
9. <u>Both (of) her</u> applications (or: <u>Her two</u> applications) have been rejected.
10. The self-service unit, <u>according to</u> the Production Manager, will be fully operational next month.

Down to Business
5

GLOWY Progress report on marketing launch in Germany Dated: 01 March

Negotiations

1. Herr Melchior will lead the negotiations with the German trading companies (03 April).
2. For this purpose, we are producing
– a written offer, with prices
– a sample of GLOWY under a German package label
– the strategy used to introduce GLOWY onto the British market
– our advertising strategy.

Sales and promotions

1. We have hired Promotional Consultants Network (= PCN)
– to recruit and train sales reps
– to develop an advertising strategy
– to get the best places on the shelves (ie find out who receives the goods; who fills the shelves).
2. Contact with the points of sale is very important. To get GLOWY onto retailers' shelves, the sales reps have to visit the various branches and introduce it to the branch managers. Once GLOWY is on the shelves, the sales reps have to take care of the product presentation by means of regular visits to the branches – on average, every four weeks. So it is important to build up a network of well-motivated reps and to send one to every branch – for each of the 16 German federal states, we need about five reps.

Logistics:

1. The first priority is to guarantee punctual delivery and the best methods of co-operating. To achieve this, we are finding out
– (from each trading company) if delivery is required to (a) a central store or (b) each branch;
– what intermediate storage facilities will be needed.

2. Petersen Spediteur are
– advising on the EDP-supported control for the distribution system
– supporting us in the negotiations with the trading companies.

Dealing with visual info
Second consultant's figures:

* Transport costs:	DM 0.11
	– based on DM 350 per pallet; 3,200 units per pallet
* Waste disposal costs (green point):	DM.0.09
	– based on 30g net packaging weight
* Promotion costs:	DM 0.30
	– based on DM 15,000 outlay
Total costs:	DM 0.50

So there is no difference between the total costs (per unit) estimated by the two consultants (both = DM 0.50).

The British-American Difference
UK: a) 999 or 112 (= not any of the numbers listed under "Gas"!); b) 01284 763111; c) 999 or 112 (= not either of the numbers listed under "Ambulance"!); d) 999 or 112 (= not either of the numbers listed under "Fire Prevention"!)

USA: a) 988-5882; b) 1-800-444-3333; c) 1 + 800-555-1212 (= "Toll-Free"); d) 1 + 411

Last but not least

NEVER TAPE MY DUO	O V E R D U E **P** A Y M E N T
CHEER SMART RAKE	M A R K E T **R** E S E A R C H
SOS THREW GIG	G R **O** S S W E I G H T
NO BAD CAR GRID	B O A R **D** I N G C A R D
QUIT CORNY ATOLL	Q **U** A L I T Y C O N T R O L
IN VACCINE OR SOUL	**C** O N S U L A R I N V O I C E
LEANEST BEACH	B A L A N C E S H E E **T**
ICE TURNIP	U N **I** T P R I C E
POST TANGO CRIES	**O** P E R A T I N G C O S T S
CAGE TITANIC SPY	S E A T I **N** G C A P A C I T Y

Collected Word Bank

2% for cash	*2% Skonto bei Barzahlung*
3 months' credit	*3 Monate Ziel*
24-hour clock	*24-Stunden Uhr*
30 days net	*30 Tage netto*
access	*Zugang*
accommodate	*unterbringen*
accommodation	*Unterkunft*
according to our estimate	*nach unserer Schätzung*
according to the contract	*vertragsgemäß*
administration	*Verwaltung*
advance order	*Vorausbestellung*
advertising campaign	*Werbekampagne*
advertising budget	*Werbeetat*
after-sales service	*Kundendienst*
against 3 months' acceptance	*gegen Dreimonatsakzept*
agency	*Agentur*
agent	*Makler, Vertreter*
agreement	*Vereinbarung*
aim	*Ziel*
air freight	*Luftfracht*
air freight charges	*Luftfrachtkosten*
air waybill (= AWB)	*Luftfrachtbrief*

airtight packaging	*luftdichte Verpackung*
allow a discount	*einen Rabatt gewähren*
amount to	*sich belaufen auf*
annual turnover	*Jahresumsatz*
answerphone	*Anrufbeantworter*
anticlockwise (BE)	*gegen dem Uhrzeigersinn*
apologise	*entschuldigen*
apology	*Entschuldigung*
area code	*Ortsnetzkennzahl*
articulated lorry (BE)	*Lastzug*
as per contract	*laut Vertrag*
at short notice	*kurzfristig*
attend	*anwesend sein*
attendance	*Anwesenheit*
attorney (AE)	*Rechtsanwalt*
award (of a contract)	*Vergabe (eines Vertrags)*
backlog	*Rückstand*
baggage cart (AE)	*Kofferkuli*
balance sheet	*Bilanz*
bank charges	*Bankgebühren*
bank overdraft	*Überziehungskredit*
banknote (AE)	*Geldschein*
bar chart	*Balkendiagramm*
bill (AE)	*fakturieren*
bill (= banknote)	*Geldschein*
bill (in a restaurant) (BE)	*Rechnung (im Restaurant)*
bill of exchange	*Wechsel*
bill of lading (= B/L)	*Konnossement*
blanket (insurance) policy	*Generalpolice*
board of directors	*Vorstand*
boarding card	*Bordkarte*
book	*buchen*
booking	*Buchung*
booth (AE)	*Stand (Messe)*
bottom line, the	*unterm Strich*
box file	*kastenförmiger Aktenordner*
break even	*kostendeckend arbeiten*
breakdown (in figures)	*Aufschlüsselung*
breakthrough	*Durchbruch*
bring sb up to date	*jdn auf dem Laufenden halten*
broadside (AE)	*Werbezettel*
brochure	*Prospekt*
broker (BE)	*Makler*
bulk order	*Mengenbestellung*
bulletin board (AE)	*Schwarzes Brett*
business application	*geschäftliche Anwendung*
business card	*Visitenkarte*
business with foreign customers	*Geschäfte mit ausländischen Kunden*
by sea	*auf dem Seeweg*
cab (AE)	*Taxi*
call collect (AE)	*R-Gespräch führen*
call confidentiality	*Einrichtung zur Vermeidung des Abhörens Ihres Gesprächs durch Dritte*
cancel an order	*eine Bestellung annullieren*
car hire	*Autovermietung*

car park (BE)	*Parkplatz*
careless	*fahrlässig*
carrier	*Frachtführer/Spediteur*
cash against documents (= CAD)	*Kasse gegen Dokumente*
cash in advance	*Vorauszahlung*
cash on delivery (= COD)	*gegen Nachnahme*
cash with order (= CWO)	*Barzahlung bei Auftragserteilung*
catalogue price	*Katalogpreis*
cause difficulty	*Schwierigkeiten verursachen*
cellular phone	*Funktelefon*
certificate of origin	*Ursprungszeugnis/Herkunftsbescheinigung*
certificate of seaworthiness	*Seetüchtigkeitszeugnis*
certified public accountant (AE)	*Wirtschaftsprüfer*
CFR (= Cost and Freight)	*Kosten und Fracht*
chairperson	*Vorsitzender*
chartered acountant (BE)	*Wirtschaftsprüfer*
check (AE)	*abhaken*
check (in a restaurant) (AE)	*Rechnung (im Restaurant)*
check in	*sich anmelden/einchecken*
checking account (AE)	*laufendes Konto*
CIF (= Cost, Insurance, Freight)	*Kosten,Versicherung, Fracht*
CIP (= Carriage and insurance paid)	*frachtfrei versichert*
claim a discount	*einen Rabatt fordern*
claim compensation	*Entschädigung fordern*
clause (in a contract)	*Klausel (in einem Vertrag)*
clearance (customs)	*Zollabfertigung*
clearance sale (BE)	*Räumungsverkauf*
close-out sale (AE)	*Räumungsverkauf*
co-operation	*Unterstützung (Zusammenarbeit)*
collect call	*R-Gespräch (= der Angerufene zahlt)*
collect on delivery (= c.o.d.) (AE)	*Nachnahme*
commercial invoice	*Handelsrechnung*
commodity sales	*Warenumsatz*
common stock (AE)	*Stammaktien*
commuter ticket (AE)	*Saisonkarte*
company (BE)	*Firma*
company logo	*Firmenlogo*
compensate	*entschädigen*
compensation (BE)	*Vergütung*
competitiveness	*Konkurrenzfähigkeit*
compile	*kompilieren*
connection	*Verbindung*
consignment	*(Waren)sendung*
consignment note	*Frachtbrief*
consolidations	*Sammelladungen*
consular invoice	*Konsulatsfaktura*
consumer	*Verbraucher*
consumer goods	*Verbrauchsgüter*
contract	*Vertrag*
contract of carriage	*Frachtvertrag*
contract of sale	*Kaufvertrag*
contracting parties	*vertragsschließende Parteien*
corporation (AE)	*Firma*
cost-sharing	*Kostenteilung*
counterclockwise (AE)	*gegen den Uhrzeigersinn*

country code	*Landesvorwahl*
CPT (= Carriage paid)	*frachtfrei*
credit card call	*Telefonanruf mit Kreditkarte*
credit card order	*Bestellung per Kreditkarte*
creditworthy	*kreditwürdig*
current account (BE)	*laufendes Konto*
custom-made (AE)	*maßgeschneidert*
customer loyalty	*Kundentreue*
customer relations	*Kundenbeziehungen*
customized	*maßgeschneidert*
customs	*Zoll*
customs invoice	*Zollfaktura*
DAF (= Delivered at frontier)	*geliefert Grenze*
damage	*Schaden/Schäden*
data	*Daten*
database	*Datenbank*
DDP (= Delivered duty paid)	*geliefert verzollt*
DDU (= Delivered duty unpaid)	*geliefert unverzollt*
deadlines	*Vertragsfristen für Leistungen*
debt collection	*Schuldeneintreibung*
debt collection agency	*Inkassobüro*
delay	*Verspätung*
delivery charge	*Liefergebühr*
delivery date	*Liefertermin*
demonstrate a model	*ein Modell vorführen*
demonstration	*Vorführung*
departure lounge	*Abflughalle*
deposit account (BE)	*Sparkonto*
DEQ (= Delivered ex quay)	*geliefert ab Kai*
DES (= Delivered ex ship)	*geliefert ab Schiff*
despatch note	*Versandschein*
diary	*Terminkalender*
directory enquiries	*Fernsprechauskunft*
disappointed	*enttäuscht*
discount	*Rabatt*
dispute	*Streitfall*
distributor	*Vertriebsagent, Verteiler*
diversified	*aufgefächert, diversifiziert*
do a deal	*ein Abkommen treffen*
do it again (BE)	*wiederholen*
do it over (AE)	*wiederholen*
document of title	*Traditionspapier*
documents against acceptance (= D/A)	*Dokumente gegen Akzept*
documents against payment (= D/P)	*Kasse gegen Dokumente*
domestic flight	*Inlandflug*
downsizing	*Stellenabbau*
draft	*Wechsel, Entwurf*
draw up a contract	*einen Vertrag aufsetzen*
duty-free	*zollfrei*
EDP (= electronic data processing)	*EDV (= elektronische Datenverarbeitung)*
EDP-supported	*EDV-gestützt*
electronic payment	*elektronische Zahlung*
elevator (AE)	*Aufzug*
enter into a contract	*Vertrag abschließen*
equipment	*Ausrüstung/Einrichtung*

eraser (AE)	*Radiergummi*
estate agent (BE)	*Immobilienmakler*
exchange rate	*Wechselkurs*
Executive Vice-President (AE)	*Geschäftsführer*
expire	*auslaufen*
expiry	*Ablauf*
express delivery	*Eilsendung*
extension number	*Durchwahl*
EXW (= Ex works)	*ab Werk*
fabricate (AE)	*herstellen*
fact sheet	*Info-Blatt*
FAS (= Free alongside ship)	*frei Längsseite Seeschiff*
fault	*Schuld*
favourable	*günstig*
FCA (= Free carrier)	*frei Frachtführer*
feasibility	*Durchführbarkeit*
fill in (BE)	*ausfüllen (Formular)*
fill out (AE)	*ausfüllen (Formular)*
financial director	*Leiter der Finanzabteilung*
financing	*Finanzierung*
firm offer	*Festangebot*
firm order	*Festauftrag*
fixed costs	*Fixkosten, Gemeinkosten*
flight schedule	*Flugplan*
flow chart	*Flussdiagramm*
FOB (= Free on board)	*frei an Bord*
folder	*Aktenmappe, Schreibmappe*
follow-up order	*Nachbestellung*
forecast	*Voraussage, Prognose*
forwarding agent	*Spediteur*
freeway (AE)	*Autobahn*
freight bill	*Frachtrechnung*
freight costs	*Frachtkosten*
freight rate	*Frachttarife*
freight service	*Frachtdienst*
freight train (AE)	*Güterzug*
fulfilment of contract	*Vertragserfüllung*
full-time	*Vollzeit*
full stop (BE)	*Punkt*
gap in the market	*Marktnische*
gas (or: gasoline) (AE)	*Benzin*
General Delivery (AE)	*postlagernd*
give an assurance	*versichern*
global village, the	*globales Dorf*
go bankrupt (AE)	*Bankrott gehen*
go into liquidation (BE)	*Bankrott gehen*
goods (plural only)	*Ware*
goods train (BE)	*Güterzug*
graphics	*Grafik*
green point	*grüner Punkt*
gross weight	*Bruttogewicht*
guarantee delivery	*Lieferung garantieren*
handling	*Beförderung*
handouts	*Prospekte, Blätter, Handouts*
have in stock	*vorrätig haben*

headed paper	*Papier mit Briefkopf*
health certificate	*Gesundheitszeugnis*
hold sb responsible for sth	*jdn für etw verantwortlich machen*
holding company (BE)	*Dachgesellschaft*
icon	*Bildsymbol*
import duty	*Einfuhrzoll*
import permit	*Importgenehmigung*
import restrictions	*Einfuhrbeschränkungen*
in working order	*funktionsfähig*
inadvertent(ly)	*versehentlich*
income tax	*Einkommensteuer*
incorporated (= Inc.) (AE)	*GmbH*
increase in turnover	*Umsatzsteigerung*
incur costs	*Kosten auf sich nehmen*
industrial site	*Industriegelände*
information bulletin	*Mitteilungsblatt*
initial order	*Erstauftrag*
inland flight	*Inlandflug*
inland transport	*Inlandstransport*
insurance	*Versicherung*
insurance certificate	*Versicherungszertifikat*
interest	*Zinsen*
interest rate	*Zinssatz*
interim payment (BE)	*Abschlagszahlung*
interim report	*Zwischenbericht*
intermediate stop	*Zwischenstop*
international call	*Auslandsgespräch*
international flight	*internationaler Flug*
inventory (BE)	*Inventar*
inventory control (AE)	*Materialwirtschaft*
invoice (BE)	*fakturieren, Rechnung*
irrevocable	*unwiderruflich*
issuing bank	*Emissionsbank*
item	*Posten*
job-sharing	*Arbeitsteilung*
jobber (AE)	*Großhändler*
joint venture	*Beteiligungsunternehmen*
keyboard	*Tastatur*
labelling	*Etikettierung*
labour charges	*Arbeitskosten, Lohnkosten*
launch	*herausbringen, auf den Markt bringen*
lawyer (AE)	*Rechtsanwalt*
leisure-time (AE)	*Freizeit*
letter of credit (L/C)	*Akkreditiv*
licensing contract	*Lizenzvertrag*
lift (BE)	*Aufzug*
likely costs	*voraussichtliche Kosten*
limited (= Ltd.) (BE)	*GmbH*
link	*verbinden*
local branch	*Filiale*
local call	*Ortsgespräch*
logo	*Logo, Firmenzeichen*
long-distance call (AE)	*Ferngespräch*
long-term aim	*langfristiges Ziel*
look into sth	*etwas untersuchen/prüfen*

lorry (BE)	*Lastwagen*
loss-leader	*Lockartikel*
luggage trolley (BE)	*Kofferkuli*
made-to-measure (BE)	*maßgeschneidert*
mail (AE)	*verschicken*
mail order	*Postversand*
mailbox (AE)	*Briefkasten*
mailing list	*Adressenliste*
mailman (AE)	*Briefträger*
main competition, the	*die Hauptkonkurrenten*
make (BE)	*herstellen*
make headway	*vorankommen, Fortschritte machen*
management	*Unternehmensleitung*
Managing Director (BE)	*Geschäftsführer*
manufacture	*herstellen*
manufacturing	*Herstellung*
market research	*Marktforschung*
market share	*Marktanteil*
marketing	*Vertrieb*
marketing costs	*Marketingkosten*
memo (= memorandum)	*Mitteilung, Notiz*
middle-term aim	*mittelfristiges Ziel*
mistake	*Fehler*
mistakenly	*irrtümlicherweise*
mobile phone	*Mobiltelefon (Handy)*
mode of transportation	*Transportart*
money order	*Zahlungsanweisung*
motorway (BE)	*Autobahn*
mouse	*Maus*
name card/tag	*Namenskärtchen/Namensschild*
negotiation	*Verhandlung*
negotiator (AE)	*Makler*
net weight	*Nettogewicht*
not to arrive on time	*nicht rechtzeitig ankommen*
note (BE)	*Geldschein*
notice board (BE)	*Schwarzes Brett*
occasional use	*gelegentliche Benutzung*
offer	*Angebot*
office premises	*Büroräume*
one-way ticket (AE)	*Einzelfahrschein*
online	*on line*
open a letter of credit	*ein Akkreditiv eröffnen*
open-ended	*offen, unbefristet*
operating costs	*Betriebskosten*
operator	*Vermittlung*
or best offer (= o.b.o.) (AE)	*Höchstgebot*
or near(est) offer (= o.n.o.) (BE)	*Höchstgebot*
ordinary shares (BE)	*Stammaktien*
our latest model	*unser neuestes Modell*
outlay	*Auslagen*
outlet	*Händler, Verkaufsstelle*
output	*Produktionsleistung*
outsourcing	*Auslagerung von Unternehmensaktivitäten*
outstanding	*unbezahlt*
overdue	*überfällig*

overdue payment	*überfällige Zahlung*
overestimate	*überschätzen*
overheads	*Betriebskosten*
overlook a delay	*über eine Verspätung hinwegsehen*
packaging	*Verpackung*
packaging material	*Verpackungsmaterial*
packing charges	*Verpackungskosten*
packing list	*Packliste*
pallet	*Palette*
paper clip	*Büroklammer*
parking lot (AE)	*Parkplatz*
part-time	*Teilzeit*
part payment (BE)	*Teilzahlung*
partial payment (AE)	*Teilzahlung*
participant	*Teilnehmer*
participate	*teilnehmen*
pay the whole bill (BE)	*für alle zahlen*
payment on receipt of goods	*Zahlung bei Erhalt der Waren*
payment on receipt of invoice	*Zahlung bei Rechnungserhalt*
payphone	*Münztelefon*
period (AE)	*Punkt*
period of contract	*Vertragsdauer*
personnel manager	*Leiter der Personalabteilung*
petrol (BE)	*Benzin*
phone booth/box	*Telefonzelle*
pick up the tab (AE)	*für alle zahlen*
pie chart	*Kreisdiagramm*
planning	*Planung*
point of delivery	*Zustellungsort*
policy meeting	*Strategie-/Grundsatzbesprechung*
portable	*tragbar*
post (BE)	*verschicken*
post code (BE)	*Postleitzahl*
postage and packing (= p&p)	*Porto und Verpackung*
postbox (BE)	*Briefkasten*
poste restante (BE)	*postlagernd*
poster	*Plakat*
postman (BE)	*Briefträger*
price reduction	*Preisnachlass*
preference shares (BE)	*Vorzugsaktien*
preferred stock (AE)	*Vorzugsaktien*
premises	*Örtlichkeit, Räumlichkeit, Grundstück*
pricing	*Preisfestsetzung*
printer	*Drucker*
product specifications	*Produktbeschreibung*
production manager	*Leiter der Fertigung*
profit margin	*Gewinnspanne*
proforma (or: pro-forma) invoice	*Pro-forma-Rechnung*
progress payment (AE)	*Abschlagszahlung*
progress report	*Fortschritts-/Lagebericht*
promotion budget	*Werbeetat*
prompt payment	*sofortige/umgehende Zahlung*
proof-of-purchase (AE)	*Kassenbon*
proposal	*Vorschlag*
proprietary company (AE)	*Dachgesellschaft*

provisional	*provisorisch*
publicity campaign	*Werbekampagne*
publicity leaflet (BE)	*Werbezettel*
punch	*Locher*
quality control	*Qualitätskontrolle*
railroad (AE)	*Eisenbahn*
railway (BE)	*Eisenbahn*
raw materials	*Rohstoffe*
ready-made (+ noun)	*Fertig- (Nomen)*
real estate agent (AE)	*Immobilienmakler*
realtor (AE)	*Immobilienmakler*
recall-voice messaging	*Einrichtung zur Aufnahme von Mitteilungen, wenn Ihr Telefon ausgeschaltet ist*
receipt	*Quittung*
recruit	*anwerben*
refreshments	*Erfrischungen*
regret sth	*etwas bedauern*
regulations	*Bestimmungen*
reimburse	*erstatten*
reliability	*Zuverlässigkeit*
reminder	*Mahnbrief, Zahlungserinnerung*
remit	*überweisen*
remittance	*Überweisung*
remuneration (AE)	*Vergütung*
repair (of goods)	*Ausbesserung*
repayment	*Rückzahlung*
repeat order	*Nachbestellung*
resources	*Ressourcen*
responsible	*verantwortlich*
retailer	*Einzelhändler*
return journey (BE)	*Hin- und Rückfahrt*
reverse the charges (BE)	*R-Gespräch führen*
review (our) options	*(unsere) Optionen überprüfen*
revocable	*widerruflich*
rewrite	*überarbeiten*
rival product	*Konkurrenzprodukt*
roam	*das Mobiltelefon bei Auslandsreisen in ausländischen Netzen benutzen*
rough calculation of costs	*Vorkalkulation*
round trip (AE)	*Hin- und Rückfahrt*
roundabout (BE)	*Kreisverkehr*
rubber (BE)	*Radiergummi*
run into difficulty	*Schwierigkeiten bekommen*
running charges	*laufende Kosten*
sales	*Verkauf*
sales clerk(AE)	*Verkäufer*
sales forecast	*Absatzprognose*
sales graph	*Absatzdiagramm*
sales receipt (BE)	*Kassenbon*
sales rep (= representative)	*Handelsvertreter*
sales target	*Verkaufsziel*
sales tax (AE)	*Mehrwertsteuer*
salesperson (AE)	*Verkäufer*
sample	*Muster*
savings account (AE)	*Sparkonto*

schedule	*Zeitplan*
screen	*Bildschirm*
season ticket (BE)	*Saisonkarte*
seating capacity	*Sitzkapazität*
selling price	*Verkaufspreis*
semi-skilled	*angelernt*
separator	*Trennfolie, Trennblatt*
service	*Dienstleistung*
session	*Sitzung*
shape up	*in Form bringen*
shelf (plural: shelves)	*Regal(e)*
shipment	*(Waren)sendung*
shop assistant (BE)	*Verkäufer*
shopping cart (AE)	*Einkaufswagen*
shopping centre (BE)	*Einkaufszentrum*
shopping mall (AE)	*Einkaufszentrum*
shopping trolley (BE)	*Einkaufswagen*
short notice	*kurzfristig*
shortage	*Fehlmenge, Engpass*
short-term aim	*kurzfristiges Ziel*
show a profit	*Profit verzeichnen*
shuttle service	*Pendelverkehr*
signing (of a contract)	*Unterzeichnung (eines Vertrags)*
silent partner (AE)	*stiller Teilhaber*
single ticket (BE)	*Einzelfahrschein*
skilled	*ausgebildet*
sleeping partner (BE)	*stiller Teilhaber*
slide	*Dia*
slide projector	*Diaprojektor*
slump	*Einbruch*
solicitor (BE)	*Rechtsanwalt*
solution	*Lösung*
spare time (BE)	*Freizeit*
special design	*Sonderanfertigung*
special sales campaign	*Verkaufssonderaktion*
specialise in	*sich spezialisieren auf*
spreadsheet	*Tabellenkalkulation*
stand (BE)	*Stand (Messe)*
standing order	*Dauerauftrag*
staple	*Heftklammer*
stapler	*Hefter*
state-of-the-art	*technisch auf dem neusten Stand*
stick to an agreement	*sich an eine Abmachung halten*
stock	*Lagerbestand*
stock-taking (BE)	*Inventar*
stock control (BE)	*Materialwirtschaft*
stocks	*Vorräte*
storage	*Lagerung*
storage facilities	*Lagermöglichkeiten*
streetcar (AE)	*Straßenbahn*
strengthen	*stärker werden*
strictly net	*rein netto*
subway (AE)	*U-Bahn*
supplier	*Lieferant/Zulieferer*
surfing	*surfen*

table	*Tabelle*
tailor-made	*maßgeschneidert*
take as a basis	*zugrunde legen*
take legal action	*gerichtlich vorgehen*
take legal steps	*rechtliche Schritte einleiten*
target group	*Zielgruppe*
tax allowance (BE)	*Steuerfreibetrag*
tax exemption (AE)	*Steuerfreibetrag*
taxi (BE)	*Taxi*
telephone directory	*Telefonbuch*
telephone number	*Rufnummer*
terms of contract	*Vertragsbedingungen*
terms of delivery	*Lieferbedingungen*
third party	*Dritter*
thru (= through) (AE)	*bis*
tick (BE)	*abhaken*
time frame	*Zeitplan*
timetable	*Zeitplan/Stundenplan/Fahrplan*
tool	*Werkzeug*
trade restrictions	*Handelsbeschränkungen*
trading partner	*Handelspartner*
trading terms	*Handelsbedingungen*
traffic circle (AE)	*Kreisverkehr*
tram (BE)	*Straßenbahn*
transfer	*umsteigen,überweisen*
transparency	*Folie*
traveller's cheque	*Reisescheck*
trial order	*Probeauftrag*
truck (AE)	*Lastwagen*
truck-trailer (AE)	*Lastzug*
trunk call (BE)	*Ferngespräch*
typography	*Schriftarten*
undelivered	*nicht geliefert*
underestimate	*unterschätzen*
Underground (BE)	*U-Bahn*
unfavourable	*ungünstig*
unit price	*Stückpreis*
units sold	*verkaufte Einheiten*
urgent	*dringend*
user-friendly	*benutzerfreundlich*
variable costs	*variable Kosten*
VAT (= Value-Added Tax) (BE)	*Mehrwertsteuer*
video (cassette) recorder	*Videogerät*
video conferencing	*Videokonferencing*
warehousing	*Lagerhaltung*
warning	*Warnung*
waste disposal costs	*Entsorgungskosten*
weaken	*schwächer werden*
wharfage	*Kaigeld*
wholesaler (BE)	*Großhändler*
word processor	*Textverarbeiter*
written offer	*schriftliches Angebot*
Yellow Pages	*Gelbe Seiten*
ZIP code (AE)	*Postleitzahl*